Positive Organizational Psychology Interventions

Positive Organizational Psychology Interventions

Design and Evaluation

Stewart I. Donaldson and Christopher Chen
Claremont Graduate University
Claremont, CA
USA

WILEY Blackwell

This edition first published 2021
© 2021 John Wiley & Sons Ltd.

The right of Stewart I. Donaldson and Christopher Chen to be identified as the author(s) of this work has been asserted in accordance with law.

Registered Office(s)
John Wiley & Sons, Inc., 111 River Street, Hoboken, NJ 07030, USA
John Wiley & Sons Ltd, The Atrium, Southern Gate, Chichester, West Sussex, PO19 8SQ, UK

Editorial Office
The Atrium, Southern Gate, Chichester, West Sussex, PO19 8SQ, UK

For details of our global editorial offices, customer services, and more information about Wiley products visit us at www.wiley.com.

Wiley also publishes its books in a variety of electronic formats and by print-on-demand. Some content that appears in standard print versions of this book may not be available in other formats.

Library of Congress Cataloging-in-Publication Data
Names: Donaldson, Stewart I. (Stewart Ian), editor. | Chen, Christopher
    (Psychology researcher), editor. | John Wiley & Sons, Inc., publisher.
Title: Positive organizational psychology interventions : design and
    evaluation / [edited by] Stewart I. Donaldson, Christopher Chen,
    Claremont Graduate University, Claremont, CA, USA.
Description: Hoboken, NJ : John Wiley & Sons, Inc., [2021] | Includes
    bibliographical references and index.
Identifiers: LCCN 2020046896 (print) | LCCN 2020046897 (ebook) | ISBN
    9781118977378 (hardback) | ISBN 9781118977361 (paperback) | ISBN
    9781118977392 (pdf) | ISBN 9781118977385 (epub) | ISBN 9781118977415
    (ebook) | ISBN 9781118977408 (mobi)
Subjects: LCSH: Positive psychology. | Organizational behavior. |
    Work—Psychological aspects.
Classification: LCC BF204.6 .P665 2021 (print) | LCC BF204.6 (ebook) |
    DDC 150.19/88—dc23
LC record available at https://lccn.loc.gov/2020046896
LC ebook record available at https://lccn.loc.gov/2020046897

Cover image: © Seita / Shutterstock
Cover design by Wiley

Set in 10/12pt Warnock by Integra Software Services, Pondicherry, India

SKY07C6CB78-478F-42AB-80B0-30B5912CA061_031021

Positive Organizational Psychology Interventions: Design & Evaluation

Stewart I. Donaldson
Christopher Chen
Claremont Graduate University

Address correspondence to: Stewart I. Donaldson, Ph.D., Claremont Graduate University, 123 E. 8th Street, Claremont, CA 91711. Telephone: 909-702-7316. E-mail: stewart.donaldson@cgu.edu.

Compliance with Ethical Standards

Conflict of Interest: All the authors declare no conflict of interests.

Ethical Approval: All procedures performed in studies involving human participants were in accordance with the ethical standards of the institutional and/or national research committee and with the 1964 Helsinki declaration and its later amendments or comparable ethical standards.

Informed Consent: Informed consent was obtained from all individual participants included in the study.

Table of Contents

About the Editors

STEWART I. DONALDSON, Ph.D., is a Distinguished University Professor, Executive Director of the Claremont Evaluation Center, and Director of The Evaluators' Institute at Claremont Graduate University (CGU). He is deeply committed to improving lives through research, evaluation, and education. Professor Donaldson works with students on a wide range of topics across several fields and programs at CGU, including the science of well-being and positive psychology; positive organizational and sports psychology; positive organizational and human resource development; positive youth development and education; and community/global health program design, monitoring, and evaluation. As an immigrant born overseas and now a naturalized US citizen, Professor Donaldson has traveled extensively and especially enjoys working on cross-cultural and international topics with students who have diverse backgrounds and perspectives from all across the globe. He was recently honored with the International Positive Psychology Association (IPPA) Inspiring Mentor Career Achievement Award (2019) and appointed Faculty Advisor of the IPPA Student Division with approximately 600 student members from 50 different countries. From 2011 to 2017, he was director and faculty mentor for approximately 50 underrepresented minority graduate students from across more than 30 different universities participating in the American Evaluation Association's esteemed and internationally recognized Graduate Education Diversity Internship (GEDI) Program. Professor Donaldson has served as chair or member on more than 100 doctoral dissertation committees at Claremont Graduate University since 1995, and more than 200 master's theses and online certificate students' culminating research and evaluation projects.

In 2007, Professor Donaldson (in collaboration with professors Mihaly Csikszentmihalyi and Jeanne Nakamura) developed the first research-focused Ph.D. and M.A. programs in positive psychology. He currently provides paid employment and supervises numerous students specializing in positive organizational psychology, positive health and sports psychology, and evaluation science. Professor Donaldson works collaboratively with his students and colleagues to publish findings from his extensive portfolio of extramurally funded research and evaluation projects. This work has been cited widely, including more than 200 peer-reviewed scientific articles, chapters, and evaluation reports, and he has published or has forthcoming 18 books, including *Applied Positive Psychology* (2011), *Scientific Advances in Positive Psychology* (2017), *Toward a Positive*

Psychology of Relationships (2018), *Positive Psychological Science* (2020), and this volume *Positive Organizational Psychology Interventions: Design & Evaluation*.

Professor Donaldson has been honored with a plethora of prestigious international, national, and regional career achievement awards. Most recently at the IPPA World Congress of Positive Psychology in Melbourne, Australia (July 2019), Professor Donaldson was honored with two career achievement awards. The 2019 IPPA Work and Organizations Division "Exemplary Research to Practice Award" was presented to Professor Donaldson for many years of exemplary research and teaching, as well as a robust cumulative contribution to evidence-based practice related to fostering positive work and organizations. He was also awarded the IPPA 2019 "Inspiring Mentor Award." The student division of the IPPA recognizes one outstanding mentor in the field of positive psychology who provides continued commitment and support to students who foster professional and academic development. Professor Donaldson was given this honor to acknowledge his many years of outstanding teaching and mentoring, and for inspiring the next generation of diverse psychological scientists to make meaningful contributions to societies across the globe.

CHRISTOPHER CHEN, M.S., is a Ph.D. student in the Organizational Behavior and Psychology program at Claremont Graduate University where he received a General Bronson Fellowship and Oskamp Student Fellowship Award. He received his M.S. in Applied Psychology with a concentration in Organizational Psychology from the University of Southern California, where he was elected as a member of The Honor Society of Phi Kappa Phi. Christopher received his B.A. in Psychology from the University of California, Riverside, and was elected for membership in the Omicron Delta Kappa Society for his academic and campus community achievements. Before becoming a student at Claremont Graduate University, Christopher worked at various organizations, such as the Los Angeles Unified School District and Boston Consulting Group. Christopher has presented his research at conferences hosted by the Academy of Management, Western Psychological Association, and Western Positive Psychological Association. His general research interests revolve around the changing nature of the workplace due to technology, career and job crafting, the protean career, as well as organizational commitment. Christopher is a Global Talent and Innovation Consultant at Accenture and Associate Director of the Claremont Accenture Talent Innovation Lab.

About the Contributors

ADRIAN BERNHARDT, M.A., is a Research Associate for Psychometrics and Statistics at Endpoint Outcomes, where he supports the psychometric evaluation and validation of patient, clinician, and observer reported outcomes. His interests lie primarily in the application of factor analysis, structural equation models, and robust estimation techniques. He holds a B.A. Honors in Psychology from California State University, Northridge, and an M.A. in Organizational Behavior and Evaluation from Claremont Graduate University.

VICTORIA (VICKI) CABRERA, M.P.A. is an organizational and positive psychology consultant, researcher, and evaluator. Her research and practice interests revolve around helping people and organizations thrive and reach their full potential, with a focus on social impact. She also serves on the Executive Committee of the International Positive Psychology Association's (IPPA) Work & Organizations Division. She received her B.A in Psychology with a concentration in Industrial/Organizational Psychology from The College of New Jersey and her M.P.A in Public and Nonprofit Management and Policy from New York University. She is currently pursuing a Ph.D. in Psychology with a concentration in Positive Organizational Psychology at Claremont Graduate University.

LAWRENCE CHAN, M.A., is a Lecturer in the Department of Psychological Sciences at Woodbury University, Los Angeles, and in the Management and Human Resources Department at California State Polytechnic University, Pomona. As an organizational consultant, he has worked with many diverse organizations, including Accenture, the LA Dodger's Foundation, and The Aspen Institute. His research interests are in positive organizational behavior, namely positive behavioral indicators of performance, and cross-cultural performance management. He received his B.A. in Psychology from the University of California, Riverside, and his M.A. in Organizational Leadership from the University of San Diego. He is currently working on his Ph.D. in Organizational Behavior at Claremont Graduate University.

SCOTT I. DONALDSON, Ph.D., is a Postdoctoral Scholar in Evaluation, Statistics, and Measurement at the University of California, San Diego School of Medicine, Moores Cancer Center. Scott received his Ph.D. in Psychology with a concentration in Evaluation and Applied Research Methods and a co-concentration in Positive Organizational Psychology from Claremont Graduate University. He received his B.A. in Psychology from the University of California, Los Angeles, and his M.S. in Organizational Psychology from the University of Southern California. His research focuses on the design and evaluation of behavioral health interventions at work.

MATT DUBIN, Ph.D., is the Founder and Principal of Dubin Consulting Group, an organizational culture and leadership development consultancy that enables organizations to create a culture of flow and peak performance. His philosophy is that each person's job should mean more than work, and organizational success depends on the mutual investment between a company and its people. From start-ups to Fortune 500 companies, Matt has worked with organizations across a variety of industries, including professional sports, tech, entertainment, fashion, law, finance, and academia. Matt completed his Ph.D. in Positive Organizational Psychology at Claremont Graduate University, where he was awarded the inaugural "Mihaly Csikszentmihalyi Dissertation Award for Excellence in Positive Psychology" for his research on cultivating flow in the workplace.

HANNAH FOSTER GRAMMER, M.A., is a Research Lab Member at the Health Psychology and Prevention Science Institute, as well as at the Social Identity Center at Claremont Graduate University. Currently, she is conducting research on strengths-based versus traditional-based goal setting during performance review meetings on performance outcomes, mediated through basic needs satisfaction as part of self-determination theory. She is working toward a Ph.D. in Social Psychology at Claremont Graduate University, with a focus on application in an organizational development context. She is interested in conservation psychology through a social and organizational development lens, specifically in terms of exploring vested interest and attitude-behavior consistency with attitudinal change approaches to achieve effective communication initiatives.

SHARON HONG, M.A., is a Management Consultant at one of the largest professional services firms, with experience in change, diversity, equity, and inclusion, future of work, culture, talent strategy, and leadership development. She earned a B.A. in Psychology at Pepperdine University and her M.A. in Psychology with a concentration in Positive Organizational Psychology from Claremont Graduate University. Her research interests focus on bringing vulnerability, authenticity, and the human touch to the workplace.

ELI KOLOKOWSKY is a Ph.D. student in Positive Organizational Psychology at Claremont Graduate University. Before coming to Claremont Graduate University, Eli graduated from Cal Poly San Luis Obispo where they received a B.S. in Psychology. Eli is interested in facilitating positive employee experiences through organizational development, and focuses on diversity, equity, and inclusion initiatives in the workplace.

JENNIFER M. NELSON, M.A., is a Freelance Organization Development and Evaluation Consultant in the healthcare industry and an adjunct professor at Azusa

Pacific University in the Leadership and Organizational Psychology department. Her passion is improving the quality of work–life for healthcare professionals so they can better serve the community and inspiring future practitioners to improve organization effectiveness for social betterment. Her research interests revolve around effective leader development, program evaluation, and positive organization development interventions. She received her B.S. in Industrial/Organizational Psychology at Central Michigan University and her M.A. in Applied Psychology with a concentration in Organizational Behavior and Evaluation.

ADRIAN REECE is a Principal Consultant in the Claremont Accenture Talent Innovation Lab. He is working towards his Ph.D. in Organizational Behavior at Claremont Graduate University. He received his B.B.A. in Industrial/Organizational Psychology from CUNY Baruch College. His current research interests surround innovation, optimal performance, measurement, and behavioral modeling. He strives to utilize data to uncover the mosaic of regular and irregular patterns that make each employee unique.

EMILY ZAVALA is a Police Service Representative with the Los Angeles Police Department working as an emergency operator and police dispatcher for the past 14 years. Guided by personal experience, her research is focused on the development of practices to preserve and enhance the well-being of first responders. She received her B.A. in Psychology from California Lutheran University and is currently working on her M.A. in Psychology with a concentration in Positive Organizational Psychology and Evaluation at Claremont Graduate University.

Preface

The 2020 global pandemic has reminded us how important it is to "follow the science" in our efforts to prevent and ameliorate our most urgent and important health, well-being, community, organizational, and societal challenges. For example, "follow the science" is the cry being heard around the world as leaders and public health professionals attempt to slow the spread and alleviate the suffering being caused by Covid-19. High-quality empirical research and evaluations are being funded at a rapid rate worldwide to determine the efficacy of treatments to reduce the severity and length of illness caused by the coronavirus, as well as to discover an effective vaccine.

The second wave of devastating consequences of the 2020 global pandemic will likely be linked to dramatic declines in well-being, performance, and organizational effectiveness. What does science tell us about enhancing and preventing declines in well-being, performance, and organizational effectiveness? This volume explores those questions by following the positive organizational psychology intervention science during the past two decades and illustrates how to use that science, as well as positive psychological science more broadly, to design and evaluate the next generation of positive organizational psychology interventions (POPIs). After summarizing what we now know from two decades of positive psychological science, including POPI science, each chapter uses aspects of that science in the design of a next-generation POPI. The final chapter emphasizes the importance of the measurement and strategic evaluation of POPIs and provides frameworks for understanding worker and organizational needs, efficacy evaluations of new POPIs, as well as measuring and evaluating the effectiveness of POPIs being implemented in the global workplace.

The editors wish to thank the chapter authors for their creativity and innovative evidence-based approaches to designing POPIs that promise to enhance and prevent declines in well-being, performance, and organizational effectiveness in these challenging times. Special thanks to the Wiley team: Jake Opie, Monica Rogers, Christina Weyrauch, Arthi Kangeyan, and Alan Everett for their amazing editorial and production work, and for efficiently and effectively managing this project. It is our hope that all this exemplary teamwork will provide you with an engaging, meaningful, and productive experience as you make your way through the chapters in this volume.

Stewart I. Donaldson
Christopher Chen
Claremont, CA

1

Designing Positive Organizational Psychology Interventions

Stewart I. Donaldson, Christopher Chen, & Scott I. Donaldson

The contemporary version of the science of positive psychology introduced by Professors Martin Seligman and Mihaly Csikszentmihalyi at the turn of the 21st century (Seligman & Csikszentmihalyi, 2000) rests on the shoulders of some of the earlier pioneers and thought leaders in the discipline and profession of psychology. Most notably, William James and Abraham Maslow introduced the concepts of optimal functioning, self-actualization, and positive psychology decades before the current perspective was launched (see James, 1908; Maslow, 1954). Nevertheless, Seligman and Csikszentimihalyi's vision and call to the next generation of psychological scientists is what led to an explosion of activity worldwide, and the development of a substantial peer-reviewed scientific literature on well-being, excellence, and optimal human functioning over the past two decades (Donaldson et al., 2020a; Donaldson et al., 2020b; Donaldson et al., 2015; Kim et al., 2018).

While there are now more than 50 regional and national positive psychology professional organizations across the world (see Kim et al., 2018), one of the largest professional organizations of positive psychologists in the world today is the International Positive Psychology Association (IPPA) with several thousand members from more than 70 countries. The IPPA describes positive psychology as a field that focuses on the study and practice of positive emotions, strengths, and virtues that make all individuals, institutions, and communities thrive, and has a three-part mission:

1. To promote the science of positive psychology and its research-based applications.
2. To facilitate collaboration among researchers, teachers, students, and practitioners of positive psychology around the world and across academic disciplines.
3. To share the findings of positive psychology with the broadest possible audience.

The IPPA currently has five divisions, with the largest division of over 1,000 members focused on positive organizational psychology (POP). The IPPA Positive Work and Organizations Division's mission is to serve as a bridge

Positive Organizational Psychology Interventions: Design and Evaluation, First Edition.
Stewart I. Donaldson and Christopher Chen.
© 2021 John Wiley & Sons Ltd. Published 2021 by John Wiley & Sons Ltd.

between research and practice and facilitate collaboration to increase the incorporation of positive psychology in academic research related to organizations and the practice of positive psychology in the organizational context, thereby positively transforming the way the world works.

Positive Organizational Psychology

Donaldson and Ko (2010) defined POP "as the scientific study of positive subjective experiences and traits in the workplace and positive organizations, and its application to improve the effectiveness and quality of life in organizations." They identified two related multidisciplinary streams of scholarship and research, positive organizational behavior (POB; Luthans, 2002) and positive organizational scholarship (POS; Cameron et al., 2003), that greatly contributed to the understanding of POP topics such as positive leadership, positive organizational development and change, positive psychological capital (PsyCap), organizational virtuousness and ethics, well-being at work, work engagement, flow at work, and the like.

Inspired by the new vision for the addition of a positive approach to psychological science, Fred Luthans, Professor of Organizational Behavior at the University of Nebraska, published his seminal work on POB in 2002 (see Donaldson et al., 2020b). He defined POB as "the study and application of positively oriented human resource strengths and psychological capacities that can be measured, developed, and effectively managed for performance improvement in today's workplace" (Luthans, 2002a, p. 59). He envisioned POB capacities, such as hope, optimism, resiliency, and self-efficacy, as something one can measure, develop, and use to improve performance (see Donaldson et al., 2020b; Warren et al., 2017).

A year later, Cameron et al. (2003) provided an even more expansive vision for POS, which is "concerned primarily with the study of especially positive outcomes, processes, and attributes of organizations and their members" (Cameron et al., 2003, p. 4). POS is focused on understanding the drivers of positive behavior in the workplace that would enable organizations to rise to new levels of achievement (Roberts et al., 2005). POS seeks to study organizations characterized by "appreciation, collaboration, virtuousness, vitality, and meaningfulness where creating abundance and human well-being are key indicators of success" (Bernstein, 2003).

Donaldson and Ko (2010) suggested that POP serves as an umbrella term that covers POB, POS, and other related labels (e.g., positive psychology at work) with regard to their research topics, foci, and the level of analysis. More recently, Warren et al. (2017) proposed the umbrella term positive work and organizations (PWO), which encourages integration among POP, POB, and POS. The unifying framework enriches traditional organizational behavior approaches, such as applied organizational psychology, organizational behavior, and management. It also influences technology, hospitality, management, law, and financial planning as a consequence of the growing popularity of the positive perspective in the workplace (Warren et al., 2017). The goal of this book is to understand specific practices, programs, and interventions that can be designed based on the large and growing body of scientific literature to improve work life and organizational effectiveness. We will broadly call these efforts positive organizational psychology interventions (POPIs). We will first briefly review the scientific evidence for positive psychology interventions (PPIs) more generally, and then discuss the effectiveness of POPIs, which are the application of PPIs in the workplace.

Positive Psychology Interventions

Donaldson et al. (under review) recently systematically reviewed and analyzed the findings from 22 meta-analyses and 231 randomized controlled trials (RCTs) designed to determine the efficacy of PPIs. They found that the science of PPIs has matured to the point where we now have numerous systematic reviews and meta-analyses to determine which PPIs are most effective under specific conditions (see Table 1.1). Most of these reviews and meta-analyses of RCTs show that PPIs, on average, do have at least small to medium-sized positive effects on important outcomes. For example, three recent meta-analyses based on numerous empirical tests and thousands of participants clearly illustrate the conditions under which PPIs can generate well-being and optimal human functioning (Donaldson et al., 2019a; Hendriks et al., 2020; Koydemir et al., 2020).

Table 1.1 Positive Psychology Intervention Meta-Analyses.

References	Title	Sample	Findings
Heekerens and Eid (2020)	Inducing positive affect and positive future expectations using the best-possible-self intervention: A systematic review and meta-analysis	34 randomized controlled trial (RCT) studies, 4,462 participants	The best-possible-self (BPS) interventions were effective positive psychology interventions (PPIs) with small effects for positive affect and optimism, with no substantial follow-up effects. Moderators included: assessment of momentary affect immediately after the intervention and conceptualizing optimism as positive future expectations instead of a general orientation in life.
Hendriks et al. (2020)	The efficacy of multi-component positive psychology interventions: A systematic review and meta-analysis of randomized controlled trials	50 RCT studies in 51 articles, 6,141 participants	Multicomponent PPIs were effective with small effects for subjective well-being and depression, small to moderate effects for psychological well-being and anxiety, and moderate effects for stress, after taking study quality and outliers into account. Moderators included region and study quality. Non-Western countries and lower quality studies found greater effects.

(Continued)

Table 1.1 *(Cont'd)*

References	Title	Sample	Findings
Koydemir et al. (2020)	A meta-analysis of the effectiveness of randomized controlled positive psychological interventions on subjective and psychological well-being	68 RCT studies of non-clinical populations, 16,085 participants	PPIs were effective with small effects for psychological well-being and subjective well-being, with small to moderate effects when targeting both types of well-being, with evidence for sustained effects at follow-up. Moderators included: longer interventions (vs shorter), traditional methods (vs technology-assisted methods), and mixed outcomes for age.
Brown et al. (2019)	The effects of positive psychological interventions on medical patients' anxiety: A meta-analysis	12 RCT studies with 1,131 participants; 11 non-randomized trials with 300 participants, patients	PPIs were effective with small to medium effects for patient anxiety, sustained eight weeks post. Moderators included: clinician-led interventions (vs self-administered) and longer interventions (vs shorter).
Carrillo et al. (2019)	Effects of the Best Possible Self intervention: A systematic review and meta-analysis	29 studies in 26 articles, 2,909 participants	BPS interventions were effective PPIs with small effects for well-being, optimism, negative affect, and depressive symptoms, as well as moderate effects for positive affect. Moderators included: older participants and shorter (total minutes of) practice. BPS was more effective than gratitude interventions for positive and negative affect outcomes.
Donaldson et al. (2019a)	Evaluating positive psychology interventions at work: A systematic review and meta-analysis	22 studies, 52 independent samples, 6,027 participants from 10 countries	Five workplace PPIs (psychological capital, job crafting, strengths, gratitude, and employee well-being) can be effective with small effects for desirable work outcomes (performance, job well-being, engagement, etc.) and with small to moderate effects for undesirable work outcomes (negative performance, negative job well-being). Moderators for both desirable and undesirable outcomes did not include the type of theory or intervention delivery method.

(Continued)

Table 1.1 (*Cont'd*)

References	Title	Sample	Findings
Howell and Passmore (2019)	Acceptance and Commitment Training (ACT) as a positive psychological intervention: A systematic review and initial meta-analysis regarding ACT's role in well-being promotion among university students	5 randomized experiments of university students, 585 participants	Acceptance and Commitment Training was an effective PPI with small effects on well-being.
Lomas et al. (2019)	Mindfulness-based interventions in the workplace: An inclusive systematic review and meta-analysis of their impact upon wellbeing	35 RCT studies, 3,090 participants	Mindfulness-based interventions were effective with moderate effects for stress, anxiety, distress, depression, and burnout, as well as small to moderate effects for health, job performance, compassion, empathy, mindfulness, and positive well-being, with no effects for emotional regulation. Moderators for health included: region, mindfulness-based stress-reduction intervention type, and age (younger vs older). Moderators for positive well-being and compassion included: gender.
Slemp et al. (2019)	Contemplative interventions and employee distress: A meta-analysis	119 studies, 6,044 participants	Contemplative interventions (e.g., mindfulness, meditation, and other practices) were effective with small to moderate effects for reducing employee distress sustained at follow-up. Moderators included: type of contemplative intervention and type of control group. Adjustments for publication bias lowered overall effects.
White et al. (2019)	Meta-analyses of positive psychology interventions: The effects are much smaller than previously reported	2 previous meta-analyses (Bolier et al., 2013; Sin & Lyubomirsky, 2009)	When small sample size bias was taken into account, PPIs were effective with small effects for well-being, with mixed effectiveness for depression. Notes need for increasing sample sizes in future studies.

(*Continued*)

Table 1.1 (*Cont'd*)

References	Title	Sample	Findings
Chakhssi et al. (2018)	The effect of positive psychology interventions on well-being in clinical populations: A systematic review and meta-analysis	30 studies, 1,864 participants with clinical disorders	PPIs were effective with small effects for well-being and depression, moderate effects for anxiety, and no significant effects for stress, with similar effects 8–12 weeks post. Moderator for well-being included: guided PPIs (vs unguided, such as self-help). Moderator for stress included: control group type. Moderators did not include: population type, intervention format (individual vs group), intervention duration (shorter vs longer), or type of PPI.
Curry et al. (2018)	Happy to help? A systematic review and meta-analysis of the effects of performing acts of kindness on the well-being of the actor	27 studies in 24 articles, 4,045 participants	Kindness interventions (e.g., random acts of kindness) were effective PPIs with small to medium effects for well-being (for the actor of kindness). Moderators did not include: sex, age, type of participant, intervention, control condition, or outcome measure.
Hendriks et al. (2018)	The efficacy of positive psychology interventions from non-Western countries: A systematic review and meta-analysis	28 RCT studies, 3,009 participants	PPIs from non-Western countries were effective with moderate effects for well-being and large effects for depression and anxiety.
Hendriks et al. (2019)[a]	How WEIRD are positive psychology interventions? A bibliometric analysis of randomized controlled trials on the science of well-being	188 RCT studies in 187 articles from 24 countries, 43,582 participants	Most PPI studies that employ RCTs come from Western Educated Industrialized Rich Democratic (WEIRD) populations. 78.2% of the RCT studies reviewed were conducted in Western countries. However, the number of non-Western publications has increased since 2012.
Dhillon et al. (2017)	Mindfulness-based interventions during pregnancy: A systematic review and meta-analysis	14 articles (some RCT and some non-RCT studies), pregnant (prenatal) participants	Mindfulness-based interventions showed no significant effects for anxiety, depression, or perceived stress in the pooled RCTs, but each showed a significant effect in the pooled non-RCTs. Further, four RCTs and four non-RCT studies showed effectiveness for mindfulness as an outcome.

(*Continued*)

Table 1.1 *(Cont'd)*

References	Title	Sample	Findings
Dickens (2017)	Using gratitude to promote positive change: A series of meta-analyses investigating the effectiveness of gratitude interventions	38 studies, 5,223 participants	Gratitude interventions can be effective with small to medium effects for well-being, happiness, life satisfaction, grateful mood, grateful disposition, positive affect, and depressive symptoms, with mixed findings for negative affect and stress, and no significant effects for physical health, sleep, exercise, prosocial behavior, or self-esteem. Moderators included: adults (vs children or college aged). Moderators did not include: gender, type of neutral comparison group, duration of the follow-up period.
Davis et al. (2016)	Thankful for the little things: A meta-analysis of gratitude interventions	32 studies in 26 articles	Gratitude interventions were effective PPIs with small effects for psychological well-being but not gratitude itself in comparison to measurement-only controls. However, gratitude interventions were effective with moderate effects for gratitude and small effects for psychological well-being, with no significant effects for anxiety, in comparison to alternate-activity conditions. Moderators did not include: type of gratitude intervention or dosage (neither days nor minutes of participation).
Weiss et al. (2016)	Can we increase psychological well-being? The effects of interventions on psychological well-being: A meta-analysis of randomized controlled trials	27 RCT studies, 3,579 participants	Behavioral interventions were effective with moderate effects for psychological well-being, with small effects at follow-up. Moderators included: clinical groups (vs non-clinical) and individual face-to-face interventions (vs self-help or group face to face). Moderators did not include: age, number of sessions, measurement instrument, and control group. Lower-quality studies found greater effects.
Theeboom et al. (2014)	Does coaching work? A meta-analysis on the effects of coaching on individual-level outcomes in an organizational context	18 studies, 2,090 participants, organizational context	Coaching was effective with moderate to large effects for goal-directed self-regulation and with small to moderate effects for performance/skills, well-being, coping, and work attitudes in an organizational context.

(Continued)

Table 1.1 *(Cont'd)*

References	Title	Sample	Findings
Bolier et al. (2013)	Positive psychology interventions: A meta-analysis of randomized controlled studies	39 RCT studies in 40 articles, 6,139 participants	PPIs were effective with small effects for subjective well-being, psychological well-being, and depression. Moderators for decreasing depression included: longer duration (four or eight weeks instead of less than four weeks), recruited as a referral from a healthcare practitioner or hospital (as opposed to recruitment at a community center, online, or a university), the presence of psychosocial problems, and individual delivery (vs self-help or group). Lower-quality studies found greater effects.
Mazzucchelli et al. (2010)	Behavioral activation interventions for well-being: A meta-analysis	20 RCT studies, 1,353 participants	Behavioral activation (BA) interventions were effective with moderate effects for well-being in both non-clinical participants and those with depressive symptoms, indicating that BA can be useful for non-clinical populations alongside its more common setting as a treatment for depression.
Sin and Lyubomirsky (2009)	Enhancing well-being and alleviating depressive symptoms with positive psychology interventions: A practice-friendly meta-analysis	51 studies, 4,266 participants	PPIs were effective with moderate effects for well-being and depressive symptoms. Moderators included: self-selection to participate in the PPI, older age, depression status, individual (vs group therapy), and relatively longer duration.

[a] A bibliometric analysis not a meta-analysis (Donaldson et al., under review).

For example, Hendriks et al. (2020) meta-analyzed 50 randomized controlled trials (RCTs) including a total of 6,141 participants to examine the efficacy of multicomponent positive psychological science interventions (MPPIs). After controlling for study quality and other important covariates, they concluded that MPPIs had an overall small effect on subjective well-being and depression, and a small to moderate effect on psychological well-being. Furthermore, they suggest MPPIs had an overall small to moderate effect on anxiety and a moderate effect on stress.

Koydemir et al. (2020) followed a more comprehensive approach in the selection of studies by including new moderators, focusing on adult non-clinical populations and increases in well-being, and comparing the effects of PPIs targeting subjective and psychological well-being (i.e., hedonism or eudaimonia) or a combination of the two. They found PPIs do increase well-being and that longer interventions showed stronger immediate effects than shorter ones, and interventions based on traditional methods were more effective than those that used technology-assisted methods.

Finally, Donaldson et al. (under review) discovered that many of the meta-analyses they reviewed underscored how important the quality of an RCT seemed to be in terms of accurately estimating PPI efficacy and the generation of outcomes. That is, lower-quality RCTs often overestimated the effects of PPIs. Therefore, Donaldson et al. (under review) developed an evaluation procedure to determine the top 3 and top 10 most successful PPIs – in terms of being tested with a high-quality RCT, having positive effects on well-being over time, and being adaptable to implementation in diverse, marginalized, and disadvantaged populations during a global pandemic. They illustrated how future efforts to generate well-being can now build upon this causal evidence and emulate the most efficacious PPIs to be as effective as possible across a diverse range of participants and settings.

Positive Organizational Psychology Interventions

Drawing from streams of science under the PWO umbrella, including POP, POB, and POS, Donaldson et al. (2019a, 2019b) set out to find which POPIs seem the most promising to date for enhancing well-being and optional functioning at work. They were able to isolate and analyze 22 of the most rigorously tested POPI studies conducted in the workplace. All of these studies (1) implemented an experimental or quasi-experimental intervention in an organizational setting (e.g., with employees, managers, teachers, nurses, staff members, etc.), (2) included pre- and post-test measures, and (3) were analyzed at the individual, team, or organizational level (Donaldson et al., 2019a, 2019b). These 22 peer-reviewed studies were included in a meta-analysis containing 52 independent samples. The total number of participants in this meta-analysis was 6,027 (n(treat) = 2,187; n(control) = 3,840), representing 10 nations (e.g., Australia, China, Netherlands, Sweden, United States, etc.).

It was found that POPIs had small to moderate positive effects across both desirable and undesirable work outcomes (e.g., job stress), including well-being, engagement, leader–member exchange, organization-based self-esteem, workplace trust, forgiveness, prosocial behavior, leadership, and calling. Furthermore, they found the following five types of POPIs to be the most successful:

- Psychological capital interventions
- Job-crafting interventions
- Employee strengths interventions
- Employee gratitude interventions
- Employee well-being interventions

The specific effects of each of the five POPIs are described in detail in Donaldson et al. (2019a).

Donaldson et al. (2019b) followed up their meta-analysis with an in-depth analysis of the theory-driven design of each POPI, and described the theory of change and theory of action for each successful POPI (see Chen, 2005; Donaldson, 2007, in press). The theory of change illustrates exactly what the POPI is expected to improve. The theory of action illustrates exactly what was done in an effort to create those improvements in work life and optimal functioning at work. Tables 1.2 and 1.3 provide details on how successful POPIs have been designed to date.

Table 1.2 POPI Theories of Change (TOC).

References	PP Theory	Change Model	Explicit TOC (Y/N)	Implicit TOC	Expected Work Outcomes	Actual Work Outcomes	Supporting Literature
Chan (2010)	Gratitude	Count-your-blessings model	N	Gratitude has a causal influence on well-being, and an effective strategy to enhance well-being is to lead people to count their blessings or to reflect on those aspects of their lives for which they are grateful.	Increase in subjective well-being consistent with gratitude interventions used in the Chinese population.	Significant decrease in emotional exhaustion and depersonalization–aspects of Maslach's burnout inventory.	(Chan, 2009; Froh et al., 2008; Lyubomirsky et al., 2005; Seligman et al., 2005, 2006; Watkins et al., 2003)
Harty et al. (2016)	Gratitude	Count-your-blessings model	N	Grateful outlook creates more positive and optimistic appraisals of one's life, higher levels of positive affect and more prosocial motivation.	Psychological capital can play an important role in performance, satisfaction, and devotion to work, resulting in less absence from work due to illness and a reduction in cynicism, deviant behavior, stress-related symptoms, and resignations.	Significant increase in job satisfaction.	(Emmons & McCullough, 2003; Seligman et al., 2005)

References	PP Theory	Change Model	Explicit TOC (Y/N)	Implicit TOC	Expected Work Outcomes	Actual Work Outcomes	Supporting Literature
Grant and Gino (2010)	Gratitude	Gratitude expressions	N	Gratitude expressions can increase helpers' prosocial behaviors by increasing their agentic feelings of self-efficacy and their communal feelings of social worth.	Prosocial behavior will increase based on the number of voluntary calls that each fundraiser made during the week before and the week after the intervention.	Significant increase in prosocial behavior.	(McCullough et al., 2001)
Kaplan et al. (2014)	Gratitude	Sustainable happiness model	N	Volitional actions can influence well-being, that is, people can intentionally facilitate cognitions and behaviors to increase their own happiness and well-being.	Research suggests that effect sizes associated with these types of interventions are larger for the components of subjective well-being (including affect) than for other psychological outcomes such as eudaimonic well-being or depression.	Significant increase in positive affective well-being and negative affective well-being.	(Boiler et al., 2013; Lyubomirsky et al., 2005)
Winslow et al. (2017)	Gratitude	Sustainable happiness model	Y	Gratitude counteracts the "negativity bias" by shifting employees' focus from negative events to positive ones.	Job-related positive and negative affective well-being and job stress will improve.	Null findings for positive affective well-being and negative affective well-being. Null findings for job satisfaction and job stress.	(Baumeister et al., 2001; Lyubomirsky et al., 2005)

(Continued)

Table 1.2 (*Cont'd*)

References	PP Theory	Change Model	Explicit TOC (Y/N)	Implicit TOC	Expected Work Outcomes	Actual Work Outcomes	Supporting Literature
Van Wingerden et al. (2016)	Job crafting	JD-R model	Y	JD-R theory postulates that job resources gain their motivational potential when employees are confronted with highly challenging job demands.	JD-R model suggests that work engagement and performance can be fostered through interventions by targeting the most important job demands and (job and personal) resources.	Significant increase in work engagement and in-role performance.	(Bakker, 2011; Bakker & Demerouti, 2014)
Demerouti et al. (2017)	Job crafting	JD-R model	N	Through proactive behaviors like job crafting, individuals are likely to become more open to the undergoing changes and adapt more successfully to these changes.	Job crafting can improve employee well-being, job characteristics, and job performance in changing settings.	Significant increases in positive affect well-being, openness to change, and adaptive performance.	(Gordon et al., 2013; Kramer et al., 2004; Van den Heuvel et al., 2015)
Van Wingerden et al. (2017) (2)	Job crafting	JD-R model	Y	The JD-R model provides a clear description of the way demands, resources, psychological states, and outcomes are associated. Additionally, personal resources can be helpful in dealing with job demands and may contribute to improved performance.	The JD-R model suggests that work engagement and performance can be fostered through interventions that stimulate participants to optimize their job demands and (job and personal) resources.	Significant increase in work engagement and in-role performance.	(Bakker, 2011; Bakker & Demerouti, 2008, 2014; Bakker et al., 2012; Demerouti et al., 2001)

References	PP Theory	Change Model	Explicit TOC (Y/N)	Implicit TOC	Expected Work Outcomes	Actual Work Outcomes	Supporting Literature
Van den Heuvel et al. (2015)	Job crafting	JD-R model	N	The content of the job-crafting intervention is based on the role of job crafting in the JD-R model.	Personal resources help to deal with adversity, goal attainment, and adaptivity.	Significant increase in leader–member exchange and a significant decrease in negative affective well-being. Null findings for positive affective well-being.	(Bakker et al., 2014; Van den Heuvel et al., 2014; Van den Heuvel et al., 2010; Xanthopoulou et al., 2009).
Van Wingerden et al., 2017 (1)	Job crafting	JD-R model	Y	The JD-R model provides a clear description of the way demands, resources, psychological states, and outcomes are associated. Additionally, personal resources can be helpful in dealing with job demands and may contribute to improved performance.	The JD-R model suggests that work engagement and performance can be fostered through interventions that stimulate participants to optimize their job demands and (job and personal) resources.	Null findings for work engagement but a significant increase in in-role performance.	(Bakker, 2011; Bakker & Demerouti, 2008, 2014; Bakker et al., 2012; Demerouti et al., 2001)

(Continued)

Table 1.2 (*Cont'd*)

References	PP Theory	Change Model	Explicit TOC (Y/N)	Implicit TOC	Expected Work Outcomes	Actual Work Outcomes	Supporting Literature
Williams et al. (2016); Williams et al. (2017)	PsyCap	IO-OI model	Y	The IO-OI model is a dual approach process model that proposes that work happiness is influenced by factors "inside" the employee and factors "outside" of the employee. Factors inside the employee are those that influence an employee's experience of work and that cannot be separated from the individual, such as attitudes, values, beliefs, emotions, and behaviors.	Seeing more virtues in others elevates organization members to behave more virtuously. The elevation proposition explains how the processes of selective exposure and confirmation bias may contribute to increasing the capacity for virtuousness at the collective level, thus building organizational social resources leading to increased work happiness.	Null findings for organizational virtuousness.	(Fisher & Boyle, 1997; Luthans Williams et al., 2015; Williams et al., 2016, unpublished; Youseff & Luthans, 2011)
Yuan (2015)	PsyCap	PsyCap microintervention model and conversation of resource theory	N	According to the conservation of resource theory, people seek to obtain, retain, and protect resources; and stress occurs when there is a net loss of resources, the threat of loss, or a	There is evidence of PsyCap among the Chinese population. PsyCap was positively associated with employer-rated performance.	Significant increase in work engagement.	(Hofboll, 2002; Luthans, 2004, 2008; Luthans et al., 2008)

References	PP Theory	Change Model	Explicit TOC (Y/N)	Implicit TOC	Expected Work Outcomes	Actual Work Outcomes	Supporting Literature
				lack of resource gain following the investment. At the same time, resource gains could buffer the negative effects of resource loss and create more opportunities for further gains. PsyCap on the other hand, just like human and social capital, can be considered as another resource that is developable and accumulative.			
Zhang et al. (2014)	PsyCap	PsyCap microintervention model	Y	The principles of PsyCap will improve organizational competitiveness.	PsyCap directly influences job engagement, job satisfaction, job performance, organizational commitment, counterproductive work behavior, and organizational citizenship behavior.	Significant increase in job performance.	(Avey et al., 2010; Luthans et al., 2006, 2007)

(Continued)

Table 1.2 (*Cont'd*)

References	PP Theory	Change Model	Explicit TOC (Y/N)	Implicit TOC	Expected Work Outcomes	Actual Work Outcomes	Supporting Literature
Williams (2010)	Strengths theory	Clifton StrengthsFinder	N	Principles can be used to govern the development of strengths, including knowing one's strengths, valuing one's strengths, assuming personal responsibility for developing the strengths, and practicing the strengths.	The intended positive effect on employee engagement is to help create a fulfilling work environment where employees (1) are not afraid of appraisals, (2) look forward to receiving performance feedback, and (3) are clear about how their strengths help them contribute to the organization.	Null findings on performance appraisals.	(Clifton & Anderson, 2006; Gable & Haidt, 2005; Kowalski, 2008; Lindbom, 2007).
Harzer and Ruch (2012)	Strengths theory	VIA framework	N	The application of individual signature strengths is related to positive experiences in life, like life satisfaction, well-being, and meaning in life as well as to positive experiences at	Individuals with a calling perceive their work as being meaningful due to helping other people or the broader society (directly or indirectly). Individuals with a calling regard their work	Significant increase in calling.	(e.g., Dik & Duffy, 2009; Elangovan et al., 2010; Harzer & Ruch, 2013, 2014; Littman-Ovadia & Steger 2010; Proctor et al., 2011; Wood

References	PP Theory	Change Model	Explicit TOC (Y/N)	Implicit TOC	Expected Work Outcomes	Actual Work Outcomes	Supporting Literature
				work, like job satisfaction, pleasure at work, meaning at work, and job performance.	to be their purpose in life rather than a means for financial rewards or career advancement.		et al, 2011; Wrzesniewski et al., 1997)
MacKie (2014)	Strengths theory	Manualization framework	N	Manualization offers the opportunity to be specific and consistent about what is meant by strengths development by requiring the coachee to rate themselves on four criteria.	Executive coaching that explicitly targets leadership development must by necessity use reliable and valid measures of leadership behavior that gather data from a wide range of stakeholders to assess the impact of the coaching intervention.	Significant increase in other-rater feedback on transformational leadership.	(Biswas-Diener et al, 2011; Bowles et al., 2007; Kauffman, 2006; Seligman, 2007)
Meyers and van Woerkom (2017)	Strengths theory	Positive-activity model	N	Engaging in positive activities, such as employing one's strengths, makes people feel good about themselves in the short term, which contributes to their longer-term well-being.	Results of prior research have supported an association between identifying and working on one's strengths and positive affect, self-efficacy as a component of PsyCap, and satisfaction with life.	Significant increase in work engagement and a significant decrease in burnout.	(Douglass & Duffy, 2015; Lyubomirsky & Layous, 2013; van Woerkom & Meyers, 2015; Wood et al., 2011; Zwart et al., 2015)

(Continued)

Table 1.2 (*Cont'd*)

References	PP Theory	Change Model	Explicit TOC (Y/N)	Implicit TOC	Expected Work Outcomes	Actual Work Outcomes	Supporting Literature
Page and Vella-Brodrick (2013)	Strengths theory	Character strengths and virtues framework	N	Individuals who use their strengths at work are more likely to be engaged and happy in their jobs. This in turn predicts other valued organizational outcomes, including business unit performance, turnover, and productivity.	Strengths can lead to increases in well-being, including lowered stress, greater self-esteem, and improved vitality and positive affect, as has been shown in longitudinal research	Null findings on work-related well-being.	(Harter et al., 2002; Wood et al., 2011)
Neumeier et al. (2017)	Well-being	PERMA	N	PERMA proposes that well-being consists of five components: positive emotions (experiencing positive emotions such as happiness, hope, and joy), engagement (being highly absorbed and interested in life activities; experiencing flow and focused	PERMA improves organizational outcomes of higher workplace well-being levels, including lower absenteeism, higher job satisfaction, less turnover intention, better organizational citizenship behavior, and higher customer satisfaction.	Significant increase in employee well-being.	(Boehm & Lyubomirsky, 2008; Bowling et al., 2010; Diener & Seligman, 2004; Layous et al., 2014b; Lyubomirsky et al., 2005a; Pelled & Xin, 1999; Wright, 2010)

References	PP Theory	Change Model	Explicit TOC (Y/N)	Implicit TOC	Expected Work Outcomes	Actual Work Outcomes	Supporting Literature
				attention, and using one's strengths), relationships (feeling valued by others and having close, mutually satisfying relationships), meaning (having a sense of purpose derived from something viewed as larger than the self), and accomplishment (striving for achievement; feelings of mastery).			
Laschinger et al. (2012)	Positive relationships	CREW program	N	CREW was designed to promote positive interpersonal working relationships among healthcare workers.	Numerous anecdotal reports of uncivil behavior in nursing settings and empirical studies indicate that high levels of supervisor and coworker incivility can have detrimental effects, such as lower productivity and organizational commitment.	Significant increases in empowerment, trust in management, and significant decreases in supervisor incivility.	(Lewis & Malecha, 2011; Osatuke et al., 2009; Smith et al., 2010)

(*Continued*)

Table 1.2 (*Cont'd*)

References	PP Theory	Change Model	Explicit TOC (Y/N)	Implicit TOC	Expected Work Outcomes	Actual Work Outcomes	Supporting Literature
Fiery (2016)	Self-compassion	JD-R-model and self-compassion	Y	The JD-R framework is considered the dominant model of work stress in the literature today and is increasingly used to explain how and why individuals may differ in their well-being in the face of similar job demands and resources.	Self-compassion is predictively and longitudinally associated with decreased stress and anxiety; it negatively predicts emotional exhaustion and positively predicts job satisfaction in preliminary cross-sectional studies among clergy and first-year pediatric residents.	Significant increase in work-related psychological flexibility.	(Bakker & Demerouti, 2014; Barnard & Curry, 2012; Neff et al., 2007; Olson et al., 2015)

Table 1.3 POPI Action Models

References	PP Theory	Intervention Exercises	Intervention Protocols	Intervention Implementers	Implementing Organization	Target Group
Chan (2010)	Gratitude	Weekly log of three good things recorded using a count-your-blessings form.	Naikan meditation-like questions through an online questionnaire	Online	Chinese University of Hong Kong	Chinese school teachers
Harty et al. (2016)	Gratitude	Observing and documenting things for which they are appreciative on five occasions.	Five-step protocol with lectures and instructional activities	Two researchers	Non-governmental organization	Physiotherapists, occupational therapists, nurses, assistant nurses, etc.
Grant and Gino (2010)	Gratitude	A director of annual giving visited the organization to thank the fundraisers for their work. She explained to the fundraisers, "I am very grateful for your hard work. We sincerely appreciate your contributions to the university."	In-person conversation	Director of annual giving	Public university	Fundraisers at a university
Kaplan et al. (2014)	Gratitude	Log at least three times per week things that they are grateful for related to their job.	Gratitude prompt	Online	Two large public universities	Staff members (e.g., administrative assistant, program coordinator, financial aid)

(Continued)

Table 1.3 (*Cont'd*)

References	PP Theory	Intervention Exercises	Intervention Protocols	Intervention Implementers	Implementing Organization	Target Group
Winslow et al. (2017)	Gratitude	At least twice weekly, participants were asked to think about and record two things in their job or work for which they are grateful (examples included supportive work relationships, sacrifices, or contributions that others have made for you, advantages or opportunities at work, and thankfulness for the opportunity to have your job in general).	Gratitude prompt	Online	Large social service agency	Agency directors
Wingerden et al. (2016)	Job crafting	First, participants acknowledged, shared, and discussed their thoughts and feelings about their careers with each other. They looked back on things they experienced at work, shared the things they like in their recent job, and discussed their future ambitions. Second, the participants practiced giving and receiving feedback, including gracefully receiving compliments. Third, they practiced refusing requests. Fourth, participants made an overview of their job tasks and their personal strengths, motivation, and possible risk factors at work.	Michigan Job Crafting Exercise	Trained facilitators	Healthcare organization	Healthcare professionals (treat hearing impairments)

References	PP Theory	Intervention Exercises	Intervention Protocols	Intervention Implementers	Implementing Organization	Target Group
Demerouti et al. (2017)	Job crafting	This intervention consisted of a one-day training that focuses on achieving individual changes at two different levels: (1) cognitions and (2) behavior (Zwaan et al., 2005). To achieve the first goal, employees are encouraged to reflect on their work situation and to recognize their work tasks and aspects of their job that they would like to change. The second goal is achieved through familiarization with the theory of job crafting and the JD-R model.	Michigan Job Crafting Exercise	Trained facilitators	Municipality	Social services municipality
Van Wingerden et al. (2017) (2)	Job crafting	The participants made an overview of their job tasks and sorted them into three categories: tasks they spent a lot of time at, tasks they had to do often, and tasks they had to do sometimes. They also designated whether they did the task individually or with others. The participants wrote the outcomes on small, medium, and large notes and stuck them on a piece of brown paper. After this, they labeled the tasks in terms of urgency and importance. Then the participants made an overview of their personal strengths, motivations, and possible risk factors in their work and matched these to their tasks. At the end of the first training session, they made a personal crafting plan.	Michigan Job Crafting Exercise	Trained facilitators	Primary schools for special education	Teachers

(Continued)

Table 1.3 (*Cont'd*)

References	PP Theory	Intervention Exercises	Intervention Protocols	Intervention Implementers	Implementing Organization	Target Group
Van den Heuvel et al. (2015)	Job crafting	The training day included background theory on the JD-R model (Bakker & Demerouti, 2007) and job crafting (Wrzesniewski & Dutton, 2001). Participants mapped their tasks, demands, and resources on a poster. Reflection on the poster helped them to identify situations at work they would like to craft. Personal crafting stories were shared and analyzed in the group. Following this, a plan with specific job-crafting goals, such as how to seek resources, how to reduce demands, and how to seek challenges, was drawn up by each participant	Michigan Job Crafting Exercise	Trained facilitators	Police district	Police officers
Van Wingerden et al. (2017) (1)	Job crafting	The job-crafting intervention consists of exercises and goal setting aimed at increasing social job resources, increasing challenging job demands, increasing structural job resources, and decreasing hindering job demands.	Michigan Job Crafting Exercise	Trained facilitators	Primary schools for special education	Teachers

References	PP Theory	Intervention Exercises	Intervention Protocols	Intervention Implementers	Implementing Organization	Target Group
Williams et al. (2017)	PsyCap	Participants are taught how to dispute negative thinking patterns with more optimistic perspectives, to foster optimism and hope; participants learn about the ABC model of cognitive-behavioral therapy (Ellis, 1957) and how to identify deeply held beliefs that may be driving unhelpful thought patterns and behaviors to build resilience; and at the end of each topic, participants identify how they could use the skill or knowledge taught in their personal and professional lives to build efficacy.	PsyCap research and materials from UPENN's Positive Psychology Center	Trained facilitators	Large independent school	Teaching and non-teaching roles
Williams et al. (2016)	PsyCap	Participants are taught how to dispute negative thinking patterns with more optimistic perspectives, to foster optimism and hope; participants learn about the ABC model of cognitive-behavioral therapy (Ellis, 1957) and how to identify deeply held beliefs that may be driving unhelpful thought patterns and behaviors to build resilience; and at the end of each topic, participants identify how they could use the skill or knowledge taught in their personal and professional lives to build efficacy.	PsyCap research and materials from UPENN's Positive Psychology Center	Trained facilitators	Large independent school	Teaching and non-teaching roles

(Continued)

Table 1.3 (Cont'd)

References	PP Theory	Intervention Exercises	Intervention Protocols	Intervention Implementers	Implementing Organization	Target Group
Yuan (2015)	PsyCap	Four training sessions each targeting an aspect of PsyCap: (1) hope using SMART goals, (2) self-efficacy using expressive writing, (3) optimism taught using the ABCDE model, and (4) resilience using risk management and resource leverage practice skills	*Happy@Work* training materials	Online	Chinese University of Hong Kong	Random employees of organizations in China
Zhang et al. (2014)	PsyCap	Then they were provided with the structured reading material and informed that they had 30 minutes to read the material independently and silently.	Structured reading materials	Trained facilitator	Beijing Normal University	Employees of five random companies in China
Williams (2010)	Strengths theory	Participants did an online strengths-identification assessment, received feedback on their respective strengths from the facilitator, and received training on how to incorporate a discussion on strengths into the organization's existing performance-appraisal interview.	Strengths-identification assessment	Online and facilitator	Non-profit community health organization	Leaders

References	PP Theory	Intervention Exercises	Intervention Protocols	Intervention Implementers	Implementing Organization	Target Group
Harzer and Ruch (2012)	Strengths theory	Participants were invited to a web-based training platform; there they learned about their four highest character strengths (derived from the rank order of the VIA-IS scales in the pretest) in step 1. In step 2 they thought about daily activities and tasks at work, and subsequently, in step 3, collected the ways they currently use their signature strengths in daily activities and tasks at work. Finally, in step 4, they developed if-then plans about how to use the four highest character strengths in new and different ways in daily activities and tasks at work.	Activities outlined by Seligman et al. (2005)	Online	University of Zurich	Diverse group of German-speaking employees in different jobs
MacKie (2014)	Strengths theory	Each coachee received six 90-min coaching sessions that followed a format articulated in their coaching manual.	Interview protocol, 360° feedback, Realise2 inventory	Executive coaches	Multinational non-profit organization	Senior managers

(Continued)

Table 1.3 (Cont'd)

References	PP Theory	Intervention Exercises	Intervention Protocols	Intervention Implementers	Implementing Organization	Target Group
Meyers and van Woerkom (2017)	Strengths theory	Before the training, participants were asked to complete a preparatory assignment (strengths identification). To this end, they received a stack of strengths cards with 24 strengths applicable in the working context and some blank cards that could be filled in individually. Participants were triggered to search for their own talents. Subsequently, participants took part in a half-day face-to-face training, which was given to 40–45 individuals at a time and was facilitated by two professional trainers.	Strengths questionnaires, feedback from third parties, and self-reflection exercises	Trained facilitator	Dutch consultancy specialized in training and development	Convenience sample of employees in implementing organization
	Strengths theory	The program consisted of six, one hour, small group-based sessions. Each session was facilitated by the first author according to a set training manuals to ensure consistency across groups. Participants focused on their strengths and learned from their best (or peak) experiences, to increase motivation and facilitative change, as	Training manual	Researcher	Large government agency	Customer service, human resources, marketing, and communications

References	PP Theory	Intervention Exercises	Intervention Protocols	Intervention Implementers	Implementing Organization	Target Group
		per appreciative inquiry (Cooperrider, 1986; Cooperrider et al., 2008). Care was taken to optimize well-being and learning outcomes for participants by facilitating sessions in a positive, supportive, and affirming environment (Joseph & Linley, 2006) and providing opportunities for autonomy and group discussion (Ryan & Deci, 2000; Vella, 2000). The facilitator recorded adherence to this approach using field notes and ratings (5-point Likert scale where 1 = poor adherence and 5 = strong adherence), which was completed at the end of each session. Notes and ratings were also taken regarding other elements of delivery, including fidelity and participant attendance. This data formed part of the process evaluation.				

(Continued)

Table 1.3 (Cont'd)

References	PP Theory	Intervention Exercises	Intervention Protocols	Intervention Implementers	Implementing Organization	Target Group
Neumeier et al. (2017)	Well-being	The PERMA framework of Seligman's well-being theory (2018) was applied to select the varied psychology interventions (PIs) for the program. For each selected PI, empirical research suggested that the exercise affects at least one of the five well-being components proposed by the PERMA framework, covering all five components in their combination in each, that could be integrated into the daily working routine in different workplace settings (i.e., self-reflective writing exercises and activities that did not require any special material or environment).	Seven PERMA-based exercises	Online	LMU Munich	Self-registered employees (online)
Laschinger et al. (2012)	Positive relationships	The CREW program organized five activities: promote respectful interactions among staff on the unit, develop skills in conflict management, team building on the unit, share successes within and outside of units, and eliminate negative communication associated with poor resources system.	CREW process manual	Trained facilitator	Hospital	Nurses

References	PP Theory	Intervention Exercises	Intervention Protocols	Intervention Implementers	Implementing Organization	Target Group
Fiery (2016)	Self-compassion	The first week's meditation, a compassionate body scan, is designed primarily to facilitate mindfulness by asking the listener to get in touch with and "just notice" bodily sensations, and is very similar to the first in a series of guided meditations implemented in the widely accepted and researched mindfulness-based stress-reduction program by Jon Kabat-Zinn (1982). The second week's meditation is grounded in the breath, again incorporating mindfulness, but also self-kindness and common humanity as listeners are asked to breathe in affection and kindness to themselves while breathing out affection and kindness toward others who are suffering. The third week's meditation is a variant of a "loving-kindness" meditation, an ancient Buddhist practice designed to increase goodwill toward the self and others.	Three guided self-compassion meditations taught in the mindful self-compassion program	Online	Animal shelter	Random sample of employees at an animal shelter

Designing Next-Generation Positive Organizational Psychology Interventions

The authors in this volume have used the science of PWO as described above, as well as the lessons from the first wave of POPI designs and evaluations to explore potential candidates for the next generation of POPIs. Each of the POPIs explored uses the best positive psychological science available (see Donaldson et al., under review) to improve the well-being and work life of diverse workers across a wide range of organizational settings.

In Chapter 2, Matt Dubin explores the concept and science of flow at work (Csikszentmihalyi, 1975, 1990). He describes the challenges modern-day employees face when trying to achieve this state of intense focus, especially in the increasingly technologically complex work environment. An in-depth overview of the FLOW POPI (Find, Learn, Own, Wrap) and associated tools to overcome these challenges is described. The FLOW POPI is designed to enhance productivity, focus, engagement, and job satisfaction in the modern workplace.

Chapter 3 focuses on the issue of engagement at work through the lenses of self-determination theory and optimal distinctiveness theory. Christopher Chen introduces JobCraft+, a POPI that integrates components of traditional job crafting and positive psychology concepts such as identification of strengths, reflected best-self activation, and relational affirmation. Using a persona approach, Chen guides the reader through the details of the JobCraft+ POPI from a participant's experience.

Chapter 4 presents an example application of POP to the traditional performance review process. Hannah Foster Grammer and Adrian Bernhardt provide an overview of the limitations inherent to the traditional performance review and related theories surrounding the proposed positive psychology-enhanced components. Through a detailed summary of the POPI, Grammer and Bernhardt weave in elements from appreciative inquiry to goal-setting theory to help strengthen the performance review process for both managers and their reviewees.

Taking a step outward to the organizational level, Chapter 5 examines the use of POP for capacity building in social impact organizations. After discussing the research underlying her POPI, such as the science of well-being (PERMA) and psychological capital, Vicki Cabrera presents a framework for positive capacity building by integrating tenets from appreciative inquiry and evaluation. Using this framework, Cabrera presents the incorporation of positive psychology topics such as mindfulness, reflected best-self activation, and appreciation into her POPI.

Chapter 6 shifts our focus to the realm of diversity, equity, and inclusion. Lawrence Chan and Adrian Reece first discuss the limitations of traditional forms of cultural competency training. Using healthcare organizations as an example, the authors build on double-loop learning theory to introduce a POPI that aims to develop the participants' cultural awareness and humility with the goal of improving positive relationships. A detailed overview of each step of the POPI and applicable tools is provided.

Continuing in the area of diversity, equity, and inclusion, Chapter 7 addresses the impacts of sexual harassment in the workplace and challenges associated with sexual harassment prevention training. By incorporating psychological concepts such as the bystander effect and positive psychological concepts such as positive deviance, Eli Kolokowsky and Sharon Hong present a novel POPI that is both more proactive and less punitive in nature compared to traditional interventions in preventing the occurrence of sexual harassment in the workplace.

Chapter 8 explores concerns regarding the well-being of civilian law enforcement employees, specifically those who take emergency calls and dispatch officers to the scene. Emily Zavala and Lawrence Chan present research showing emergency call dispatchers experiencing heightened levels of stress, burnout, and peritraumatic/posttraumatic stress disorder, while also experiencing lower levels of job satisfaction and work–life balance. Several POPIs aimed at increasing psychological capital and mindfulness among law enforcement officers are discussed, with the authors proposing similar POPIs for emergency call dispatchers.

Chapter 9 examines the principles of positive leadership and leader development programs. Using the ADDIE (Analyze, Design, and Develop, Implement, and Evaluate) training model, Jennifer Nelson presents a POPI for the further development of positive leaders. Nelson provides a detailed overview of each phase of the intervention along with their components, such as strength assessments, goal setting, building psychological capital, creating high-quality relationships, and reflective journaling.

Stewart I. Donaldson, Scott I. Donaldson, and Christopher Chen discuss the importance of the measurement and evaluation of POPIs in Chapter 10. They discuss the distinction between efficacy and effectiveness evaluations of POPIs and provide detailed examples of how measurement and evaluation procedures can be developed across all types of investigations and settings. They conclude that the future success of POPIs is highly dependent on the use of appropriate measurement and evaluation approaches.

Conclusion

This volume was designed to provide readers with a summary of developments during the past two decades that have led the emerging area of POP, and to present the state of the science related to efficacy and effectiveness of POPIs. In the chapters ahead, you will learn about new applications of the science of POP, the theory-driven and research-based design of new POPIs, and state-of-the-art measurement and evaluation approaches critical to the success of future PPIs designed for the contemporary global workplace. We wish you many insights related to your own work, well-being, and meaningful life contributions as you explore the future of positive psychology applied to work in the forthcoming chapters.

References

*References marked with a single asterisk indicate interventions included in Table 1.1.
**References marked with a double asterisk indicate interventions included in Table 1.2.
***Table 1.2 supporting literature available upon request

Bakker, A. B., & Demerouti, E. (2007). The job demands resources model: State of the art. *Journal of Managerial Psychology*, *22*(3), 309–328.

Bernstein, S. (2003). Positive organizational scholarship: Meet the movement: An interview with Kim Cameron, Jane Dutton, and Robert Quinn. *Journal of Management Inquiry*, *12*(3), 266–271.

Boiler, L., Haverman, M., Westerhof, J. G., Riper, H., Smit, F., & Bohlmeijer, E. (2013). Positive psychology interventions: A meta-analysis of randomized controlled studies. *BMC Public Health*, *13*, 119–119.

*Brown, B., Gude, W. T., Blakeman, T., Veer, S. N., Ivers, N., Francis, J. J., … Daker-White, G. (2019). Clinical performance feedback intervention theory (cp-fit): A new theory for designing, implementing, and evaluating feedback in health care based on a systematic review and meta-synthesis of qualitative research. *Implementation Science*, *14*(1), 1–25.

Cameron, K., Dutton, J., & Quinn, R. (2003). *Positive organizational scholarship: Foundations of a new discipline* (1st ed.). San Francisco, CA: Berrett-Koehler.

*Carrillo, A., Rubio-Aparicio, M., Molinari, G., Enrique, Á., Sánchez-Meca, J., & Baños, R. M. (2019). Effects of the best possible self intervention: A systematic review and meta-analysis. *PLoS One*, *14*(9), e0222386.

*Chakhssi, F., Kraiss, J. T., Sommers-Spijkerman, M., & Bohlmeijjer, E. T. (2018). The effect of positive psychology interventions on well-being in clinical populations: A systematic review and meta-analysis. *BMC Psychiatry*, *18*(1), 211.

**Chan, D. (2010). Gratitude, gratitude intervention and subjective well-being among Chinese school teachers in Hong Kong. *Educational Psychology*, *30*(2), 139–153.

Chen, H. T. (2005). *Practical program evaluation: Assessing and improving planning, implementation, and effectiveness*. Thousand Oaks, CA: Sage.

Cooperrider, D. L. (1986). *Appreciative inquiry: Toward a methodology for understanding and enhancing organizational innovation*. (Doctoral dissertation). Case Western Reserve University.

Cooperrider, D., Whitney, D. D., Stavros, J. M., & Stavros, J. (2008). *The appreciative inquiry handbook: For leaders of change*. Berrett-Koehler Publishers.

Csikszentmihalyi, M. (1975). *Beyond boredom and anxiety*. Washington, DC: Jossey-Bass Publishers.

Csikszentmihalyi, M. (1990). Literacy and intrinsic motivation. *Daedalus*, *199*(2), 115–140.

*Curry, O. S., Rowland, L. A., Van Lissa, C. J., Zlotowitz, S., McAlaney, J., & Whitehouse, H. (2018). Happy to help? A systematic review and meta-analysis of the effects of performing acts of kindness on the well-being of the actor. *Journal of Experimental Social Psychology*, *76*, 320–329.

*Davis, D. E., Choe, E., Meyers, J., Wade, N., Varjas, K., Gifford, A., ... Worthington, E. L., Jr. (2016). Thankful for the little things: A meta-analysis of gratitude interventions. *Journal of Counseling Psychology, 63*(1), 20–31.

**Demerouti, E., Xanthopoulou, D., Petrou, P., & Karagkounis, C. (2017). Does job crafting assist dealing with organizational changes due to austerity measures? Two studies among greek employees. *European Journal of Work and Organizational Psychology, 26*(4), 574–589.

*Dhillon, A., Sparkes, E., & Duarte, R. V. (2017). Mindfulness-based interventions during pregnancy: A systematic review and meta-analysis. *Mindfulness, 8*(6), 1421–1437.

*Dickens, L. R. (2017). Using gratitude to promote positive change: A series of meta-analyses investigating the effectiveness of gratitude interventions. *Basic and Applied Social Psychology, 39*(4), 193–208.

Donaldson, S. I. (2007). *Program theory-driven evaluation science: Strategies and applications.* New York, NY: Psychology Press.

Donaldson, S. I. (in press). *Theory-driven evaluation science: Culturally responsive and strengths focused applications.* New York NY: Psychology Press.

Donaldson, S. I., Cabrera, V., & Gaffaney, J. (under review). *Following the positive psychology intervention science to generate well-being in a global pandemic.* Manuscript submitted for publication.

Donaldson, S. I., Csikszentmihalyi, M., & Nakamura, J. (2020a). *Positive psychological science: Improving everyday life, health, work, education, and societies across the globe* (2nd ed., Ser. Series in Applied Psychology). Abingdon, OX: Routledge, Taylor & Francis Group.

Donaldson, S. I., Dollwet, M., & Rao, M. A. (2015). Happiness, excellence, and optimal human functioning revisited: Examining the peer-reviewed literature linked to positive psychology. *Journal of Positive Psychology, 10*(3), 185–195.

Donaldson, S. I., Donaldson, S. I., & Ko, I. (2020b). Advances in the science of positive work and organizations. In S. I. Donaldson, M. Csikszentmihalyi, & J. Nakamura (Eds.), *Positive psychological science: Improving everyday life, health and well-being, work, education, and society* (2nd ed.). New York, NY: Routledge Academic.

Donaldson, S. I., Heshmati, S., & Donaldson, S. I. (in press). A global perspective on well-being and positive psychological science: Systematic reviews and meta-analyses. In A. Kostic (Ed.), *Positive psychology: An international perspective.* London: Wiley.

Donaldson, S. I., & Ko, I. (2010). Positive organizational psychology, behavior, and scholarship: A review of the emerging literature and evidence base. *Journal of Positive Psychology, 5*, pp. 177–191.

*Donaldson, S. I., Lee, J. Y., & Donaldson, S. I. (2019a). Evaluating positive psychology interventions at work: A systematic review and meta-analysis. *International Journal of Applied Positive Psychology, 4*, 113–134.

Donaldson, S. I., Lee, J. Y., & Donaldson, S. I. (2019b). The effectiveness of positive psychology interventions in the workplace: A theory-driven evaluation approach. In V. Z. Llewellyn & S. Rothmann (Eds.), *Theoretical approaches to multi-cultural positive psychology interventions* (pp. 115–159). Cham, Switzerland: Springer International.

Ellis, A. (1957). Rational psychotherapy and individual psychology. *Journal of Individual Psychology, 13*(1), 38–44.

**Fiery, F. M. (2016). *Exploring the impacts of self-compassion and psychological flexibility on burnout and engagement among animal shelter staff: A moderator analysis of the jobs-demands resources framework and a randomized controlled field trial of a brief self-guided online intervention* (Doctoral dissertation). The University of North Carolina at Charlotte. ProQuest Dissertations Publishing.

**Grant, M. A., & Gino, F. (2010). A little thanks goes a long way: Explaining why gratitude expressions motivate prosocial behavior. *Journal of Personality and Social Psychology, 98*(6), 946–955.

**Harzer, C., & Ruch, W. (2012). When the job is a calling: The role of applying one's signature strengths at work. *Journal of Positive Psychology, 7*(5), 362–371.

Harty, B., Gustafsson, J., Björkdahl, A., & Möller, A. (2016). Group intervention: A way to improve working teams' positive psychological capital. *Work, 53*(2), 387–398.

*Heekerens, J. B., & Eid, M. (2020). Inducing positive affect and positive future expectations using the best-possible-self intervention: A systematic review and meta-analysis. *The Journal of Positive Psychology*. doi:https://doi.org/10.1080/174 39760.2020.1716052

*Hendriks, T., Hassankhan, A., Schotanus-Dijkstra, M., Bohlmeijer, E., & De, J. (2020). The efficacy of multi-component positive psychology interventions: A systematic review and meta-analysis of randomized controlled trials. *Journal of Happiness Studies, 21*(1), 357–390.

*Hendriks, T., Schotanus-Dijkstra, M., Hassankhan, A., Graafsma, T., Bohlmeijer, E., & de Jong, J. (2018). The efficacy of positive psychology interventions from non-western countries: A systematic review and meta-analysis. *International Journal of Wellbeing, 8*(1), 71–98.

*Hendriks, T., Warren, M. A., Schotanus-Dijkstra, M., Hassankhan, A., Graafsma, T., Bohlmeijer, E., & de Jong, J. (2019). How weird are positive psychology interventions? A bibliometric analysis of randomized controlled trials on the science of well-being. *The Journal of Positive Psychology: Dedicated to Furthering Research and Promoting Good Practice, 14*(4), 489–501.

*Howell, A. J., & Passmore, H.-A. (2019). Acceptance and commitment training (act) as a positive psychological intervention: A systematic review and initial meta-analysis regarding act's role in well-being promotion among university students. *Journal of Happiness Studies, 20*(6), 1995–2010.

James, W. (1908). *The meaning of truth*. New York, NY: Longman Green and Company.

Joseph, S., & Linley, P. A. (2006). *Positive therapy: A meta-theory for positive psychological practice*. Routledge.

Kabat-Zinn, J. (1982). An outpatient program in behavioral medicine for chronic pain patients based on the practice of mindfulness meditation: Theoretical considerations and preliminary results. *General Hospital Psychiatry, 4*(1), 33–47.

**Kaplan, S., Bradley-Geist, J., Ahmad, A., Anderson, A., Hargrove, A., & Lindsey, A. (2014). A test of two positive psychology interventions to increase employee well-being. *Journal of Business and Psychology, 29*(3), 367–380.

Kim, H., Doiron, K., Warren, M. A., & Donaldson, S. I. (2018). The international landscape of positive psychology research: A systematic review. *International Journal of Wellbeing, 8*(1), 50–70.

*Koydemir, S., Sökmez, A. B., & Schütz, A. (2020). A meta-analysis of the effectiveness of randomized controlled positive psychological interventions on subjective and psychological well-being. *Applied Research in Quality of Life*, 1–41. doi:https://doi.org/10.1007/s11482-019-09788-z

**Laschinger, H. K. S., Heather, K., Leiter, P. M., Day, A., Gilin-Oore, D., & Mackinnon, P. S. (2012). Building empowering work environments that foster civility and organizational trust: Testing an intervention. *Nursing Research, 61*(5), 316–325.

*Lomas, T., Medina, J. C., Ivtzan, I., Rupprecht, S., & Eiroa-Orosa, F. J. (2019). Mindfulness-based interventions in the workplace: An inclusive systematic review and meta-analysis of their impact upon wellbeing. *The Journal of Positive Psychology, 14*(5), 625–640.

Luthans, F. (2002). Positive organizational behavior: Developing and managing psychological strengths. *Academy of Management Executive, 16*, 57–72.

**MacKie, D. (2014). The effectiveness of strength-based executive coaching in enhancing full range leadership development: A controlled study. *Consulting Psychology Journal: Practice and Research, 66*(2), 118–137.

Maslow, A. H. (1954). *Motivation and personality*. New York, NY: Harper.

Mazzucchelli, T. G., Kane, R. T., & Rees, C. S. (2010). Behavioral activation interventions for well-being: A meta-analysis. *The Journal of Positive Psychology, 5*(2), 105–121.

Meyers, M., & van Woerkom, M. (2017). Effects of a strengths intervention on general and work-related well-being: The mediating role of positive affect. *Journal of Happiness Studies: An Interdisciplinary Forum on Subjective Well-Being, 18*(3), 671–689.

**Neumeier, L., Brook, L., Ditchburn, G., & Sckopke, P. (2017). Delivering your daily dose of well-being to the workplace: A randomized controlled trial of an online well-being programme for employees. *European Journal of Work and Organizational Psychology, 26*(4), 555–573.

**Page, K., & Vella-Brodrick, D. (2013). The working for wellness program: RCT of an employee well-being intervention. *Journal of Happiness Studies: An Interdisciplinary Forum on Subjective Well-Being, 14*(3), 1007–1031.

Roberts, L. M., Spreitzer, G., Dutton, J., Quinn, R., Heaphy, E., & Barker, B. (2005). How to play to your strengths. *Harvard Business Review, 83*(1), 74–80.

Ryan, R. M., & Deci, E. L. (2000). Intrinsic and extrinsic motivations: Classic definitions and new directions. *Contemporary Educational Psychology, 25*(1), 54–67.

Seligman, M. E. P., & Csikszentmihalyi, M. (2000). Positive psychology: An introduction. *American Psychologist, 55*, 5–14.

Seligman, M. E. P., Steen, T. A., Park, N., & Peterson, C. (2005). Positive psychology progress: Empirical validation of interventions. *American Psychologist, 60*(5), 410–421.

Sin, N., & Lyubomirsky, S. (2009). Enhancing well-being and alleviating depressive symptoms with positive psychology interventions: A practice-friendly meta-analysis. *Journal of Clinical Psychology, 65*(5), 467–487.

*Slemp, G. R., Jach, H. K., Chia, A., Loton, D. J., & Kern, M. L. (2019). Contemplative interventions and employee distress: A meta-analysis. *Stress and Health: Journal of the International Society for the Investigation of Stress, 35*(3), 227–255.

Theeboom, T., Beersma, B., & van Vianen, A. E. M. (2014). Does coaching work? A meta-analysis on the effects of coaching on individual level outcomes in an organizational context. *The Journal of Positive Psychology, 9*(1), 1–18.

**Van den Heuvel, M., Demerouti, E., & Peeters, M. (2015). The job crafting intervention: Effects on job resources, self-efficacy, and affective well-being. *Journal of Occupational and Organizational Psychology, 88*(2), 1–22.

**Van Wingerden, J., Bakker, A., & Derks, D. (2017). The longitudinal impact of a job crafting intervention. *European Journal of Work and Organizational Psychology, 26*(1), 107–119.

**Van Wingerden, J., Derks, D., & Bakker, B. A. (2017). The impact of personal resources and job crafting interventions on work engagement and performance. *Human Resource Management, 56*(1), 51–67.

Vella, J. (2000). A spirited epistemology: Honoring the adult learner as subject. *New Directions for Adult and Continuing Education, 2000*(85), 7–16.

Warren, M. A., Donaldson, S. I., & Luthans, F. (2017). Taking positive psychology to the workplace: Positive organizational psychology, positive organizational behavior, and positive organizational scholarship. In M. A. Warren & S. I. Donaldson (Eds.), *Scientific advances in positive psychology (pp. 195–227)*. Westport, CT: Praeger.

*Weiss, L. A., Westerhof, G. J., & Bohlmeijer, E. T. (2016). Can we increase psychological well-being? The effects of interventions on psychological well-being: A meta-analysis of randomized controlled trials. *PLoS One, 11*(6), e0158092.

*White, C. A., Uttl, B., & Holder, M. D. (2019). Meta-analyses of positive psychology interventions: The effects are much smaller than previously reported. *PLoS One, 14*(5), e0216588.

Williams, K. B. (2010). *The influence of a strengths-based intervention on the performance-appraisal process* (Doctoral dissertation).

**Williams, P., Kern, M., & Waters, L. (2016). Exploring selective exposure and confirmation bias as processes underlying employee work happiness: An intervention study. *Frontiers in Psychology, 7*(878), 1–13.

**Williams, P., Kern, M., & Waters, L. (2017). The role and reprocessing of attitudes in fostering employee work happiness: An intervention study. *Frontiers in Psychology, 8*(28), 1–12.

**Wingerden, J., Bakker, A., & Derks, D. (2016). A test of a job demands-resources intervention. *Journal of Managerial Psychology, 31*(3), 686–701.

**Winslow, C. J., Kaplan, S. A., Bradley-Geist, J. C., Lindsey, A. P., Ahmad, A. S., & Hargrove, A. K. (2017). An examination of two positive organizational interventions: For whom do these interventions work? *Journal of Occupational Health Psychology, 22*(2), 129–137.

Wrzesniewski, A., & Dutton, J. E. (2001). Crafting a job: Revisioning employees as active crafters of their work. *Academy of Management Review, 26*(2), 179–201.

**Yuan, Q. (2015). *Evaluating the effectiveness of a psychological capital development program on mental health, engagement, and work performance* (Doctoral dissertation). The Chinese University of Hong Kong. ProQuest Dissertations Publishing.

**Zhang, X., Li, Y., Ma, S., Hu, J., & Jiang, L. (2014). A structured reading materials-based intervention program to develop the psychological capital of chinese employees. *Social Behavior and Personality: An International Journal, 42*(3), 503–515.

Zwaan, J., Van Burik, M., & Janssen, T. (2005). *Draaiboek persoonlijke effectiviteit; assertiviteitstraining voor mensen in organisaties.* (Unpublished manuscript). Schouten and Nelissen, Zaltbommel.

2

Flow

Sustaining Focus at Work in the Age of Distraction

Matthew Dubin

The ability to focus attention on a single endeavor at work is becoming a more elusive experience as individuals grapple with the effects of a digitally-driven society. Digital devices have become a ubiquitous feature of the modern workplace, with 96% of US workers having access to a computer, smartphone, or tablet (Harter, Agrawal, & Sorenson, 2014). Having consistent access to smartphones has also blurred the traditional separation between work and one's personal life, since individuals are now able to perform work-related tasks from any location at any time (Kossek & Lautsch, 2012; Kreiner et al., 2009; Major & Germano, 2006, as cited in Derks et al., 2015).

This rise of digital technology has had a profound impact on people's ability to focus their attention. The human attention span has decreased to eight seconds according to a study by Microsoft Corporation of 2,000 Canadians over 18 years of age (as cited in Borreli, 2015), which is four seconds less than the 12-second attention span found in the year 2000. Additionally, open-office workspaces, where individuals work with no physical barriers from their coworkers and there are very few closed-off offices, have increased the possibility of distraction throughout the day, where individuals can easily interrupt each other's focus due to enhanced accessibility.

The inability to focus one's attention is in direct contrast to the experience of flow; the subjective optimal experience of being completely immersed in an activity (Csikszentmihalyi, 1975, 1990). With the average US working adult now working 47 hours per week (according to Gallup, as cited in Saad, 2014), there is ample opportunity for individuals to experience flow at work. However, Gallup reports that only 32.5% of Americans are engaged at work, which they define as those "who are involved in, enthusiastic about and committed to their work and workplace" (Gallup, 2017). Although flow and Gallup's operationalization of employee engagement are not the same, they share the overlapping element of involvement with work, and Csikszentmihalyi (2003) has suggested that experiencing flow on the job is an essential element of employee engagement. This intervention is designed to provide individuals and teams with the knowledge, resources, strategies, and support to experience flow consistently both individually and collectively, and ultimately lead more fulfilling, focused, and satisfying work lives. Through a combination of discovery, assessments, workshops, and coaching, this intervention will provide participants with a comprehensive

Positive Organizational Psychology Interventions: Design and Evaluation, First Edition.
Stewart I. Donaldson and Christopher Chen.
© 2021 John Wiley & Sons Ltd. Published 2021 by John Wiley & Sons Ltd.

framework to experience flow more consistently as an individual and create a more flow-conducive culture for their team members.

The Theory of Flow

Csikszentmihalyi (1975) first thought of the preliminary flow concept when observing artists (mainly painters) work. He noticed that when these artists were absorbed in their work, they no longer seemed to require survival necessities such as sleep or food; they were completely and totally engrossed in the task at hand. Interestingly, Csikszentmihalyi noticed that when the painting was complete, the project no longer seemed to be of interest and they merely moved on to the next project. In subsequent research, Csikszentmihalyi observed individuals engaged in tasks in other domains, such as dancers, rock climbers, and surgeons. He noticed that, regardless of domain, they all seemed to have similar optimal experiences of complete involvement in what they were doing. They all seemed to engage in the activity for its own sake, what Csikszentmihalyi calls an autotelic experience (auto means self; telos means goal; Csikszentmihalyi, 1990). Csikszentmihalyi (1990) conceptualized flow to be an authentically enjoyable experience; one that increases an individual's complexity and strengthens the self, transcending activities solely focused on providing pleasure or done only for financial benefit. Any activity, such as work, listening to music, having a conversation with someone, or thinking, can provide a flow experience if it contains a certain set of parameters and characteristics, which are as follows.

The Balance Between Perceived Skill and Challenge

When one is in flow, her skills matches the opportunity for action (Csikszentmihalyi, 1990; Moneta & Csikszentmihalyi, 1996; Nakamura & Csikszentmihalyi, 2002; Nakamura & Dubin, 2015). If one's level of skill exceeds the opportunity for action, boredom will be the likely result. However, if the challenge exceeds one's capacity for action, this will likely lead to anxiety. For example, if an individual who has no experience in public speaking is asked to give a presentation in front of the entire company without rehearsing beforehand, this will likely be an intensely anxiety-provoking experience.

When an individual engages in a flow task, her skills will inevitably increase, which will lead them to seek increasingly complex challenges to maintain the flow experience in that given activity. For example, if public speaking became a flow activity for the individual in the example above, they may pursue more complex challenges such as speaking in front of larger audiences or speaking on a more diverse set of topics without the aid of PowerPoint slides.

Clear Goals and Immediate Feedback

In flow, there is most likely a well-defined goal accompanied by immediate feedback, which informs individuals of their progress in pursuit of that goal (Csikszentmihalyi, 1990; Nakamura & Csikszentmihalyi, 2002; Nakamura &

Dubin, 2015). When feedback is instant, flow is more likely to occur since they are more likely to stay engaged in the task without external thoughts flooding the mind (Linsner, 2009).

The nature of goals and feedback can vary widely. While some short-term goals take days or weeks, goals can often take months or years to accomplish. This does not necessarily inhibit the flow experience. On the contrary, a clear long-term goal can provide an avenue for one to experience flow on an enduring basis.

Concentration

A hallmark of flow is complete concentration in the flow activity; intense absorption and involvement in the task at hand. In Csikszentmihalyi's (1975, 1990) research he discovered that when individuals experience flow, they forget about potential negative thoughts and distractions and are able to invest all of their psychic attention in the flow task. This sense of intense concentration ideally eliminates the psychic entropy one often feels when unable to devote their attention to external stimuli (Csikszentmihalyi & Csikszentmihalyi, 1988). While concentrating fully on any external stimuli can temporarily reduce psychic entropy, what differentiates the flow task from other activities is that it builds complexity and ultimately strengthens and completes the self (Csikszentmihalyi, 1990).

The Merging of Action and Awareness

When one is in flow, there is a merging of action and awareness. All of one's attention is given to the activity, and actions feel automatic. Even when the task requires considerable mental or physical effort, during flow it feels effortless, as if the individual is part of the activity (Csikszentmihalyi, 1990; Nakamura & Csikszentmihalyi, 2002).

Loss of Self-Consciousness

With deep concentration and the merging of action and awareness, one's attention is fully invested in the task. As a result of this, one no longer gives attention to the self, and instead individuals often report feeling unified with the environment (Csikszentmihalyi, 1990). A considerable amount of psychic energy is given to the self in daily life, whether one is protecting the self from social and environmental threats or worrying about how one is coming across to other people. When the other flow parameters are met and one can completely invest attention in the task, any threat, worry, or concern comes directly from the activity itself, for that is all that matters in the moment (Csikszentmihalyi, 1985).

Sense of Control

When in the midst of a flow experience, individuals feel a sense of control over their actions and can instinctively react to what comes next during the task (Nakamura & Csikszentmihalyi, 2002). This sense of control is not necessarily the same as actual control. Nevertheless, the individual perceives that they are in control throughout the flow activity and does not fear losing control like individuals often do in daily life (Csikszentmihalyi, 1990). Although control is perceived, one's sense of actual control over a flow activity grows considerably as they builds their skills.

Losing Track of Time

In most cases, according to Csikszentmihalyi's (1975, 1990) research, time seems to move much faster than usual, with hours passing in what feels like minutes. The activity itself has its own rhythm and mechanisms to convey progress that usually does not conform to a specific time sequence. For example, when a doctor experiences flow while performing a surgery, they have a clear goal, mechanisms for feedback, and feel total involvement in the task. With these flow parameters in place, it is likely she will lose track of time during the surgery and will know when the surgery is complete without the assistance of a clock.

Intrinsic Motivation

While the above components are key aspects of the flow experience, a vital condition for individuals to experience flow in any capacity is that they are intrinsically motivated to pursue the flow activity (Abuhamdeh & Csikszentmihalyi, 2009; Csikszentmihalyi, 1975, 1990; Csikszentmihalyi & Rathunde, 1993; Linsner, 2009; Nakamura & Csikszentmihalyi, 2002). Intrinsic motivation is conceptualized by Deci and Ryan (1985) as taking part in something because one inherently enjoys it or finds it interesting. In contrast, extrinsic motivation refers to taking part in something because of the external reward or outcome that it provides. In the context of flow, one pursues the flow task for its own sake because of the optimal experience it provides; simply being able to take part in the task is the reward.

In other words, flow is an autotelic experience that is worth pursuing even without the presence of an external reward (Csikszentmihalyi, 1990; Nakamura & Dubin, 2015). Some activities that are pursued for what Csikszentmihalyi (1990) calls "exotelic" (i.e., extrinsically rewarding) reasons eventually become autotelic. For example, an individual may initially pursue a career as a lawyer because of the potential salary they could make, and eventually may find they love learning about and practicing law, thus turning aspects of their job into a flow experience. Csikszentmihalyi (1975, 1997, 2002) has indicated that one who has an autotelic personality will be more likely to experience flow on a consistent basis than others due to the ability and desire to pursue tasks for their own sake (Nakamura & Csikszentmihalyi, 2002).

Flow at Work

Although flow can occur in any domain, it can be argued that its potential and prevalence are greater at work than in almost any other context. However, many Americans seek to avoid work when given the choice of how to spend their time. Csikszentmihalyi (1990) noted that the most pursued leisure activity in the United States at that time (television watching) rarely produces flow, and those on the job are about four times as likely to experience flow compared with individuals watching television. Csikszentmihalyi and LeFevre (1989) found that individuals were far more likely to experience flow while working (54%) than during leisure activities (18%). Csikszentmihalyi (1990) calls this the paradox of work: While most individuals would prefer to spend their time in leisure and avoid work, they report having some of their most positive experiences at work, while often reporting low moods during their leisure time (Csikszentmihalyi & LeFevre, 1989). One explanation is that flow at work could be accompanied by stress that would lead one to prefer leisure pursuits (Nakamura & Csikszentmihalyi, 2009; Rheinberg et al., 2007).

However, a deeper examination into the nature of work suggests why flow seems to occur more often in this domain. Many jobs inherently possess flow's parameters and characteristics, such as the opportunities to use one's skills, the presence of challenge, immediate feedback, clear goals, and the potential for total concentration (Csikszentmihalyi, 1990, 2003; Fullagar & Kelloway, 2009, 2013). The more complex and intrinsically motivating a job is, the more likely flow becomes and the more likely an individual will want to further pursue their work (Crooke, 2008; Csikszentmihalyi, 1997; Csikszentmihalyi & LeFevre, 1989; Harackiewicz et al., 1998). Csikszentmihalyi (1990, 2003) suggested that business leaders should design and structure jobs to provide employees with ample opportunity to experience flow, and employees should seek ways to develop autotelic personalities to pursue challenges, develop skills, and set goals that will enable them to experience flow on a more regular basis.

Antecedents and Outcomes of Flow at Work

While flow at work is similar to flow in any context, Bakker (2005) characterized flow in the workplace as being a *short-term* peak experience where one is completely involved in what they are doing, accompanied by flow's other usual components such as time distortion and the merging of action and awareness. In his study of flow's antecedents at work, Bakker (2005) found that the job characteristics of autonomy, social support, and feedback predict flow's occurrence at work. Resources, both at the personal (i.e., self-efficacy) and organizational (i.e., social support, clear goals, innovation) level, have been found to increase flow's prevalence at work (Fullagar & Kelloway, 2013; Salanova et al., 2006) and flow on the job has been found to decrease work exhaustion (Zito et al., 2015).

Other job characteristics suggested to increase flow at work include skill variety and the significance of the work task (Demerouti, 2006; Donaldson & Ko, 2010; Fullagar & Kelloway, 2009). Specific job activities that have been found to predict flow include problem solving, planning, and evaluation (Nielsen & Cleal, 2010). A study that examined 10 working days of participants via a diary found that day-specific flow experiences were found to mediate the relationship between affective commitment and a worker's day-specific well-being, as well as help employees more effectively deal with demands on self-control (Rivkin et al., 2016). Furthermore, flow at work has been found to be associated with employee creativity and to act as a mediator between authentic leadership and employee creativity (Zubair & Kamal, 2015). For individuals who are high in conscientiousness, frequent flow experiences have been found to improve both in-role and extra-role performance (Demerouti, 2006), and flow is associated with motivation, positive mood, and enjoyment in the context of work (Donaldson & Ko, 2010; Fullagar & Kelloway, 2009; Martin & Jackson, 2008).

This author's dissertation researched the flow experiences of individuals working in the knowledge economy and found the flow enablers, inhibitors, and strategies listed in Table 2.1.

By utilizing general flow research and the findings of Dubin's (2018) dissertation research, the current intervention was designed.

Table 2.1 Summary of Flow Enablers, Inhibitors, and Strategies from Dubin's (2018) Dissertation.

1) Factors Important for Enabling Flow		2) Factors Important for Inhibiting Flow	
Headphones and noise levels	• Wearing headphones/earbuds • Noise level distractions	People interruptions	• In-person interruptions • Technology interruptions
Having a clear direction	• Know what to do and where to go	Urgent tasks/ priorities	• Boss priorities • Tasks
Positive leadership	• Setting example • Providing autonomy • Providing challenge	Suboptimal personal state	• Psychological • Physical
Optimal personal state	• Physical • Pressure of deadline • Psychological	Nature of projects	• Lack of clarity • Lack of control
Impact of coworkers	• Contagious flow • Collaborating with others		

3) Strategies to Facilitate Flow at Work	
Organizing time and tasks	• To-do list • Timing tasks • Block out calendar for "flow" time • Prioritizing tasks
Managing technology use	• Put phone away • Managing notifications • Focus apps • Printing • Delete apps
Mental health and wellness	• Take a break • Food/beverage • Exercise • Meditation • Yoga • Sleep • Balance

(Continued)

Table 2.1 *(Cont'd)*

Change location	• Work away from office • Separate room in office
Leadership	• Respect • Feedback • Autonomy
Wearing headphones/ listening to music	• Headphones/music at work
Being prepared and having a direction	• Satisfaction of being productive • Meetings • Establishing a clear direction

Positive Organization Development Intervention

An intervention to enhance flow in organizations must impact all aspects of the employee experience. Therefore, it is essential to work with both team leaders to enable them to create a flow-conducive culture and individual contributors to support their ability to implement flow-enabling strategies into their own daily routines at work. Success of this intervention, or any organization development intervention, depends on the full involvement and buy-in from all stakeholders.

The objectives of this intervention are:

- To educate team members about the nature of psychological concept of "flow" or optimal experience.
- To provide team members with the knowledge, skills, tools, and strategies to alter both their own and their direct reports' (if applicable) work to experience flow more consistently.
- To increase job satisfaction, work engagement, and performance through increasing flow at work.

The intervention is titled the FLOW intervention (Figure 2.1), with FLOW serving as an acronym for Find, Learn, Own, and Wrap to describe its four phases. In total the intervention is expected to last six months (one month for the FIND phase, two months for the LEARN phase, two months for the OWN phase, and one month for the WRAP phase).

Figure 2.1 The FLOW Intervention Process.

Phase 1: FIND

The first segment of the intervention is designed to find out how consistently team members currently experience flow via a quantitative survey and qualitative interviews. The survey is designed to assess their level of flow at work, as well as their level of job satisfaction and work engagement.

Interview Guide

The interview guide is based on Dubin's (2018) dissertation interviews. Those interviews were originally based on Jackson's and Jackson and Robert's interviews with elite athletes (Jackson, 1992a, 1992b; Jackson & Roberts, 1992), as well as Allison and Duncan's interviews with women in work and non-work settings (Allison & Duncan, 1988). It was used as part of the author's dissertation as well (Dubin, 2018). In Jackson and Roberts' interviews, athletes were asked about their flow experiences within their specific domain, as well as the enablers, inhibitors, and disruptors of flow. In Allison and Duncan's study, they conducted semi-structured interviews exploring the nature of the flow experience among professional women. The interview guide was also inspired by Csikszentmihalyi's original qualitative flow studies (Csikszentmihalyi, 1975) that asked individuals to describe their flow experiences.

General Flow Experiences at Work
Adapted from language from Csikszentmihalyi's (1975, 1988) original flow studies, individuals will be asked to think of a time at work where they experienced flow.

Projects
Team members will then be asked if there are specific types of projects where they experience flow more than others, designed to ascertain whether certain projects are more flow conducive than others.

Enablers, Inhibitors, and Disruptors (General)
As previously done with elite athletes (Jackson, 1992a, 1992b), team members will be asked what aspects of their jobs enable, inhibit, and disrupt their flow experiences at work.

Flow Strategies
Finally, individuals will be asked what strategies they have implemented to increase focus and absorption in their work.

Quantitative Measures

Flow
To measure flow, the survey will use the Work-Related Flow Inventory (Bakker, 2005), which measures flow based on Bakker's (2005) three aspects of flow at work: short-term peak experiences marked by absorption, intrinsic motivation, and enjoyment. This inventory was deemed appropriate for this intervention, since participants are being asked about flow in the context of work, and was found to have strong factorial validity, construct validity, and reliability (in seven samples, coefficients fell between 0.75 and 0.86 for absorption, 0.88 and 0.96 for

enjoyment, and 0.63 and 0.82 for intrinsic motivation). Items are asked on a 7-point Likert scale ranging from 1 (never) to 7 (always).

Job Satisfaction

The Work–Life Satisfaction Scale (Grawitch et al., 2013) was adapted from Diener et al. (1985). Satisfaction With Life Scale will be utilized to measure job satisfaction in the pre-/post-test of the intervention. The Work–Life Satisfaction Scale contains five items that were measured on a 7-point Likert scale ranging from 1 (strongly disagree) to 7 (strongly agree). A sample item includes: "So far I have gotten the important things I want in my work life." These items have a Cronbach's alpha of 0.86 (Grawitch et al., 2013).

Work Engagement

The Utrecht Work Engagement Scale (UWES, short version; Schaufeli et al., 2002) will be used in the intervention as well. The UWES contains nine items on a 6-point Likert scale ranging from 1 (a few times a year or less) to 6 (every day). The modified version of the measure that will be used in this intervention has a median Cronbach's alpha of 0.92 across 10 countries and robust factorial validity (Schaufeli et al., 2006). The following is a sample item: "At my work, I feel bursting with energy."

Phase 2: LEARN

During the LEARN phase of the intervention, the team will be educated about the flow concept, as well as related topics that directly impact employee flow experience. Six 90-minute workshops will be conducted.

Week 1: Individual Flow

The team will be educated about the background, conditions, and characteristics of the flow concept both in general and specifically within the work setting. The workshop will be interactive and be a combination of lecture, discussion of strategies to enter flow, and practice.

Week 2: Group Flow

The team will learn about the characteristics of group flow, how it differs from individual flow, and discuss how to experience collective flow in team projects and meetings.

Week 3: Emotional Intelligence

Emotional intelligence "is the ability to perceive emotions, to access and generate emotions so as to assist thought, to understand emotions and emotional knowledge, and to reflectively regulate emotions so as to promote emotional and intellectual growth" (Mayer & Salovey, 1997). The team will learn about the facets of emotional intelligence and strategies to be more emotionally intelligent at work. The purpose of this workshop is for individuals to better understand how to regulate their own emotions, as well as the emotions of others, to be in the right frame of mind to experience flow consistently at work. If individuals can be more aware of what makes themselves and their coworkers tick (e.g., the type of environment that enables flow for each person), and alleviate frustrations and tensions, flow can become a more readily accessible experience.

Week 4: Autonomy

Autonomy is one of the core preconditions to experience flow at work. For this module, people managers and individual contributors will be split into separate groups. People managers will learn skills and strategies to delegate effectively and avoid micromanaging. Individual contributors will learn skills and strategies to create higher levels of autonomy in their own work.

Week 5: Feedback

Since immediate feedback is one of the core preconditions of the flow experience, and is such a powerful aspect of the employee developmental experience, it is necessary for the topic to stand on its own in the intervention process.

For this week, the group will be split into people managers and individual contributors. People managers will go through a two-hour workshop on how to give effective, in-the-moment feedback for both task-specific projects, as well as big-picture developmental feedback (e.g., communication skills).

Individual contributors will go through a separate workshop on how to ask for feedback, receive feedback, and have the skills to give themselves feedback so individuals aren't as reliant on external factors to know whether they are performing well. Receiving immediate feedback is necessary to experience flow, and external sources (e.g., the manager) will not always be available to give immediate feedback throughout the course of a project.

Week 6: Work–Life Integration

Modern technology that allows individuals to work from any location at any time has enabled workers to more seamlessly integrate their work with the other aspects of their life, a lifestyle that has been termed in the popular literature "work–life integration" (Friedman, 2014; Gebhard, 2015; Schwabel, 2014; Vanderkam, 2015). Hogan & Hogan (2007) differentiate work-like integration from work–life balance in the following terms:

> First, rather than talk about 'work–life balance', which implies a 50:50 investment (or an even distribution of energies) in two separate domains, we suggest use of the term 'work–life integration'. The goal of work–life integration is: to have a satisfying, healthy, and productive life that includes work, love, and play; that integrates a range of life activities with attention to personal and interpersonal development; that fosters the psychological skills necessary for an expansion of energy associated with multiple role engagement; and that permits the construction and experience of a meaningful life defined by reference to unique wishes, interests, and values.

> *(p. 247)*

In this workshop, the team will learn about how work–life integration differs from work–life balance and discover strategies to enhance their own levels of work–life integration. The purpose of this module is for individuals to better manage their energy in their various life roles to structure their days in a way that enables them to experience flow more consistently. They will also learn how to more effectively manage their technology use both in the office and at home.

Phase 3: OWN

In this phase, the team will begin "owning" the information and practicing the new skills they have learned on a daily basis. Overall, this phase will last for four months. During this phase, the practitioner will conduct a one-on-one check-in session with each team member after 30 days to see what areas have improved and what still needs work. Updated strategies will be discussed to continue enhancing each individual's daily flow experiences.

Phase 4: WRAP

During this final phase, the purpose is to meaningfully close and measure the program. First, a two-hour team-wide "wrap" workshop will be conducted. During this workshop, a recap of the original six modules will be provided to enhance learning outcomes, and individuals will discuss each topic, what has improved, and what should be tweaked.

To measure the impact of the intervention, post-workshop feedback questionnaires will be given each week to see how well participants learned the topics of that week and whether they're able to apply it to their daily work. Subsequently, at the end of the program, each team member will take a follow-up assessment that contains the same scales as the pre-implementation assessment (i.e., flow, job satisfaction, work engagement). Also, to assess whether the team has internalized methods of applying changes to their own and direct reports' work to facilitate flow, the survey will ask questions such as "On a 1–5 scale, to what extent have you changed your day-to-day work routine?"

Ideal Conditions for Implementation

Ideally, the FLOW intervention would first take place with a specific team in a large organization, or with all staff members in a small organization (under 30 people). When introducing this intervention, it is best to start with a specific, smaller group, then expand it to more staff members once the implementer has a better idea of what strategies were most effective and what tweaks to make within the context of that specific organization.

The next condition that is ideal to implement the FLOW intervention is to work with a team leader who is fully committed to each phase of the process. While the expertise of the practitioner is essential, any intervention is only effective is there is full buy-in from the team's leader. Second, a foundational level of trust should exist between employees and the group's leader. During the FIND phase of the project, participants are considerably more likely to give honest, direct feedback if they trust the confidentiality of the process and that their responses will not be used against them in any way.

Another ideal condition for implementation is for the team leader to announce the project to the team and share the project's overall goals (enhance flow, team effectiveness, and job satisfaction). Team members should have a full understanding of the intended benefits of the project to increase their investment.

Ideally, the team should not have gone through any major personnel changes in the three months prior to the project (onboarding or offboarding a significant portion of the team). If the team has gone through any major recent transitions, it is not an ideal time to introduce an intervention that will take time and energy while they're still grappling with internal change.

Strengths and Limitations

The FLOW intervention has several key strengths that are designed to enhance its impact. First, it is grounded in both internal research (interviews with the organization's team members) and external research (pre-existing research on the flow concept and its application at work). The internal research will create a more relevant, impactful experience for participants, since the practitioner will have in-depth knowledge of the team's culture, strengths, and limitations.

Second, this intervention is customized with specific content to benefit both leaders and individual contributors. This should enable individuals to feel empowered to create their own flow experiences and enable leaders to create more flow-conducive environments for the individuals that report to them. Third, the program is being evaluated using scientifically validated scales, which should create a more accurate picture of the program's impact.

A few limitations exist as well that should be kept in mind. First, the intervention is very time intensive and much of the program takes place via in-person workshops. As a result, it would be difficult to scale this program to impact hundreds or thousands of employees simultaneously. Second, flow is a difficult concept to measure because it is a subjective experience. While individuals will assess their level of flow at work via a quantitative survey, this does not perfectly capture the in-the-moment nature of a flow experience. Lastly, this intervention is specifically designed for knowledge workers working on a team in an office. Therefore, this particular intervention may not be generalizable across all industries and work structures (e.g., factory workers, teachers, remote workers, etc.).

Conclusion

This FLOW intervention is designed to directly address the psychic entropy that many workers now feel with the advent of digital technology on daily experience. Modern knowledge workers are able to work from anywhere at any time, and are often inundated with a plethora of digital and in-person distractions throughout each working day. By working with each member of a team to systematically address the various issues that currently inhibit them from experiencing flow, and providing knowledge, tools, and strategies for them to experience flow more consistently, this intervention can hopefully serve as a powerful tool that teams can utilize to enhance productivity, focus, engagement, and job satisfaction in the 21st-century workplace.

References

Abuhamdeh, S., & Csikszentmihalyi, M. (2009). Intrinsic and extrinsic motivational orientations in the competitive context: An examination of person–situation interactions. *Journal of Personality, 77*(5), 1615–1635.

Allison, M. T., & Duncan, M. C. (1988). Women, work, and flow. In M. Csikszentmihalyi & I. S. Csikszentmihalyi (Eds.), *Optimal experience: Psychological studies of flow in consciousness* (pp. 118–137). New York: Cambridge University Press.

Bakker, A. B. (2005). Flow among music teachers and their students: The crossover of peak experiences. *Journal of Vocational Behavior, 66,* 26–44.

Borreli, L. (2015, May 14). *Human attention span shortens to 8 seconds due to digital technology: 3 ways to stay focused.* Retrieved from http://www.medicaldaily.com/human-attention-span-shortens-8-seconds-due-digital-technology-3-ways-stay-focused-333474

Crooke, M. W. (2008). *A mandala for organizations in the 21ˢᵗ century.* (Doctoral dissertation.) Claremont Graduate University, Claremont, CA.

Csikszentmihalyi, M. (1975). *Beyond boredom and anxiety.* San Francisco: Jossey-Bass.

Csikszentmihalyi, M. (1985). Emergent motivation and the evolution of the self. *Advances in Motivation and Achievement, 4,* 93–119.

Csikszentmihalyi, M. (1990). *Flow: The psychology of optimal experience.* New York: HarperCollins.

Csikszentmihalyi, M. (1997). *Finding flow: The psychology of engagement with everyday life.* New York: HarperCollins.

Csikszentmihalyi, M. (2003). *Good business: Leadership, flow, and the making of meaning.* New York: Viking.

Csikszentmihalyi, M., & Csikszentmihalyi, I. S. (Eds.). (1988). *Optimal experience: Psychological studies of flow in consciousness.* New York: Cambridge University Press.

Csikszentmihalyi, M., & LeFevre, J. (1989). Optimal experience in work and leisure. *Journal of Personality and Social Psychology, 56,* 815–822.

Csikszentmihalyi, M., & Rathunde, K. (1993). The measurement of flow in everyday life: Toward a theory of emergent motivation. *Nebraska Symposium on Motivation, 40,* 57–97.

Deci, E. L., & Ryan, R. M. (1985). *Intrinsic motivation and self-determination in human behavior.* New York: Plenum.

Demerouti, E. (2006). Job characteristics, flow, and performance: The moderating role of conscientiousness. *Journal of Occupational Health Psychology, 11*(3), 266–208.

Derks, D., van Duin, D., Tims, M., & Bakker, A. B. (2015). Smartphone use and work-home interference: The moderating role of social norms and employee work engagement. *Journal of Occupational and Organizational Psychology, 88,* 155–177.

Diener, E., Emmons, R. A., Larson, R. J., & Griffin, S. (1985). The satisfaction with life scale. *Journal of Personality Assessment, 49,* 71–75.

Donaldson, S. I., & Ko, I. (2010). Positive organizational psychology, behavior, and scholarship: A review of the emerging literature and evidence base. *Journal of Positive Psychology, 5*(3), 177–191.

Dubin, M. (2018). *Experiencing flow at work as a digital native in an accelerated knowledge Economy.* (Unpublished doctoral dissertation.) Claremont Graduate University.

Friedman, S. (2014, October 7). *What successful work and life integration looks like.* Retrieved from https://hbr.org/2014/10/what-successful-work-and-life-integration-looks-like.html

Fullagar, C., & Kelloway, E. K. (2009). Flow at work: An experience sampling approach. *Journal of Occupational and Organizational Psychology, 82,* 595–615.

Fullagar, C., & Kelloway, E. K. (2013). Work-related flow. In A. Bakker & K. Daniels (Eds.), *A day in the life of a happy worker* (pp. 41–57). London: Psychology Press.

Gallup. (2017). *Gallup daily: U.S. employee engagement.* Retrieved from http://www.gallup.com/poll/180404/gallup-daily-employee-engagement.aspx

Gebhard, N. (2015, May 29). *Why you should forget work–life balance.* Retrieved from https://www.fastcompany.com/3046781/why-you-should-forget-work-life-balance

Grawitch, M. J., Maloney, P. W., Barber, L. K., & Mooshegian, S. E. (2013). Examining the nomological network of satisfaction with work–life balance. *Journal of Occupational Health Psychology, 18,* 276–284.

Harackiewicz, J. M., Barron, K. E., & Elliot, A. J. (1998). Rethinking achievement goals: When are they adaptive for college students and why? *Educational Psychologist, 33*(1), 1–21.

Harter, J., Agrawal, S., & Sorenson, S. (2014, April 30). *Most U.S. workers see upside to staying connected to work.* Retrieved from http://www.gallup.com/poll/168794/workers-upside-staying-connected-work.aspx

Hogan, M., & Hogan, V. (2007). Work–life integration. *The Irish Psychologist, 22*(10), 246–254.

Jackson, S. A. (1992a). Athletes in flow: A qualitative investigation of flow states in elite figure skaters. *Journal of Applied Sport Psychology, 4,* 161–180.

Jackson, S. A. (1992b). *Elite athletes in flow: The psychology of optimal sport experience.* (Doctoral dissertation.) The University of North Carolina at Greensboro, Greensboro, NC.

Jackson, S. A., & Roberts, G. C. (1992). Positive performance states of athletes: Toward a conceptual understanding of peak performance. *The Sports Psychologist, 6*(2), 156–171.

Kossek, E. E., & Lautsch, B. A. (2012). Work–family boundary management styles in organizations: A cross-level model. *Organizational Psychology Review, 2,* 152–171.

Kreiner, G. E., Hollensbe, E. C., & Sheep, M. L. (2009). Balancing borders and bridges: Negotiating the work-home interface via boundary work tactics. *Academy of Management Journal, 52,* 704–730.

Linsner, S. H. (2009). *Transformational leadership and "flow": The mediating effects of psychological climate.* (Doctoral dissertation.) Kansas State University, Manhattan, KS.

Major, D. A., & Germano, L. M. (2006). The changing nature of work and its impact on the work-home interface. In F. Jones, R. J. Burke, & M. Westman (Eds.), *Work–life balance: A psychological perspective* (pp. 13–38). New York: Psychology Press.

Martin, A. J., & Jackson, S. A. (2008). Brief approaches to assessing task absorption and enhanced subjective experience: Examining "short" and "core" flow in diverse performance domains. *Motivation and Emotion, 32,* 141–157.

Mayer, J. D., & Salovey, P. (1997). What is emotional intelligence? In P. Salovey & D. J. Sluyter (Eds.), *Emotional development and emotional intelligence: Educational implications* (pp. 3–34). Basic Books.

Microsoft Canada Consumer Insights. (2015). *Attention spans.* Retrieved from https://advertising.microsoft.com/en/../microsoft-attention-spans-research-report.pdf

Moneta, G. B., & Csikszentmihalyi, M. (1996). The effect of perceived challenges and skills on the quality of subjective experience. *Journal of Personality, 64*(2), 275–310.

Nakamura, J., & Csikszentmihalyi, M. (2002). The concept of flow. In C. R. Snyder & S. J. Lopez (Eds.), *Handbook of positive psychology* (pp. 89–105). New York: Oxford University Press.

Nakamura, J., & Dubin, M. (2015). Flow in motivational psychology. In J. D. Wright (Ed.), *International encyclopedia of the social & behavioral sciences* (2nd ed., pp. 260–265). Waltham, MA: Elsevier.

Nakamura, J., & Csikszentmihalyi, M. (2009). Flow theory and research. In S. J. Lopez & C. R. Snyder (Eds.), *Oxford library of psychology. Oxford handbook of positive psychology* (pp. 195–206). Oxford University Press.

Nielsen, K., & Cleal, B. (2010). Predicting flow at work: Investigating the activities and job characteristics that predict flow states at work. *Journal of Occupational Health Psychology, 15*(2), 180–190.

Rheinberg, F., Manig, Y., Kliegl, R., Engeser, S., & Vollymeyer, R. (2007). Flow during work but happiness during leisure time: Goals, flow-experience, and happiness. *Journal of Work and Organizational Psychology, 51,* 105–115.

Rivkin, W., Diestel, S., & Schmidt, K. H. (2016). Which daily experiences can foster well-being at work? A diary study on the interplay between flow experiences, affective commitment, and self-control demands. *Journal of Occupational Health Psychology,* Advance online publication. doi: https://doi.org/10.1037/ocp0000039.

Saad, L. (2014, August 29). *The "40-hour" workweek is actually longer – By seven hours.* Retrieved from http://www.gallup.com/poll/175286/hour-workweek-actually-longer-seven-hours.aspx

Salanova, M., Bakker, A. B., & Llorens, S. (2006). Flow at work: Evidence for an upward spiral of personal and organizational resources. *Journal of Happiness Studies, 7,* 1–22.

Schaufeli, W. B., Bakker, A. B., & Salanova, M. (2006). The measurement of work engagement with a brief questionnaire: A cross-national study. *Educational and Psychological Measurement, 66*, 701–716.

Schaufeli, W. B., Salanova, M., Gonzalez-Roma, V., & Bakker, A. B. (2002). The measurement of engagement and burnout: A two sample confirmatory factor analytic approach. *Journal of Happiness Studies, 3*, 71–92.

Schwabel, D. (2014, January 21). *Work life integration: The new norm*. Retrieved from http://www.forbes.com/sites/danschawbel/2014/01/21/ work-life-integration-the-new-norm/#240472be2184

Vanderkam, L. (2015, March 6). *Work-life balance is dead – Here's why that might be a good thing*. Retrieved from http://fortune.com/2015/03/06/ work-life-integration/

Zito, M., Cortese, C. G., & Colombo, L. (2015). Nurses' exhaustion: The role of flow at work between job demands and job resources. *Journal of Nursing Management, 24*(1), 12–22.

Zubair, A., & Kamal, A. (2015). Authentic leadership and creativity: Mediating role of work-related flow and psychological capital. *Journal of Behavioural Sciences, 25*(1), 150–171.

3

Crafting Your Best-Self

Integrating Job Crafting and Positive Psychology Interventions

Christopher Chen

Tanya Roberts received her bachelor's degree in communications from a Los Angeles area university where she was an outstanding student and President of the Communications Club. While in college, she started working at the local Los Angeles office of a mid-sized professional services firm as a summer intern and moved to New York City after she was offered a full-time position at the firm's headquarters. This is her third year as a full-time marketing and communications specialist at the firm. However, while she was motivated and productive during her first two years at the firm, she has recently felt much less engaged at work and spends most of her time on her personal social media instead. As a result, her productivity has greatly decreased, and these issues are beginning to be brought up during her quarterly performance management reviews. *Why is Tanya so disengaged at work even though she has her dream job and is on track in a career she has defined for herself?*

While there are many contextual factors in play, one of the root causes of Tanya's reduced motivation and disengagement at work is that her basic human needs are no longer being met. To help Tanya, and the other 85% of people worldwide who suffer from disengagement at work (Gallup, 2017), I introduce a job-crafting intervention (JobCraft+) centered around strengths, relational self-affirmation, best-self activation, and future work-self salience. The intent of this intervention is to encourage job-crafting behaviors among employees by providing them with the resources that enable both short- and long-term changes to address this fulfillment of their basic human needs. Furthermore, the combination of activities in this intervention has been shown through research to increase employee engagement, motivation, proactiveness, and well-being, while also increasing team/organizational effectiveness and decreasing turnover.

Theoretical Framework

The phenomenon of disengagement at work can be explained by self-determination theory and optimal distinctiveness theory. Both theories postulate that people are only able to be truly engaged and experience well-being when their basic human needs are met. Self-determination theory identifies these needs as autonomy, relatedness, and competence (Ryan & Deci, 2000). Ryan and Deci identified these three needs through their research into factors that enhance or undermine self-regulation, intrinsic motivation, and well-being.

Autonomy is described as the need for one to feel in control of their life and being able to act in accordance with their authentic self (Ryan & Deci, 2000). For example, Tanya was free to take on roles that promoted her personal and professional development while in college. However, as a salaried employee, Tanya now feels obligated to take on all the tasks that she is assigned, regardless of their relevance to her continued professional development. Furthermore, while Tanya envisions herself becoming the Director of the Marketing and Communications department of the firm someday, she feels that her current role does not offer the opportunities that give her the required experience needed to proceed with her career. All these factors contribute to feelings of decreased autonomy for Tanya. Relatedness is described as the fundamental need to interact and be socially connected with others (Ryan & Deci, 2000). Tanya had built up a broad network of friends and professional contacts while going to school and working in Los Angeles. However, after moving to New York City, she feels increasingly distant from her previous social circles. As a result, Tanya turns to social media as a means to cling to and stay relevant in her previous social circles, while unknowingly sacrificing the high-quality relationships she could be building with her coworkers in the New York office. Further compounding this problem, because of her aspirations to rise in the organization, Tanya sees her coworkers as competition and feels increasingly isolated, which causes feelings of decreased relatedness. Competence is described as the urge to experience mastery and successfully drive the outcomes of one's work (Ryan & Deci, 2000). While Tanya was an outstanding student in college, her feelings of competence have plummeted after she began working full time at the firm. Though Tanya developed strong marketing and communication knowledge and skills during her four years in college, most of her time in her job is spent on doing tasks such as answering emails, scheduling meetings, and editing presentations. As such, she does not see a difference between the responsibilities and the tasks she was doing during her summer internship and the current full-time position she holds. Furthermore, even though she enjoys editing presentations for better clarity, she rarely feels that her contributions are appreciated. Through the lens of self-determination theory, all these factors culminate in the downward trend of Tanya's basic human needs being neglected.

Optimal distinctiveness theory states that the balance between the need for validation and similarity to others (inclusiveness) and the need for uniqueness and individuation (distinctiveness) is a fundamental human need (Brewer, 1991). This set of needs is not binary, but such that a happy, satisfied individual should feel included in their social groups yet also retain a strong sense of uniqueness. Furthermore, individuals differ in their baseline needs for inclusiveness and distinctiveness based on their personality traits and prior experiences (Brewer, 1991). In Tanya's case, she has always had a higher need for distinctiveness, and this need was met by being the President of the Communications Club while in college. During her summer internship, she also experienced a very high level of distinction as everyone wanted to meet and work with the new intern in the office. And while this situation repeated itself when she was a newly transferred employee at the New York office, the interest in her has gradually waned along with Tanya's feelings of distinctiveness. Further compounding this lack of distinctiveness is the fact that everyone in her firm has very generic job titles. As such, Tanya's basic human needs from the perspective of optimal distinctiveness are also being neglected, leading to her reduced motivation and increased disengagement at work. Taking into account these factors in Tanya's and other employee's cases, JobCraft+ was designed so that participants are given the proper tools and inspired to engage in job crafting such that they modify their job tasks, interactions with others, and cognitive perceptions to satisfy these basic human needs.

Research

Job crafting was chosen as the primary component of JobCraft+ due to its strong fit with the self-determination theory framework. Wrzesniewski and Dutton (2001) described the motivation for job crafting arising from employees' needs for control over job and work meaning, positive self-image, and human connection with others, which coincide with the basic human needs of autonomy, competency, and relatedness. Job crafting is defined as "the physical and cognitive changes individuals make in the task or relational boundaries of their work" (Wrzesniewski & Dutton, 2001, p. 179), and has been shown to increase both individual and team-level engagement and performance (Tims et al., 2013). The three components of job crafting, as defined by Wrzesniewski and Dutton (2001), involve (a) changing the type, scope, and number of job tasks, (b) changing the amount and quality of interactions with other people encountered during the job, and (c) changing the way employees perceive their jobs. The first component of this job-crafting framework would help employees increase their feelings of autonomy and competency at work, the second component increases feelings of relatedness, while the third component may help increase autonomy, competency, and relatedness by reframing the way an employee perceive aspects of the job so that it brings more meaning to their lives. Similarly, Tims et al. (2013) broke down the components of job crafting into (a) changing oneself or the work context so that there is a better fit between the person's unique attributes and their work environment, and (b) increasing the resources offered by the organization and decreasing hindering job demands that interfere with career goals. Successful job crafting leads to positive changes in the design of the job and the social environment at work, which results in more meaningful work, better work identity, and, most importantly, better person–role fit.

While job crafting addresses the basic human needs through the perspective of self-determination theory, JobCraft+ also incorporates positive psychology interventions that complement job crafting and target the need for optimal distinctiveness. The use of strength-based interventions has been comprehensively studied and there is strong evidence of the resultant positive effects on employees. A meta-analysis conducted by Gallup in 2015 found that employees who took a strength assessment that made them aware of their strongest natural talents enjoyed a 9%–15% increase in work engagement (Asplund et al., 2016). Furthermore, a longitudinal study by Cable et al. (2013) on strength-based approaches for on-boarding processes found the use of a strength-based approach during the process to predict better long-term performance and less employee turnover. The knowledge of one's strengths highlights the uniqueness of each employee and the value they bring to the team, which increases the level of felt distinctiveness and competence.

Relational self-affirmation, a process where an employee "capitalizes on one's pre-existing personal network of relationships (friends, family, and coworkers) who write narratives about times the individual made a distinct contribution," is linked to better team performance through an improved ability to participate in information exchange (Lee et al., 2016, pp. 4–5). This intervention serves to achieve two goals. First, the gathering of narratives from the employee's social and work network increases the feelings of relatedness and inclusiveness. Second, the content of the collected narratives that highlight when the employee made a distinct contribution promotes feelings of competency and distinctiveness. As such, relational self-affirmation is an important complement to reflected best-self exercises in achieving best-self activation.

Best-self interventions involve asking employees to reflect on and discuss a specific time when they were acting the way they were "born to act." These activities help the employee discern times when they were able to be their authentic selves, which, in turn, leads to increased feelings of autonomy and distinctiveness. Best-self activation occurs when a person's mental representation of their best-self becomes salient and easily accessible (Cable et al., 2015). In a series of experimental and applied longitudinal studies by Cable et al. (2015), best-self activation was found to be linked to a variety of short- and long-term positive outcomes that include: lower stress and burnout, increased positive affect, increased creative problem-solving ability, and increased performance under pressure.

Future work-self salience, the degree to which aspirations and hopes of one's future work identity are clear and easy to imagine (Strauss et al., 2012), serves two important roles in JobCraft+. First, because "a salient future work-self generates a motivating discrepancy, enables the exploration of new possibilities, and invokes mental simulation of the future" (p. 582), feelings of autonomy related to one's career will be increased. Second, future work-self salience has been found to have a positive long-term effect on proactive career behaviors. Since job crafting can be considered a proactive career behavior, future work-self salience will serve to motivate the employee to continue the practice of job crafting long after the JobCraft+ intervention. Figure 3.1 provides a summary of how the sub-interventions in JobCraft+ address the aforementioned psychological constructs.

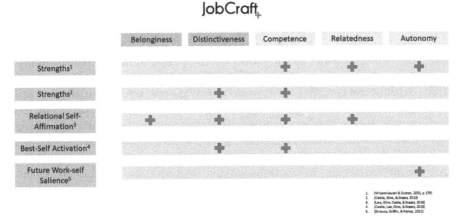

Figure 3.1 Psychological Framework of JobCraft+.

Intervention

JobCraft+ is widely applicable across all job roles and industries, given some limitations that will be discussed at the end of this chapter. However, knowledge workers and professionals would experience the greater effects from this intervention as their jobs are typically more ambiguous and easier to modify without greatly impacting the workstream of others. For example, in many manufacturing jobs, great care must be taken when changing the way one works so that all safety guidelines are met and that it does not disrupt the manufacturing process.

The intervention consists of three phases (Figure 3.2), spread across two days. Prior to the start of the intervention, it is important to meet with the organization's leadership team to determine the number of participating employees, the degree of job crafting that is allowed, and the type of strength assessment to be included. While I recommend using Gallup's *StrengthsFinder*, especially if it is already integrated into the organization, it can be a costly endeavor for a smaller organization. VIA Strengths can be used as a free/low-cost alternative. Using the Tanya persona as an exemplar participant, the steps and the experience of the intervention will be explained in detail.

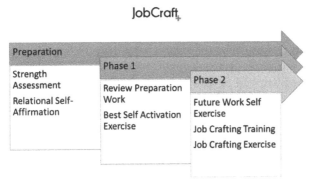

Figure 3.2 Overview of JobCraft+ Phases.

Preparation

During the preparation phase, which occurs one week before the on-site JobCraft+ workshop, participants are asked to take a strength assessment and reach out to at least three, but no more than five people in their personal/professional network to request narratives focusing on a time when the participant has made a distinctive contribution at work or similar contexts. The participant will be sent an email script along with a personalized link that they can share with the three to five people they've identified. By clicking on the link, the respondents will be able to submit their narratives through a form onto a secure server. It is important that at least two out of the five respondents are coworkers that the participant has regular interactions with, so that accurate insights are gained regarding the participant's contributions in their current role. Furthermore, it is recommended that at least one respondent be from a context outside of the current workplace so that diverse viewpoints can be gathered.

> With the encouragement of her supervisor, Tanya decides to sign up for the JobCraft+ workshop that is being offered through the firm to try to address her performance issues. Immediately after signing up for the workshop, she receives a welcome email with details of the workshop schedule and preparation work, a code to take the StrengthsFinder assessment, and an email script with a link for narrative submissions. Tanya chooses to ask George, one of her close friends from college, Mary, her current supervisor, and Bob, a coworker on her team, to provide the narratives.

Phase 1: Best-Self Activation

The first phase of JobCraft+ will start off with introductions and an ice breaker to build rapport and psychological safety. Each participant then receives a personalized workbook that contains detailed agendas for both days, their strengths report, the narratives received from each respondent, all the resources to be covered, and blank worksheets to be filled out during the course of the workshop. The participants will be first asked to review the themes identified in their strengths report. A trained facilitator will then instruct the participants in a workshop on how to use strengths and briefly go over each individual strength in the report. As part of the relational self-affirmation component, the participants will individually read their received narratives and highlight any connection between the narratives and their strengths. Following this, the participants will be split up into groups where they will discuss their findings. It is of vital importance that the facilitator establish guidelines that promote a psychologically safe atmosphere by this point so that the participants will feel comfortable sharing their findings.

After a short break, the participants will engage in a reflected best-self exercise by answering the following request on their worksheet: "Reflect on a specific time – perhaps on a job, perhaps at home – when you were acting the way you were *born to act*," using their strengths report and collected narratives as inspiration. After completing this portion of the exercise, the participants will return to their groups and work together to create a realistic image of each participant's best work-selves, which will be recorded in the workbook. The discussion will then focus on the specific contexts and aspects of their jobs that contribute to or detract from each participant's ability to be their best-self at work.

> While Tanya already knows many of the people in the workshop, she is glad to take part in the ice breaker exercise as it decreases the tension in the room. Eating a light breakfast, Tanya looks through her strengths report and finds her top five strengths to be: Achiever, Communication, Responsibility, Relator, and Input. With a bit of trepidation, Tanya reviews the narratives that she has received. She is happy to hear from George, who reminisces about her successes as President of the Communication Club when they were in college together. Tanya is especially surprised to see Bob, whom she considers as her competition, write about the time when Tanya talked with him while he was going through a rough patch, and saved him from quitting the firm. Furthermore, she appreciates the story that Mary, her supervisor, shares about how Tanya's design changes on an external slide impressed the CEO of a company so much that they became the firm's client.
>
> After some light-hearted conversation with her workshop cohort over lunch, Tanya writes about the experience where she pulled together a team and helped all the other student organizations develop marketing strategies when she was President of the Communication Club as reflective of her best-self. Tanya then consolidates all that she has learned and works with her groupmates to create an image of herself when she is at her best. Finally, Tanya identifies that being on a need-to-know basis, not being able to see the outcomes of her work, the lack of professional development opportunities, and her perception of her coworkers as competitors are detractors to being her best-self at work. She also concludes that tight deadlines, the ability to know more about the recipient of her work, and having a close group of teammates are contributors to her ability to be at her best.

Phase 2: The Mastery Experience

During the second phase, participants will be asked to review the images of their best-selves that they have constructed during the previous phase. Using their best-self as a foundation, the participants will individually imagine a realistic version of their future work-selves in five and ten years. Coming back together into groups, the participants will share their future work-self images and brainstorm paths they can take to reach these goals, focusing on the barriers they may encounter and the skills and experience they would need.

The facilitator would then teach the participants how to job craft. They would first cover the modification of task boundaries, in which employees may choose to do more, fewer, or different tasks than defined by their job roles. Second, they would discuss the altering of relational boundaries, in which employees choose to change the number and quality of interactions with others. Finally, they would talk about changing cognitive boundaries, in which employees choose to perceive their current job roles in more meaningful ways.

For the mastery experience, the employees would then get back together into groups to help each other create a job-crafting plan by implementing all the knowledge about themselves that they've gained from the previous exercises. This process would involve setting objective goals and timelines as to how they would like to implement each element of their job-crafting plan. The facilitator would conclude the workshop by asking a few volunteers to share their job-crafting plans with the entire room. By the end of the workshop, the participants will have achieved best-self activation, future work-self salience, and gained efficacy in creating and executing a job-crafting plan.

> Tanya reviews the characteristics of her best work-self and immediately feels a sense of competency. She then tries to imagine her future work-self. Using the image of her best-self as a template, she realizes that she would not be ready for a director position in five years; however, she does see herself becoming the Director of the Marketing and Communications department after ten years in the firm. After further brainstorming, Tanya can see herself realistically becoming a senior manager in the marketing department in five years. She shares these versions of her future work-self with her group to get their feedback regarding the paths she will have to take. One barrier she immediately identifies is the lack of high-quality relationships she has with her supervisor and her coworkers. Tanya also realizes that she lacks the project management experiences needed to become a manager.
>
> After learning about how to job craft, Tanya gets to work creating her job-crafting plan. Because she finds responding to emails and other administrative tasks draining, she decides to block off a portion of her morning and afternoon for these tasks so that she can focus on the work that she finds meaningful. Tanya also plans to ask her supervisor if she could assist with the planning of future projects to gain project management experience and also to obtain a more holistic view of the projects she is working on. She also decides on a plan to actively reach out for feedback so that she can see the outcomes of her work. From the insights she gained during the relational affirmation exercise, Tanya realizes that she needs to stop perceiving her coworkers as competitors and make an effort to develop professional relationships with them. She plans to attend all optional meetings and make an effort to communicate in-person instead of only through email whenever possible. Furthermore, she plans to propose the idea of having a team lunch every week, so she can develop deeper relationships with her teammates. The narrative from Tanya's supervisor also changes her perception of her work. While she had previously thought of the slide design as a meaningless task, she now sees the importance of her efforts to the success of the firm. She creates a goal to always think of how her work would affect a client's view of the firm whenever she is feel-

ing unmotivated. Tanya is the first to volunteer and proudly share with the room her job-crafting plan. She leaves the workshop feeling re-energized and confident in her job-crafting abilities.

Limitations

While JobCraft+ can benefit employees in all roles and organizations across all industries, there exist several limitations that can affect the effectiveness of this intervention. First, leadership buy-in is crucial. If the leadership of an organization is vehemently against the idea of job crafting, they may actively undermine the process and even punish employees who engage in the practice. Second, some forms of job crafting may be more difficult to achieve for certain roles. As alluded to previously, it is much harder to change task boundaries as a manufacturing floor worker than a knowledge worker because of the structure of the job. Third, while supervisors can encourage employees to attend JobCraft+, it should never be used as punishment for poor performance. Forcing an employee to attend JobCraft+ undermines the fundamental human need for autonomy and the intervention as a whole. Fourth, JobCraft+ is not a solution for systematic employee disengagement. If widespread patterns of employee disengagement are occurring, this is indicative of a structural or managerial problem and top-down job redesigns or more holistic organizational change solutions must be considered. Fifth, while JobCraft+ can lead to higher employee retention rates, there also exists a possibility that after participating in the best-self and future work-self exercises, some employees may realize that their job is not a good fit for them and consequently leave their role or even the organization. Finally, the client organization's culture must be supportive of employee well-being. If the culture of the organization assigns little value to well-being, there will be low engagement and participation during the exercises, which would greatly reduce the effectiveness of the intervention.

Conclusion

Disengagement in one's job in a well-functioning organization manifests due to complex reasons that are often unique to each employee. By targeting the fundamental human needs of autonomy, relatedness, competence, belongingness, and distinction, JobCraft+ is an intervention that is at once relatable across different populations of people and work contexts, while also prompting the creation of bespoke solutions that meet each individual's unique needs and goals. Building upon the tried and true method of job crafting, JobCraft+ utilizes complementary positive psychological interventions to help participants gain a better understanding of themselves, encourages proactive work behaviors, and empowers them to become more engaged and truly thrive at work.

References

Asplund, J., Harter, J. K., Agrawal, S., & Plowman, S. K. (2016). *The relationship between strengths-based employee development and organizational outcomes 2015 strengths meta-analysis.* Gallup. https://www.gallup.com/cliftonstrengths/en/269615/strengths-meta-analysis-2015.aspx

Brewer, M. B. (1991). The social self: On being the same and different at the same time. *Personality and Social Psychology Bulletin, 17,* 475–482. doi:https://doi.org/10.1177/0146167291175001

Cable, D., Lee, J. J., Gino, F., & Staats, B. R. (2015). How best-self activation influences emotions, physiology and employment relationships. *Harvard Business School Working Paper,* doi:http://doi.org/10.2139/ssrn.2662057

Cable, D. M., Gino, F., & Staats, B. R. (2013). Breaking them in or eliciting their best? Reframing socialization around newcomers' authentic self-expression. *Administrative Science Quarterly, 58,* 1–36. doi:http://doi.org/10.1177/00018392 13477098

Gallup. (2017). *State of the global workplace.* New York, NY: Gallup Press.

Lee, J. J., Gino, F., Cable, D. M., & Staats, B. R. (2016). Preparing the self for team entry: How relational affirmation improves team performance. *Harvard Business School,* doi:http://doi.org/10.2139/ssrn.2753160

Ryan, R., & Deci, E. (2000). Self-determination theory and the facilitation of intrinsic motivation. *American Psychologist, 55,* 68–78. doi:http://doi.org/10.1037/0003-066X.55.1.68

Strauss, K., Griffin, M. A., & Parker, S. K. (2012). Future work selves: How salient hoped-for identities motivate proactive career behaviors. *Journal of Applied Psychology, 97,* 580–598. doi:http://doi.org/10.1037/a0026423

Tims, M., Bakker, A. B., Derks, D., & van Rhenen, W. (2013). Job crafting at the team and individual level: Implications for work engagement and performance. *Group & Organization Management, 38,* 427–454. doi:http://doi.org/10.1177/1059601113492421

Wrzesniewski, A., & Dutton, J. E. (2001). Crafting a job: As active employees revisioning crafters of their work. *Academy of Management Review, 26,* 179–201. doi:http://doi.org/10.2307/259118

4

Positive Performance Reviews Using Strengths-Based Goal Setting

Hannah Foster Grammer & Adrian Bernhardt

Strengths-based goal setting (SBGS) is a synthesis of positive organizational development (POD) and social psychology. In the organizational context, this is when employees set personal goals that are self-derived, based on their talents and aptitudes, as opposed to traditional goal setting that is based on deficits or weaknesses. Integrating this positive type of goal setting into performance review meetings (PRMs) is based on a culmination of theory and research in both positive and social psychology fields on motivation in the workplace and the related underlying drivers of performance. Drawing on self-determination theory (Ryan & Deci, 2000) and its premise that people have three basic psychological needs that are the basis for motivation to modify behavior and actions, we propose that SBGS will increase dependent levels of performance, compared to using a traditional approach. This effect is predicted to be mediated through meeting these basic needs.

Background

Today's global economy is characterized by rapid growth and uncertainty. Employees face higher demands than in the past, including stress related to meeting competitive deadlines and pressure to adapt to a continually changing environment. Notably, long hours, workforce gaps, insufficient organizational support, social care cuts, and a culture of blame from top-down pressures and serial reorganization contribute to this fragile system (Lemaire & Wallace, 2017). These factors can lead to systematic dissonance between employers and employees, impacting well-being, motivation, engagement, and performance dynamics. Creating a high-functioning workplace, where human talent is maximized to its fullest potential and where employees are intrinsically motivated to engage with tasks and the environment, is challenging and dependent on a multitude of factors.

Positive Organizational Psychology Interventions: Design and Evaluation, First Edition.
Stewart I. Donaldson and Christopher Chen.
© 2021 John Wiley & Sons Ltd. Published 2021 by John Wiley & Sons Ltd.

In addition to experiencing overhead pressures and self-scrutiny of performance, most employees undergo periodic PRMs with their superiors. A performance appraisal or review is an evaluation of an individual's performance on job-related dimensions. While varying in subtle formatting differences based on the organization, the basic structure and intent are the same. Namely, performance reviews are intended for two multifaceted purposes. The first is administrative; results from these meetings are used to make decisions about incentives (such as promotions, raises, and increases in responsibility) and for consequences (such as pay cuts, demotions, and terminations) (Latham, 2009a; Rotundo, 2009). The second purpose is both developmental and motivational. Performance reviews are executed as a process for increasing motivation to improve performance and contribute to organizational objectives (Latham, 2009a).

As essential tools for individual development and documentation, reviews are often conducted in one-on-one, vis-à-vis meetings between managers and subordinates. A central idea with these meetings is their potential utility as support mechanisms to contribute to the available resources a company can provide employees to mitigate feelings of burnout by conversely improving future performance, promoting growth, and increasing engagement (Rotundo, 2009). Therefore, performance reviews are one of the most widely used management tools to align employee behaviors and performance with overall business strategy and represent a crucial human resource function within organizations (Cummings & Worley, 2015).

Although PRMs represent an element to employee development, they often do precisely the opposite of what they are intended to do because it can be difficult to maintain a balanced discourse surrounding positive and negative information (Bouskila-Yam & Kluger, 2011; McCunn, 1998). Traditional PRMs have been found to discourage and demotivate rather than encourage and motivate employees due to several reasons (Latham, 2009a). Bowman (1999) concluded that more often than not performance reviews are given by reluctant managers and received by unreceptive employees. This finding demonstrates the perceptual negativity associated with performance reviews from both perspectives.

Gabris and Ihrke (2001) found a relationship between poor-quality performance reviews and increases in employee burnout. Namely, decisions to leave the firm that contributed to turnover rates stemmed from perceptions of procedural injustice, miscommunication, and resulting misunderstandings, and overall job dissatisfaction (Eberly et al., 2009; Rotundo, 2009).

One component to performance evaluation systems that might be strategic to consider is the method by which these appraisals are communicated during one-on-one evaluation meetings. This focus on communication dynamics is vital because effective communication increases perceptions of justice, trust, confidence, and overall productivity. Engaging in two-way, double-loop communication could increase the quality of appraisal meetings (Moynihan, 2005). Managers who model the ability to listen, clarify, explain, and empathize with subordinates' perceptions and emotions could increase the quality of PRMs, and ultimately dependent positive organizational outcomes (Latham, 2009a; Rotundo, 2009). A wealth of research demonstrates that the linkage between performance reviews and increases in performance is mediated by objective and supportive feedback (Cummings & Molloy, 1977; Cummings & Worley, 2015; Manz & Sims, Jr, 1987; Mintzberg, 1975; Sayles, 1964; Walton & Schlesinger, 1979; Weisbord, 1985). This connection underscores the importance of ensuring high-quality communication within PRMs. In particular, to take full advantage of employees' performance potential, feedback should include information on what employees should continue doing based on what is currently working and personal strengths, and upon what they should improve and cultivate. Useful feedback communicates to employees where they should direct their energy and attention, reducing potential ambiguity from unclear expectations and directing this energy more productively toward business objectives (Jawahar, 2010; Rotundo, 2009). This can be a sensitive area of discussion because previous negative experiences with PRMs may create negative bias toward these interactions.

While the accuracy of appraisal in reviewing performance is essential, it is insufficient by itself for effective review. Managers need to possess strong interpersonal skills, especially when appraisals to be discussed contain negative information. Tziner and Murphy (1999) found that managers felt so uncomfortable communicating performance data that they would give all subordinates high ratings despite variations in actual performance. Despite this inertia of widespread challenges, including negative perceptions and outcomes, organizations continue to use PRMs as fundamental instruments for managing employees.

Furthermore, the evaluative nature of performance reviews can contribute to adverse psychological outcomes for employees, termed "evaluation anxiety" (Donaldson et al., 2002), where the PRM process is so unpleasant that it impedes potential progress and optimal performance. However, these repercussions can be mitigated in part because they are conversely related, as job satisfaction and productivity are substantially correlated (Judge et al., 2001), as are both job satisfaction and commitment with turnover intentions, and actual turnover (Tett & Meyer, 1993). By definition, job satisfaction is the "pleasurable or positive emotional state resulting from the appraisal of one's job or job experience" (Locke, 1976, p. 1300), so it would seem that positive personal experiences at work are important to retention intentions. Thus, investigation of some of the determinants of greater performance and retention by looking at the underlying mechanisms behind what motivates people to perform autonomously at their best could be beneficial to increasing our understanding of this very interrelated issue.

What drives employees to perform at their highest capability, extending their best-selves of their own volition? What motivates them to engage in behaviors and actions that make them feel self-capable? Why do people feel an inherent need to integrate themselves within their social context through assimilation? We will attempt to explore these questions by first examining one perspective on the basic driving force behind behavior that can potentially explain the connection to performance outcomes.

The social and organizational psychology theories and models surrounding the related issues have many years of empirical support that lend credence to their credibility as established methods of practice. Choosing a practice from such a broad range of possible options was particularly challenging, but easier when the scope was narrowed to include only one or two aspects of organizational development to increase performance and return on investment (ROI) results.

Additionally, the surrounding literature attempting to answer the fundamental question in this chapter through related social constructs such as social identification (Tajfel & Turner, 1986), upward social comparison (Festinger, 1954), group membership (Hogg, 2010), entitativity (Campbell, 1958), norms (Cialdini & Trost, 1998), superordinate goals (Sherif, 1958), leader–member exchange (Graen et al., 1982), attribution (Kelley, 1967), personality traits (Allport & Allport, 1921), attitudes (Allport, 1935), self-efficacy (Bandura, 1982, 1997), hierarchy of needs (Maslow, 1943), and drives (Hull, 1943), among others, is replete but lacks clarity on the root causal link between motivation and performance. Thus, while each holds their own as meritorious representations of their respective fields, and given the intended direction for this intervention, we will use a syncretization of several theories and models to create a more holistic approach to our research. Examining the topic presented with a transdisciplinary lens accommodates all desired elements and incorporates the best practices of each field and related driving theory.

Prior Theory and Research

Traditional PRMs orientate meetings around finances and quantitative performance, with less emphasis on the human component and personalized plans for improvement. This disconnect between employer and employee can create a sense of unfulfillment or dissatisfaction with oneself and role within the organization, causing more opportunities for disengagement, demotivation, lower well-being, and burnout (Upadhaya et al., 2014). A possible approach to addressing these issues could be to evaluate the fundamental needs of employees and the organization as a way to establish a starting point for restructuring this review process.

Self-Determination Theory

Basic Psychological Needs

Decades of research on the underlying mechanisms of human functioning and behavior led to the development of self-determination theory (SDT) by Ryan and Deci (2000). In addition, it is widely used as a foundational basis for many theories in disciplines extending beyond social psychology, such as organizational psychology, positive organizational psychology, policy, evaluation, and public health, to name a few. SDT is a meta-theory comprised of six mini-theories and posits that people have three universal, basic, and innate psychological needs as the basis for fostering positive processes. These three needs include the desire for *competence* (Harter, 1978; White, 1963), *autonomy* (DeCharms, 1968; Deci, 1975), and *relatedness* (Baumeister & Leary, 1995; Reis, 1994). *Competence* is the belief that one can positively impact their surroundings and outcomes, *autonomy* pertains to feeling control, i.e., self-determination, over one's actions, and *relatedness* is the internalized account of connection strength between internal-ized values and extrinsic regulations within the social environment to maintain closeness with others (Deci & Ryan, 2014, p. 19; Ryan, 1995).

The SDT perspective on basic needs satisfaction (BNS) may seem character-istically similar to other theories, such as Maslow's (1943) premise that needs are hierarchically ordered, or McClelland's (1965) idea that needs can be acquired through positive reinforcement achievement through learning and socialization. While some aspects of these and other related theories may be true, SDT is distinct in that it suggests that all of the needs are important and that they are "*innate*, fundamental propensities" (Van den Broeck et al., 2010, p. 983). The regulatory processes determining the degree (rather than the per-ceived importance or strength) to which these needs can be satisfied affects the quality of mental health and behavior (Deci & Ryan, 2000), is a self-perpetuat-ing process, and is the greatest predictor for optimal functioning and well-being (Deci & Ryan, 2014; Van den Broeck et al., 2010, p. 983). Deci and Ryan (2000) said themselves that the basic needs are the key to understanding motivation:

> The specification by SDT of the three fundamental needs for competence, relatedness, and autonomy was not simply an assumptive or a priori pro-cess but instead emerged from inductive and deductive empirical pro-cesses. We found that without the concept of needs we were unable to provide a psychologically meaningful interpretation and integration of a diverse set of research results in the areas of intrinsic motivation, which we consider to be a basic, lifelong psychological growth function (Deci & Ryan, 1980), and internalization, which we consider to be an essential aspect of psychological integrity and social cohesion (Ryan et al., 1985).
>
> *(p. 232)*

The underlying axiom is that people generally strive toward growth and actively take steps to overcome challenges and gain useful experiences that guide agency. More specifically, inherent growth tendencies depend on BNS, and the extent to which BNS is achieved, more positive outcomes are predicted (Deci & Ryan, 2014). Furthermore, BNS can affect domains such as motivation (e.g., Deci & Ryan, 2008; La Guardia & Patrick, 2008; Ryan et al., 2006; Ryan et al., 2008; Ryan & Deci, 2009; Soenens & Vansteenkiste, 2010), learning (e.g., Guay et al., 2008; Stipek, 2002), engagement (e.g., Meyer & Gagné, 2008), commitment (e.g., Meyer & Maltin, 2010), performance (e.g., Baard et al., 2004), and ultimately well-being (e.g., Niemiec et al., 2009; Nix et al., 1999; Reis et al., 2000).

Furthermore, the organismic–dialectical perspective of SDT clarifies that these needs are complementary rather than antagonistic, as well as equally vital and interrelated (Sheldon et al., 2001). However, different needs have been linked to different predictors and outcomes (Brien et al., 2010; Brien et al., 2012; Gagné et al., 2009; Greguras & Diefendorff, 2009). While each basic need has been sepa-rately linked to certain outcomes, the focus of this intervention follows the understanding that all needs are universally needed to self-determine. Individual variances are concomitants of the degree to which these needs are prioritized and satisfied, but ultimately they come together in an interconnected balance, and satisfaction of all three needs may predict positive, related results (Clifton et al., 2002). Specific outcomes are highlighted below.

Motivation

More specifically, meeting these needs requires the activation of motivation, which is defined as "a set of energetic forces that originates both within as well as beyond an individual's being, to initiate work-related behavior, and to determine its form, direction, intensity, and duration" (Pinder, 1998, p. 11). There are two overarching types of motivation: *intrinsic* and *extrinsic*. Ryan and Deci (2000) describe *intrinsic* motivation as "the prototypic manifestation of the human tendency toward learning and creativity" (p. 69), where "the fullest representations of humanity show people to be curious, vital, and self-motivated … to learn; extend themselves; master new skills; and apply their talents responsibly" (p. 68). Contrastly, *extrinsic* motivation stems from external sources and is predominant in the workplace. Reasoning is instrumental toward compliance, such as gaining rewards and avoiding punishments (external regulation), or toward self-control, such as boosting one's ego or avoiding feeling guilty (introjection). It can also be because the task at hand holds personal importance, such as conscious valuing, or because the task is fully assimilated to one's values and needs (integration). Regarding integration, while it does share some characteristics of intrinsic motivation it is still considered extrinsic because the task or goal trying to be achieved originates from outside the self. There is also a third motivation variable, *amotivation*, which is simply unwillingness or lack of motivation.

Gagné and Deci (2005) conceptualized motivation as a continuum based on self-regulation, where integrated extrinsic motivation is seen as the ideal type of motivation for the work context because it possesses the highest level of reflection (Dworkin, 1988). This is because the behavior is autonomous and self-governed as a result of a choice that is fully volitional, and the task at hand is phenomenologically salient. Additionally, intrinsic motivation is inherently autonomously regulated. At the other end of the spectrum, extrinsic motivation can be controlled or impersonal, in which case it is not intrinsic or autonomous. Many work environments function around controlled motivation excitation (e.g., bonuses, quota fulfillment demands, job stake-related threats, and supervisory approval). Whereas autonomous motivation is correlated with well-being and higher performance, controlled motivation is correlated with burnout and turnover intentions (Gagné & Deci, 2005; Van den Broeck et al., 2008). Unifying autonomous self-determination with the three basic needs and fitting it into the PRM context, research shows the importance of autonomy to intrinsic and extrinsic motivation as a way to shift from a more external perceived locus of causality and internalize external agendas as personally meaningful and self-derived.

Engagement

According to this theory, need satisfaction is a precursor to higher performance, and actions that satisfy these needs on dispositional and situational factors and that are intrinsically and autonomously motivated because they are enjoyable or inherently interesting lead to higher levels of well-being and positive affect (Ryan et al., 1996; Sheldon & Elliot, 1999, in Gagné, 2014). This process of internalized, self-regulation, and autonomous motivation is what Ryan and Deci (2000) termed *engagement*, which enhances feelings of autonomy and increases volitional persistence, behavioral effectiveness, and task performance (Macey & Schneider, 2008; Ryan & Deci, 2000). Macey and Schneider conceptualize engagement as a state, trait, and behavioral tendency involving having a strong affective tone of high involvement, energy, and sense of self-presence. These two definitions operationally overlap; however, the former focuses more on behavioral affect and the latter on task performance (Meyer & Gagné, 2008, p. 61). In the work context, engagement is a multidimensional construct. It is centered on positive regard toward the given work environment, which includes job satisfaction, job involvement, and organizational commitment (Harter et al., 2002; Macey & Schneider, 2008). Additionally, research shows that these constructs are correlated and possess similar affectivity, including energy, enthusiasm, activation, and passion (Le et al., 2010). As such, they are sensitive to each other and require a well-structured balance for salience. Thus, it is clear that it is an important factor to consider in developing needs-satisfaction-centered performance review processes.

In fact, according to Bakker et al. (2011), "virtually all studies on work engagement offer evidence for the benefits of the experience" (p. 17). Studies show that the benefits of having engaged employees are numerous and include having psychological capital, higher self-esteem, optimism, and goal persistence. Furthermore, Katie Bailey, a professor at the University of Sussex who studies employee engagement, said, "the overwhelming weight of evidence is that people who are engaged with their work enjoy higher levels of wellbeing and morale, they're more satisfied with their work, they perform better, and organizations with a highly engaged workforce also tend to be better performing and to have a workforce with higher levels of commitment and lower levels of turnover" (Limb, 2015). However, most work systems are structured in a way that creates an environment for extrinsic motivation, which reflects a desire to avoid punishment and gain rewards, boost self-efficacy, attain goals, and where the external forces that drive motivation may produce desired outcomes but perhaps at the expense of personal well-being. While this is not always the case, the idea of going beyond focusing on finances and shifting autonomous motivation from extrinsic to intrinsic is of particular importance for companies, since research shows that the latter is more powerful in terms of increasing engagement, and, optimally, better performance.

Commitment

Furthermore, higher levels of engagement from autonomous regulation can also lead to a greater sense of commitment to task completion and the organization (Ryan & Deci, 2000). Commitment is an important concept for companies because of its implications for retention rates as an outcome, whereas the dominant outcome in organizational commitment research was retention. Meyer and Herscovitch describe commitment as "a mind-set that can take different forms and binds an individual to a course of action that is relevant to a particular target"

(Meyer & Herscovitch, 2001, p. 310). Commitment can stem from feeling a sense of obligation (normative), from feeling a need to stay at an organization (continuance), or from a desire to stay because of strong emotional attachment (i.e., affective commitment) and impacts motivation orientation to the specific task (Meyer & Herscovitch, 2001). Thus, promoting affective commitment is key to fostering intentions to stay and perform beyond what is required. Several workplace factors that are instrumental to developing strong affective and normative commitment to organizations include support from organization members (Rhoades & Eisenberger, 2002), transformational leadership through transactional leadership (Meyer et al., 2002), and goal setting (Cummings & Worley, 2015). Furthermore, Meyer (2014) states that "Each of the factors has been subjected to considerable research in its own right, and therefore there is a large body of evidence to draw on to identify specific management policies and practices" (p. 45). Organizational-level benefits of fully engaged employees include affective and normative commitment that reflects a moral sense of duty to stay and contribute to the organization's success (Gellatly et al., 2006; Meyer & Parfyonova, 2010). Figure 4.1 is provided for reference as a logic model that summarizes the theory and its related effects.

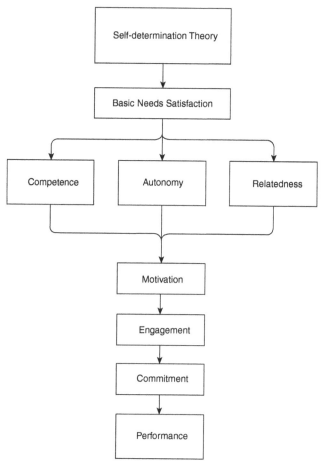

Figure 4.1 Theory Effects.

Traditional Process

One way that employers can increase performance is through goal setting that is positive and productive. Goal setting is often implemented as a business strategy, based on the well-established goal-setting theory by Latham and Locke (2007) that provides a framework of the most verifiably valid and practically applicable ways of increasing motivation (e.g., Earley & Lee, 1992; Gauggel, 1999; Locke & Latham, 1990; Miner, 1984; Mitchell & Daniels, 2003; Pinder, 1998; Prigatano et al., 1997; Weinberg, 1994). This process involves managers and employees collaboratively establishing goals that are defined by several principles and at different organizational levels. More specifically, it is a theory of motivation in the workplace with widespread applicability and states that the simplest and most direct reason for individual performance outcome differences is because of performance-related goal variance (Latham & Locke, 1991). A key concept in this theory is that goal setting, in and of itself, has affective and cognitive benefits pertaining to the mechanisms of motivation, including effort, persistence, and choice (Locke, 2009). For goal setting to be successfully motivationally driven, it must be SMART: specific, measurable, attainable, relevant, and time bound (Locke, 1968; Weinberg & Gould, 2007). Goals must also be challenging, provided with feedback for progress accountability, maintained, and adequately supported through available resources to remove obstacles and achieve success.

A noteworthy question with goal setting is how to sustain goal salience and engagement during implementation. Goal setting in the workplace is often a prescriptive process that undergoes personalization for internalization (Locke & Latham, 2002). Overarching organization objectives are often parsed into department goals, which are then dispersed by superiors to help make them manageable for individuals' attainment. Setting personal goals that are aligned with the needs of the company is a common practice in many business types and has the potential to be a crucial step in successful self-regulation that leads to gains in performance. Traditional goal setting (TGS) is stimulated by focusing on deficits in competency, where professional development is centered on reducing these shortcomings. Even when efforts are made to improve, they are usually undermined by gaps in performance, possibly causing ramifications for relationships in the organization, such as decreased morale, self-esteem, self-efficacy, teamwork, and fulfillment (Coens & Jenkins, 2000; Markle, 2000; Proctor et al., 2011), not to mention that it seems counterintuitive to SDT and BNS as the premise of well-being and engagement. This relationship between setting goals based on weaknesses and direct effects on BNS highlights the importance of implementing a management strategy that addresses the needs of both employer and employee and is an agency-promoting mechanism targeted toward expanding individual potential rather than a narrow, single-loop process.

Appreciative Inquiry

A mentioned above, one such organizational mechanism of leveraging psychological capital is through appreciative inquiry (AI), of which the study was marked as the precursor to a rise of interest in studying POD and strengths in management (Bushe, 2013). This relatively contemporary approach to planned change examines the defined areas of importance in organizations through discovering and understanding its best elements, i.e., its strengths, to develop the destined vision for change for delivery (Cooperrider & Sekerka, 2006; Cooperrider & Srivastva, 1987). By recognizing the potential gains available through exploring current assets, organizations can strategically leverage talent from within, thereby reducing new-hire and outside resources expenses and increasing ROI.

A common area of disconnect between superiors and subordinates is surrounding the issue of expectations. Goals are not formed unilaterally but are a suggestion of anticipatory reality that is based on collective action. Role ambiguity surrounding expectations is a systemic issue and has a direct negative effect on performance (Tubre & Collins, 2000). A copious amount of research on these expectation effects offers support for AI and shows that people tend to act in a way that confirms their expectations, termed self-fulfilling prophecy by Merton (1968), and that positive expectations produce positive outcomes (Cooperrider, 1990; Eden, 1988; Rosenthal & Jacobson, 1968). Relating it to BNS, this research seems to indicate that the mere expectation of completing a goal based on self-perceived competence is enough to increase the likelihood of actual success. When an open environment is encouraged to reveal expectations, amalgamations of perspective can generate a new future that fosters appreciation.

Appreciative Dialogue

On a dyadic level, this strategy would be concentrated into appreciative dialogue (AD) to help move people toward better performance in a way that is constructive and appears more authentic. During a goal-setting session, managers might utilize AD to learn employee strengths, knowledge, talents, and skills, as well as assess current well-being. AD could be implemented in a variety of goal-related areas, including to evaluate employee data, build rapport, and facilitate discussion of past success stories, shared visions, and exercise constructive creativity when generating goals (Gergen et al., 2001). As a positive dimension of support, it could also be given to provide a resource for the relatedness dimension to BNS and to act as a buffer for any negative affect employees might experience due to job demands and stressors. Furthermore, while it is easier said than done, AD can be a uniting practice that managers could model to show caring, compassionate support, forgiveness, inspiration, meaning, respect, integrity, and gratitude (Cameron et al., 2011). When goal setting incorporates AD through dynamic managerial leadership to create SBGS, it has a higher rate of successful attainment (Bakker et al., 2011).

Seven Cs of Caring Conversations

Central to the concept of AD is how this dialogue is executed. While the focus of this intervention is on the efficacy of SBGS, it might be helpful to provide an example of content for this context. One proposed method of facilitation attempts to further maximize a positive impact on employer–employee interactions by adding a third element that is comprised of seven ways to show intentional interpersonal efforts: being curious, considerate, courageous, compromising, connecting, collaborative, and celebratory (Dewar & Nolan, 2013; Edel & Belinda, 2016). Originally created for the field of healthcare, where there is a constructionist emphasis on narrative, applicability for the seven Cs of caring conversations can be generalized to fit many different work contexts due to its flexible, personalizable design. Essentially, this is the stage where seeding the vocabulary and language is especially pertinent in reconstructing interpersonal behavior to fit the organization's shared, superordinate goals (Garcea & Linley, 2011). Simply being aware of personal strengths is insufficient for promoting change and increasing productivity. Rather, establishing a positive work culture to foster growth from personal goal setting attainment can impact the very thought processes behind goal generation, and ultimately action (Minhas, 2010). Showing compassionate support to employees can go a long way in terms of how they react to instruction and on their willingness to produce higher-quality performance, and this model serves as a specific example of a possible approach to empowering goal-setting sessions for success to provide organizations with a competitive edge.

Strengths-Based Goal Setting

Finally, changing the fundamental structure of goal setting from a weaknesses orientation to one around strengths could help employees satisfy all three basic needs within a self-determined perspective replicate and expand their best performance (Meyers et al., 2015). There is a growing movement within organizational development psychology to find positive-centered solutions to solve work-related issues, pioneered by Peterson and Seligman's (2004) research on strengths and virtues. While there is a plethora of research on strengths identification, there is little available on their application in goal setting, and even less linking it to BNS in SDT. Furthermore, studies comparing the effects of TGS with SBGS are very limited, presenting a unique opportunity to explore this comprehensive approach. The available studies that are most closely aligned with the theoretical undergirding for the current study are the Hiemstra and Van Yperen (2015) study on strength- versus deficit-based self-regulated learning strategies, and the Linley et al. (2010) study on signature strengths associated with goal progress. While they both look at SBSG in terms of BNS, the former study focuses on effort intention outcomes, and the latter study focuses on BNS and well-being outcomes. Neither study uses the context of PRMs or assesses actual performance differences.

The unique theoretical perspective behind the proposed direction of research suggests that SBGS, which is directed toward satisfying the basic needs, augment engagement and well-being (Ryan & Deci, 2000). Whereas traditional employee goal development focuses on fixing deficits, SBGS helps employees identify positive traits to place them in the best position to grow individually and increase the frequency of positive work experiences (Clifton & Harter, 2003).

The SBGS process begins with discerning an individual's talents and incorporates any relevant knowledge and skills needed to refine these talents into a productive asset that benefits both the organization and the individual. This approach suggests that people develop more efficiently when utilizing given talents integrated with skills and knowledge (Asplund & Blacksmith, 2011). It is important to distinguish that talents are innate and reliable features of personality that represent the best of oneself. They can be conceptualized as the foundation around which skills and knowledge can be tailored for the best opportunity for growth. However, due to their inherent status, they are less malleable because skills are honed through practice and training and do not occur naturally, and knowledge is something that can be acquired (Aguinis et al., 2012). Furthermore, orienting goals around strengths does not ignore the significance of weaknesses or abandon discussion of them. Rather, focusing on strengths can provide a sense of direction, perhaps partially due to the verisimilitude of positive expectations regarding goals that are set around these strengths. It could also produce greater gains, including goal-directed behavior, feelings of accomplishment, positive affect, self-efficacy, and the motivation to set higher and higher goals (Govindji & Linley, 2007; Hodges & Asplund, 2010; Proctor et al., 2011). This recognition of the potential for greater gains by leveraging positive attributes and aptitudes can help employees compensate for their weaknesses, and possibly overcome them.

The potential utility of using an SBGS strategy can extend beyond the intrapersonal landscape to interpersonal relationships, where employees with identified strengths can work more efficiently with partners who complementarily support these weaknesses (Aguinis et al., 2012). This concept can also be applied to job design and allocating employees to jobs that better fit their strengths to optimize organizational functioning and efficiency through improved communication, effective teamwork, and strengthened workplace relationships (Connelly, 2002; Robison, 2003; Smith & Rutigliano, 2003).

The Performance Review Meeting Process

The decision of when to implement SBGS within an intervention is critical to maximizing the chance of successful execution. While SBGS alone can be an effective intervention, its utility could be increased when integrated within a natural context. One commonly existing system for delivery of performance information, during which time is designated for employees to design derivative goals, is a PRM. Business quotas with impinging employee expectations are perennial, so translating controlled and externally regulated objectives to a format that can bring personalized relevance through capitalization of strengths could make PRMs the perfect setting to target individual growth (Locke & Latham, 1990).

However, just as it is the case with TGS that is focused on weaknesses, typical PRMs emphasize areas in which to improve from a lack-of-competency perspective. This traditional approach is criticized by researchers and practitioners as highly aggregated and quantitative, with little direction for improvement (Aureli, 2010; Johnson & Kaplan, 1987; Kaplan & Norton, 1992; Neely et al., 1995) because many PRM programs focus on performance outcomes that rely on financial measures assessment, but an understanding of financial reports is often thwarted by a lack of technical knowledge, leading to confusion, frustration, dissatisfaction, and inability to adjust to competitive changes (Ghalayini & Noble, 1996; Kennerley & Neely, 2003; Van Woerkom & De Bruijn, 2016). This is partially because traditional PRMs were intended for middle and higher-level management, with the focus on monitoring performance with lagging metrics to reactively minimize costs, rather than on proactively and preventatively strategizing improvement. While performance provides a straightforward measure of progress, the process of reviewing this information with employees might benefit from restructuration and reshaped conceptualization of potential use.

A learning forum that presents goals quantitatively is less likely to organically produce desired routines and is less preferred over qualitative discourse (Mintzberg, 1975; Moynihan, 2005). Furthermore, because customer demands are always changing, low cost is only one of the factors companies use to stay ahead in a competitive market. Therefore, a fixed PRM format might benefit from concentrating on quality, reliable deliverables, flexible capacity, and greater effective human capital employment (Skinner, 1986). Fortunately, the need for management reforms has been recognized, and PRM programs have started to evolve beyond being a bureaucratic practice and now include prioritizing tailored employee development as companies realized the importance of employee well-being effects on performance (e.g., Choong, 2013, 2014; Forrester & Adams, 1997; Ikramullah et al., 2016; Marchand & Raymond, 2008; Najmi et al., 2005; Neely et al., 1995; Pádua & Jabbour, 2015; Wieland et al., 2015).

PRMs could offer an ideal platform for SBGS if they incorporate some positive aspects into the planning process by initiating and enhancing any effects from goal setting. Particularly, an ideal condition would be the inclusion of a participatory management style that emphasizes ongoing coaching and informal recognition for personal and organizational goal achievement (Latham, 2009a).

The beauty of conducting goal setting during PRMs is that goal commitment is not produced in a void, but rather depends on learning and coaching (Latham & Wexley, 1994). According to Latham, ongoing coaching is one of the most powerful tools managers can use to increase individual and team performance. Since goal setting depends on positive outcome expectancies, managers who engage in ongoing coaching can help employees see the link between their behaviors toward achieving goals and positive outcomes (e.g., favorable performance reviews, compensation, positive feedback, career advancement, contributing to firm success). As such, this could increase goal-directed behaviors and improve performance, tying into the principle that goal setting improves performance (Rotundo, 2009).

This in turn could help nurture autonomy, provide social support through encouraging managerial conversations, increase perceived competence through goal accomplishment, and promote an environment in which employees can flourish (Deci & Ryan, 2000; Fernet et al., 2012; Gagné, 2014; Tafvelin & Stenling, 2018; Van den Broeck et al., 2008). Leveraging these positive attributes often requires some level of managerial leadership activation to help employees identify and develop their strengths, and indeed could be crucial to goal attainment success (Deci et al., 2001). As such, much research has been conducted on ways to create a positive leadership model that facilitates well-being and optimal performance (e.g., Asplund & Blacksmith, 2011). By establishing what works through analyzing the current situation and building on available data, supervisors can foster employee growth by focusing on strengths derived from relevant constraints (Mengis & Eppler, 2008).

More specifically, Bowers and Lopez (2010) identified three constructs that are necessary for strengths capitalization: strengths reinforcement, success experiences, and continual social support. The potential for increasing motivation derived from SBGS depends on employee commitment, which can be increased through managerial coaching and encouragement to set SBGS (Latham & Wexley, 1994). When managers supply support for autonomy, it creates an autonomy causality orientation where employees feel more BNS in not only autonomy, but also in the areas of competence and relatedness (Deci et al., 1989). By prioritizing the satisfaction of employees' basic needs, managers are creating an environment that enables optimal performance and participation enjoyment, making the workplace more conducive to growth, higher intrinsic motivation, improved well-being, and increased functioning (Baard, 2002; Coens & Jenkins, 2000; Ryan & Deci, 2000). Furthermore, by showing recognition of the importance of autonomous functioning, managers also helped to satisfy employees' need for relatedness, which in one study was analyzed as the strongest predictor of performance (Baard et al., 2004).

At least in Western society, many organizations have been built around the long-standing cultural belief on expressing emotions that manager and worker efficiency are matters of rational activity (Fineman, 1996, p. 545; Lakoff & Johnson, 1980; Putnam & Mumby, 1993). However, decision-making is neurobiologically controlled by emotions (Damasio et al., 1996), but arousal requires using communication cues that are culturally shared, such as body language, language nuances, and cognitive labels, to understand the socially significant meaning (Fineman 1996, p. 546; see also Ekman, 1984; Sugrue, 1982). Thus, it seems reasonable to shift this rationality-ruling paradigm to one that capitalizes on individual strengths to foster connections. Objectively, this strategy appeals to both rational and emotional reasoning orientations because the process of personal development through positive interpersonal interactions builds rapport and attends to basic needs satisfaction.

The reasoning behind this strengths-based design is that people possess an inherent need to accomplish tasks and achieve excellence, and employees who feel included in the process and perceive that their employer is interested in them personally, taking the time to help them self-discover and cultivate individual strengths, are much more likely to pay the company back with the desired engagement, work ethic, and commitment (Asplund & Blacksmith, 2011; Van Woerkom et al., 2015). A meta-analysis conducted by researchers at Gallup saw statistically significant differences in levels of engagement between employees who received strengths-based feedback and those who did not ($d = 0.33$), with subsequent positive implications on turnover, productivity, and profits (Levine & Spreitzer, 2012). Furthermore, in a study conducted by Jawahar (2010), results of structural equation modeling provide strong support for the importance of feedback because 81% of the variance in performance was explained by the accuracy of, and satisfaction with, feedback ($N = 256$). Thus, feedback that is perceived as positive can be beneficial for employees because it achieves BNS, particularly on the competence dimension (Mouratidis et al., 2008). SBGS that is administered during PRMs can increase quality two-way communication to produce focused, improved performance, and can make the process easier for both parties while maintaining the desired objectives. These results, along with data from other studies, indicate how vital strengths-based feedback and goal setting are to levels of motivation, engagement, well-being, and performance, especially on the relatedness dimension of BNS, as well as its long-standing reliability as a positive management tool (Baard et al., 2004; Rechter, 2010; Van Woerkom & Meyers, 2015).

A Synthesized Approach

It is easily observable that study of increasing motivation, engagement, commitment, well-being, and performance is vast, with a constellation of theories, models, and concepts that practitioners and organizations can implement to improve financial and employee outcomes. Practitioners should identify the strategic imperative that would best fit the organization's business model and cultural composition. While not intended as a panacea for organizational issues, sometimes the simplest interventions affect the greatest amount of change, and the basic principle behind SBGS is to create a reflexive and sustainable tool that capitalizes on available talent by helping employees satisfy basic needs. It can be nurtured longitudinally as a systematic idea woven into the very fabric of the organization itself and implemented at the individual level by attending to the rich diversity of unique strengths to enact change. Figure 4.2 is a logic model and is provided for reference.

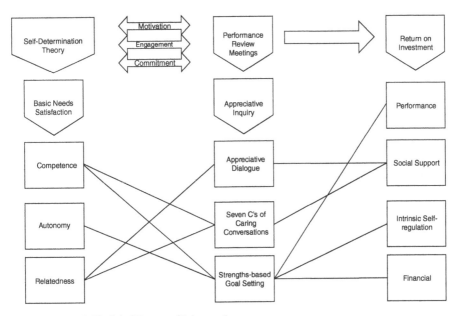

Figure 4.2 Logic Model of Proposed Intervention.

In sum, SBGS infused within PRMs is a transdisciplinary approach based on a synthesis of theoretical and applied research. It would be a small shift in focus that could produce a ripple effect throughout the organization and yield significant results for increasing intrinsic motivation and self-regulated engagement by satisfying the basic psychological needs derived from SDT. BNS can be met through setting goals that are derived from strengths rather than weaknesses. Supervisor support is an important component of goal fulfillment success, ergo, employee-set, and manager facilitated, SBGS could enhance autonomy and lead to goal completion. This in turn could increase perceived competency and high efficacy, creating a self-perpetuating cycle of positivity. A prime setting for supportive supervisor interactions is PRMs, and a positive PRM process that uses AD and the seven Cs can help create a supportive environment that fosters focused development. Lastly, BNS that is a result of collective collaboration aligned to fit organizational outcomes can contribute to the entire process through a new pedagogy by increasing motivation, engagement, commitment, well-being, and ultimately performance.

Intervention

Previous literature shows the effectiveness of focusing on employee strengths through positive interactions with managers during PRMs. However, the field of psychology as a whole has only uncovered the tip of the Freudian iceberg on the discovery of human nature and functioning. To date, no research has been conducted that provides an experimental comparison of TGS and SBGS in PRMs within an SDT *and* AI context. Furthermore, what research is available does not describe specific steps or techniques for implementation. In reviewing the current body of literature on this topic, these sentiments were echoed by other researchers. For example, Couturier and Sklavounos (2019) state:

> These studies introduce the notion of dialogue as an important success factor in the context of performance management. However, they fail to provide specific advice on how to carry out performance dialogue in such a way that information is not only collected, but also used within the sense-making process, and for the creation and dissemination of knowledge. Most articles go only as far as presenting general guidelines for an effective performance dialogue. More specifically, the importance of a structured communication around meetings is mentioned or highlighted by most authors previously cited as playing a critical role, yet this concept has not been further developed.
>
> *(p. 4)*

General Scope

The proposed intervention will utilize SBGS as an integration of the recognized AI and AD components, which is facilitated through questions framed by the seven Cs of caring conversations. The core of this idea is exemplified in the following simple mediation model (Figure 4.3).

Mediation Model

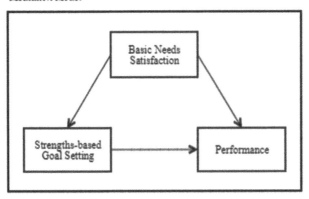

Figure 4.3 Mediation Model.

The basic process is as follows: during a PRM, employees will be asked to design goals based on their strengths. Performance would ideally be measured incrementally three months before and three months after the intervention using performance and survey-response data to discern any perceived longitudinal efficacy. Of course, time intervals between assessments would be flexible, depending on the organization's needs. Upon review of the literature, we believe that SBGS, as opposed to TGS, will produce greater results in increasing employees' motivation, engagement, commitment, well-being, and performance, evidenced by the changes in measured data. Clients could even try a smaller-scaled intervention with a preliminary pilot study to test the simple mediational effects to determine if this intervention would be a good fit for the organization.

Implementation Process

To start, the premise of this intervention is that it is intended to produce maximum ROI through the most efficient means. The program provided by the proposed process should facilitate learning that can be transferable, self-sustainable, and translate across departments. In other words, this intervention can be seen as a tool that, once provided, can be easily referenced and taught to others within the organization. Thus, the mediation model above would serve as the technical basis from which to reference when explaining the reasoning for the intervention to a potential client. It could also be condensed into a supplementary resource that organizations can use in the future.

As noted above, commonly applied human resource performance management processes more often than not are characterized by poor implementation and suboptimal, even harmful, outcomes. To address these inadequacies, we are proposing a structured, pragmatic training intervention for managers and other relevant stakeholders, designed to facilitate both learning and application of the principles of SBGS through AD to produce optimally motivated performance and well-being. This top-down approach is meant to have wide and flexible applicability to produce vertical and horizontal learning. As such, potential ROI is continual and exponential and could help to increase the organization's competitive advantage within respective industries.

Preliminary Assessment

First and foremost, a needs assessment should be conducted to make well-informed decisions on how to proceed. It can reveal weaknesses to the proposed intervention that can serve as constructive feedback to modify and refine the program to best fit the organization's needs.

The point of contact, or a chosen company representative, will work closely with organizational development practitioners and human resource executives to conduct a needs assessment to identify a gap between the expected and actual effects of the current performance review system. Data collection can be conducted through surveys and interviews with organization members. For example, surveys and interviews may ask questions such as "What are your experiences with the current process?", "What is your level of satisfaction regarding performance appraisals?", "Have PRMs assisted you in any way? If so, in what ways?" If current experiences and effects do not align with expectations, then we recommend proceeding with the intervention.

One possible preliminary question we may include is to ask if the organization previously had experience using a similar intervention in the past. The reason for this is because contextual information and results from previous exposure could help us understand the projected utility and effectiveness of our intervention. Additionally, access to clear and objective financial documents can be included in the review process to track financial indicators concerning the application of current performance appraisals. If correlations do not meet expectations, this may indicate inadequate components to the review process. This activity may even reveal a negative relationship between financial indicators and PRMs. In this event, we believe the organization might benefit from our proposed intervention. Of course, reviewing performance and any available BNS data would also be part of the needs assessment to determine if changes in current trends that align with expectations are feasible with our intervention. We strongly recommend due diligence before applying any intervention to ensure organizational readiness and successful transfer of training back to the organization. In summary, if the needs assessment indicates a gap between expected and actual effects, then we recommend proceeding with our intervention.

Presentation

The performance review meeting process (PRMP) will facilitate manager learning and application through a workshop format. The workshop will be in the form of a group conference. This intervention is comprised of a two-day, large-scale workshop. Managers and other relevant stakeholders will be invited to attend, and influential executives across the organization will also be encouraged to attend. Executive participation will model essential leadership support and commitment to the intervention, as well as legitimize the importance of the intervention due to the need for an improved PRMP. Throughout the workshop, we as the interventionists will be modeling positive open interactions and providing theory-grounded tools to help managers set stretch goals for themselves to implement these principles from the top down.

The intervention will use a modified version of AI based on the POD approach to identify strengths of the current process and to collectively investigate how these components can be incorporated into our recommended positive process. Prepackaged interventions rarely satisfy the needs of stakeholders; therefore, taking a context-based approach that is tailored to the company's financial needs while incorporating the humanistic components that drive performance, such as using AD to identify employee strengths, is critical to establishing a clear ROI. This will increase the chance of meeting stakeholder needs and result in higher buy-in because stakeholders will perceive the intervention as a modification instead of a complete change. The intervention is summarized by the steps below.

Workshop Procedure

First Day

1. Attendees will be instructed to find someone in the room (preferably someone they do not interact with often) with whom to engage in appreciative interviews regarding the strengths and positive experiences with the current process.
2. Attendees will be instructed to join two other groups (i.e., forming a group of six) and discuss common positive experiences with the current process. These groups will be tasked with writing down three common themes.
3. Groups will submit three positive themes. A facilitator will aggregate these themes into broader overarching themes and relay the gathered information to attendees.
4. POD practitioners, in combination with key human resource executives, will introduce the principles and practices associated with AD and SBGT. Expected positive organizational outcomes will be presented, and brief executive summaries of the literature and expected outcomes will be provided to each attendee.
5. As a large group, attendees will utilize AD to provide ideas of how current positive themes can be integrated with SBGS and which other systems (e.g., information systems, span of control, organizational structure) will need to be modified to support the new system. Managers can then share their experiences with evaluation meetings and reflect on the most effective techniques. After the large group meeting, common themes from this discussion will be summarized for further exploration and other planned change efforts. This information will be given to attending executives as well as disseminated to executives not in attendance after the workshop concludes. This intervention is intended to revamp the process. Other systems may need to be adjusted but are outside the scope of the PRMP. At the very least this will increase learning and empower stakeholders with information concerning misalignments.

Second Day

1. Attendees will then be asked to partner with other attendees to engage in provided PRM simulations and apply the components of AD, SBGS, and identified themes from step 3. This step will engage stakeholders in learning by doing because up to this point the intervention has been focused on exploration and theory. Attendees will move around the room, alternating between subordinate and manager roles. Attendees will engage in five simulations as subordinates and five simulations as managers.

2. Attendees will be asked to reflect on their positive experiences during these simulations and discuss them with at least three other attendees. They will then share lessons learned, and how they will apply what they have learned back in the workplace. As a final step, attendees will be asked to create action plans for themselves by writing down how they will apply what they have learned in the workplace in a practical step-by-step fashion. Placing the learning that occurred during the workshop in their particular everyday contexts will reduce the ambiguity of implementation and increase transfer to the workplace. This activity will be framed as managers setting goals for themselves to experience firsthand the positive effects of PRM. Additionally, participants will be provided with a take-home version of the intervention for personal reference and guide for those who might have been unavailable to attend.

Based on the amassed evidence for SBGS, BNS, and PRMs effects as individual components, combining them into the intervention's design should produce optimal results with the addition of an interaction of variables along each axis of the aforementioned, hypothetical mediation model (Fritz & MacKinnon, 2007, 2008). By providing training to managers and other stakeholders, they can disperse the program tools they learned to institute dynamic change across the organization.

Ideal Conditions for Implementation

The efficacy of organization development interventions depends on the in-depth diagnosis and the extent to which organizational needs are met. Interventions should be designed to fit organizational contingencies to realize anticipated outcomes (Cummings & Worley, 2015).

As previously mentioned, prepackaged interventions rarely meet an organization's needs because organizations represent a complex web of interactions that result in distinct cultures and processes. Generic off-the-shelf interventions may appeal to management due to false promises of fast, easy, and cost-effective implementation but rarely include an initial context-based needs assessment to target the root cause of deficiencies (e.g., organization-, group-, and individual-level misalignments). Also, standardized interventions assume homogeneity across organizations in terms of task and interpersonal processes that are in reality unique and highly contingent (Salas & Stagl, 2009). To address these concerns, we added a component to our intervention that attempts to mold itself to the context by engaging organization members in designing the intervention to fit their unique context by using a modified large group AI framework (Cummings & Worley, 2015).

Despite attempts to maximize generalizability, the proposed intervention's core principles of goal setting and strengths-based feedback assume a particular context. In the following sections, we will explicate to the best of our knowledge ideal conditions for implementation as well as strengths and limitations.

Leadership and overall organizational support for the intervention are crucial for the horizontal and longer-term vertical transfer of training back to the workplace. If the application of new knowledge, skills, and abilities is not encouraged or seen as pointless, then the intervention will have little effect on individual and firm performance. In an unsupportive climate, the training recipient will revert to previous ways of operation, costing the organization time and money. Leadership support is critical because leaders can either contribute to a climate for learning or prevent the application of new behaviors. For a training intervention to be successful, there must exist a supportive climate (Salas & Stagl, 2009). A supportive climate may consist of organizational culture emphasizing the values of performance, learning, and risk taking. Employee autonomy and flexibility are also essential characteristics of a supportive climate; the principles of goal setting assist employees in directing their focus and attention toward goal-directed behaviors (i.e., self-regulation) to meet challenging goals. According to SDT alluded to above, increases in the internal regulation of behaviors thereby increases intrinsic motivation to perform that behavior (Ryan & Deci, 2000), indicating the essentiality of autonomy for persistent goal-directed behaviors. In combination, autonomy and goal setting will produce motivated, engaged, and higher-performing employees.

Overall dissatisfaction with the current performance review process will likely be an ideal condition. Member acceptance and energy toward a planned change effort often requires a negative view of current conditions to stimulate readiness to change. If management and employees are satisfied with the current review process, then there exists little to no reason to implement our intervention. Management can stimulate an impetus for change by disseminating the results of a needs assessment with organization members or other related negative implications from maintaining an ineffective review process.

Variable pay for a performance compensation system is another ideal condition that will complement the principles of goal setting. In addition to positive emotions of pride and accomplishment associated with meeting challenging goals, compensation should be linked to goal attainment (Latham, 2009b). In and of itself, a properly implemented pay-for-performance compensation system will lead to increased individual and firm performance (Durham & Bartol, 2009). Goal setting and a variable pay-for-performance compensation system can have powerful effects on firm performance. Variable pay-for-performance systems do not permanently increase base pay; additional pay linked to positive deviance must be re-earned. A particular type of variable pay-for-performance system is especially relevant to goal setting, the lump-sum bonus. Lump-sum bonuses are a form of variable pay where individuals are given bonuses for achieving particular goals (Durham & Bartol, 2009).

Depending on task interdependence, goals can be set, and lump-sum bonuses can be distributed for either individual or team task performance. To implement a variable pay system the organization must have objective measures of performance to base decisions on bonus allocation, which represents a potential limitation. Goal setting depends on goal commitment, which is comprised of self-efficacy and outcome expectancies. In clearly linking compensation with goal achievement, employees will expect positive financial outcomes along with other positive non-financial outcomes (Latham, 2009b). This is primarily the reason why a variable pay-for-performance system would be ideal for goal-setting principles.

Lastly, the existence of a participatory management style throughout the organization would be an ideal condition for implementation, in particular, a participatory management style emphasizing ongoing coaching and informal recognition. In addition to periodic performance reviews, individuals and teams need ongoing coaching to achieve goals and firm objectives (Latham, 2009a). In a study, employee productivity increased by 88% due to managers fostering employee confidence by communicating with them daily that they possessed the ability to attain challenging goals (Olivero et al., 1997). Effective performance management goes far beyond performance reviews; information conveyed during reviews should not be a surprise to either the manager or the employee. Ongoing coaching is one of the most powerful tools managers can use to increase individual and team performance (Latham, 2009a). Ongoing coaching is an ideal condition, especially when utilizing the principles of goal setting. Goal commitment depends on learning and coaching (Latham & Wexley, 1994). The manager can help employees see how achieving goals will lead to positive outcomes (e.g., favorable performance reviews, compensation, positive feedback, career advancement, contributing to firm success). As mentioned above, goal setting depends on positive outcome expectancies. Managers engaging in ongoing coaching will be better able to help employees see the link between their behaviors toward achieving goals and positive outcomes. When employees see the link between their performance and positive outcomes, this will increase goal-directed behaviors and improve performance; this is a central component of how goal setting improves performance (Rotundo, 2009).

Strengths and Limitations

Despite attempts to maximize generalizability, the proposed intervention's core principle of SBGS assumes a particular context of a PRM. In the following subsections, we will explicate to the best of our knowledge potential strengths and limitations. As it is the case with most research, strengths and limitations are part and parcel of the process. A metaphor to conceptualize strengths and limitations is a double-edged sword. The interrelatedness between strengths and weaknesses makes it so that while a factor can be a strength, it can simultaneously also be a limitation for the same reasons that it is a strength. Some of these relationships are more obvious, and others are more exploratory. While in-depth, the detailed list provided below is not exhaustive and precedes any possible future insights.

Due to the self-refining process of research, many of the measures mentioned above pose as strengths in and of themselves due to their individual long-standing reliability. This in turn could contribute to the fortitude of this intervention's theoretical and methodological foundation. Verily, only in a 100% controlled environment can one say for certain that the proposed methods used in this program will execute flawlessly with all desired and no undesired outcomes. However, practice in and of itself has limitations, and this intervention is no exception. Nevertheless, the vetting process for selecting the most accurate body of literature attempted to address potential gaps in logic flow or methodology. Ergo, results from this intervention may still exhibit the potential power of SBGS as a managerial tool that practitioners and businesses can implement to promote positive change.

Strengths

Central to this positive approach to traditionally negative PRMs is its flexible nature. While still in the theoretical stage, the application is pragmatic rather than ideological because it is prioritizing performance that stems from well-being to provide business benefits and deliverables. This proposed process is built around the client's criteria and needs and can be tailored accordingly. Therefore, it can accommodate many organizational designs, from local non-profit to global Fortune 500 organizations.

In both types of organizational design, time and money are valuable resources that are not easily given, especially when meeting the bottom line can take precedence over self-care. Oftentimes, it is difficult to devise a plan of strategic change that relays the necessary information and still allocates enough time in which to deliver the intervention. Furthermore, when pecuniary resources might already be strained due to poor performance and turnover, seeking help outside of departments such as human resources shows that addressing the issue is important enough to invest in outside expertise. This sensitivity to companies' time and monetary constraints is exhibited in the succinct program design, where findings reports will be provided after the training concludes. Any potential time-ROI will afford the organization the ability to reference the results perhaps for training purposes or future research exploration. Furthermore, results should be relatively straightforward, allowing for maximum efficiency through easy dissemination during any top-down training. It can create an informational chain that sustains the new program, and possibly even survive a shift in management.

Since time is a notable constraint for many organizations, our proposed PRM format can accommodate many types of meeting frequency setups, such as annual or monthly. The key is for management to touch base with employees and show that they care. Being supportive in a constructive way that is conducive to individual growth can have a positive impact on employee mental health. When well-being is increased, employees, and possibly even managers, may feel increased morale and BNS, contributing to the cycle of positivity on the related dimensions of motivation, engagement, commitment, and performance. Even the mere act of focusing on personal strengths can have an impact on one's current state of being. Of course, from an employer's perspective, ROIs are usually well received and show that both parties can experience benefits from this project. Furthermore, these ripple effects are linked to reduced burnout rates and higher retention intentions, which could serve as a significant strength across the organization.

In addition to benefits for managers and employees, SBGS within PRMs can provide financial gains for the organization, including saving money on training new employees due to turnover and providing financial incentives for retention. Directing positive employee behavior can be time consuming and pose as a bureaucratic nightmare when efforts attempting to manage diverse incentive packages would be more valuably placed elsewhere, which is often why this issue is given little attention or ignored. While not always a necessary factor, when it is relevant the company might perceive reassessing investing in employee extra-role behavior on performance-related dimensions as an asset and increase employees' connection to it. Some of the world's best organizations leverage the power of their human capital to increase individual and organizational growth and performance (Fleming & Asplund, 2007; Hodges & Asplund, 2010). According to Trice et al. (1984), if positive extra-role behavior can be generated voluntarily rather than through reward system incentives or role prescriptions, the cost to the organization is decreased. Using employee strengths as forward-looking performance measures for continuous improvement can also increase organizational effectiveness and reduce vulnerability to instability in the markets (Upadhaya et al., 2014).

Further program design strengths include: wide eligibility; easily disseminated information through a top-down approach; possibly compounded ROI; optional pilot procedures that can be built into the program to establish pre-test levels of BNS and performance for longitudinal post-test comparisons; relatively short training length; and supplementary materials for convenient reference.

Overall, the implications for this intervention are rich with the potential to positively impact PRM systems and organizations. Furthermore, the surrounding literature is replete with supporting evidence for veracity. This process could allow for maximization of resources provided by PRMs, build rapport between managers and employees, provide an effective tool to develop employee strengths, and allow opportunities for positive, open discussion around these strengths.

Limitations

Sometimes, ideal conditions are not always possible and thus depend upon certain components to be aligned for the process to work. This program contains a plethora of limitations replete with potentially deleterious effects. In the case of the organization, even if executives are willing to allow outside expertise, they, along with their teams, must be willing and able to accept and implement the program. This is when having a clear chain of command might be useful to positively reinforce the revised process, where top executives can keep sight of objectives given the relative data.

One significant factor is that organizations have different definitions and measures of performance. Performance is both a qualitative and quantitative construct, and emphasis on either is based on how it reflects each unique role or job description within a company that could vary in another company. Furthermore, the assigned values around performance can contrast between organizations, where time, bonuses, and commission might all be incorporated into measurement. Data may be standardizable, but this is why context is important to assess the best way to measure performance so that the method used reflects the subtle nuances that both qualitative and quantitative contexts can provide.

Even though the intervention considers brevity as an asset, it could also pose as a threat to validity if it does not elicit any effects. Furthermore, another source of variability lies in the different time intervals that organizations use when scheduling PRMs. Longer periods between PRMs, such as annual reviews, could affect the degree of the intervention's effectiveness. A factor that might contribute to this is vested interest (Crano, 1995; Sivacek & Crano, 1982), where perceiving the activities as low in relevance or importance might affect receptiveness and follow-through effort. This idea ties into the metaphor of strengths and limitations as a double-edged sword and presents an example of the difficulty associated with designing a methodologically sound intervention.

In terms of practical application, not only do plan procedures need to be carried out and maintained, they require a certain degree of authenticity and genuity for the successful transfer of dialogue. A possible limitation that is not accounted for in this intervention is leader inability to appropriately connect with employees or relate AD to facilitate goal generation. Leadership and overall organizational support for the intervention are crucial for the horizontal and longer-term vertical transfer of training back to the workplace. If the application of new knowledge, skills, and abilities is not encouraged or seen as pointless, then the intervention will have little effect on individual and firm performance in terms of executing key concepts learned from the training program. In an unsupportive climate, the training recipient will revert to previous ways of operation, costing the organization time and money. Leadership support is critical because leaders can either contribute to a climate for learning or prevent the application of new behaviors. Therefore, a supportive climate should be established for a training intervention to be successful (Salas & Stagl, 2009).

A supportive climate may consist of organizational culture emphasizing the values of performance, learning, and risk taking. Employee autonomy and flexibility are also essential characteristics of a supportive climate, the principles of goal setting assist employees in directing their focus and attention toward goal-directed behaviors (i.e., self-regulation) to meet challenging goals. According to SDT, alluded to above, increases in the internal regulation of behaviors thereby increases intrinsic motivation to perform that behavior (Ryan & Deci, 2000), indicating the essentiality of autonomy for persistent goal-directed behaviors. In combination, autonomy, and goal setting will produce motivated, engaged, and higher-performing employees. Thus, if a supportive environment can be achieved, it may help to counter this possible limitation.

Furthermore, the application of the program depends on at least some transparency and openness between dyads. Employees might not be open to dialogue due to prior (possibly negative) experiences or lack of established relationships with their superiors (e.g., trust, organizational justice, etc.), thereby blocking a potentially productive session. This could stem from personal reasons to social influencers such as personal static, internal politics, and culture (Ferris et al., 2017). Even if these conditions are met, effectiveness is sensitive to the designated reward structures to incentivize goal completion as well as alignment of other systems (e.g., pay, horizontal structure). Fortunately, goals that are internally motivated are less costly for companies and produce better results overall, alleviating reliance on pay-for-performance structured systems (Trice et al., 1984).

A prominent consideration in terms of some of the mediating process is the dark side of engagement. "Virtually all studies on work engagement offer evidence for the benefits of the experience" (Bakker et al., 2011, p. 17). However, engagement is not the opposite of burnout, and employees who experience full engagement can also feel burned out. There is indeed a delicate balance between passionately working that is not overengagement or workaholism. Too much engagement could lead to work–life imbalance, poorer physical and mental health, and strained personal relationships (Beal et al., 2005; Geurts & Demerouti, 2003; Halbesleben et al., 2009; Martin & Clore, 2001). Examples of negatively related measures include high self-esteem that could lead to planning fallacy (Buehler et al., 1994; Pezzo et al., 2006) and unrealistically optimistic expectations related to inappropriate goal persistence (Armor & Taylor, 1998), overconfidence that hinders performance (Vancouver et al., 2002; Vancouver et al., 2001), and creativity that might lead to frustration and diminished productivity if efforts are unfocused (Ford & Sullivan, 2004). Therefore, managers need to ensure the right amount of engagement encouraged during PRMs to create homeostasis of well-being.

There are also some limitations in employees' cognitive orientation that extend beyond Nisbett and Wilson's (1977) concerns for accessing higher-order cognitive processes. In a world of uncertainty and change, people tend to focus on the negative (negativity bias) (Baumeister et al., 2001; Rozin & Royzman, 2001). Ironically, this is also possibly reflected in the considerable length of the limitations section compared to the strengths portion of this chapter. Returning to the discussion of people, this could pose as a roadblock toward positive progress. Even if the basis of conversation is built on the principle that it is not possible to look at the positive without also evaluating the negative (Bright et al., 2011), some make the counterargument that behind every positive is a negative (Fineman, 2006). However, AI does not ignore the negative but rather embraces the polarities of this paradigm. The proposed approach shifts focus onto the heart of the matter behind these forces, giving vitality and value to organizations, by discovering dynamic connections and providing transformational change, and provides a mitigating stopgap for a cycle of perpetual perceptions of dissatisfaction and unfulfilling work (Bushe, 2010). AI through AD can be utilized in a plethora of situations a business might face but can be particularly beneficial when pessimism is most prevalent, regardless of the source of the cause. There are many ways to approach a situation, but a PRM program that incorporates SBGS can be a valuable resource for searching for the answer to issues while simultaneously presenting opportunities for learning and growth through a positive perspective.

In terms of potential utility for future applications, unfortunately, addressing these limitations takes time, and time is a precious resource. A logistical consideration is that companies that have a large employee population may not be able to afford as much time as would be optimal for quality one-on-one time with each employee, thereby sacrificing quality over quantity. In this case, managers may have to target specific employees or groups with this intervention based on who would have a higher need for the treatment. Furthermore, if employees are encouraged to take the survey outside of company time, participation might be given grudgingly, thereby affecting data.

It is important to note that the application of SBGS within PRMs is not useful for all organizations and should be evaluated for feasibility. Throughout this goal construction process during PRMs, managers specifically focus on strengths, thus omitting goal setting around weaknesses. While AI through AD is a successful tool for planned change, it is not necessarily a good fit for every organization, especially those built around improving weaknesses. Sometimes the area of interest that needs to be addressed extends beyond the scope of AI and requires further investigation with different, specialized models. Additionally, people are unique individuals and respond differently to various methods of intervention. Positive-based, inquiry-directed dialogue may evoke feelings of disconnect that the particular negative experiences are invalid or less meaningful, possibly repressing or deterring potentially important information disclosure and meaningful conversations (Egan & Lancaster, 2005; Miller et al., 2005; Pratt, 2002). Therefore, to determine if the intervention works, it is recommendable that the organization include performance measurements. However, since no two organizations are alike and there are numerous confounding and blocked variables, psychometricians and financial analysts might encounter performance measurement effects on performance (Pavlov & Bourne, 2011). Furthermore, the intervention and outcome connections would greatly benefit from supporting research, potentially through pilot studies and small-scale implementation. Even still, this approach is Western culture centered and may not have as high an impact regarding other types of organization culture interrelations.

In any case, due diligence to determine best-fit pairing is strongly recommended before applying any intervention to ensure organizational readiness and successful transfer of training back to the organization. The efficacy of organization development interventions depends on the in-depth diagnosis and the extent to which organizational needs are met. Interventions should be designed to fit organizational contingencies to realize anticipated outcomes (Cummings & Worley, 2015). As previously mentioned, prepackaged interventions rarely meet an organization's needs because organizations represent a complex web of interactions that result in distinct cultures and processes. Generic off-the-shelf interventions may appeal to management due to false promises of fast, easy, and cost-effective implementation but rarely include an initial context-based needs assessment to target the root cause of deficiencies (e.g., organization-, group-, and individual-level misalignments). Also, standardized interventions assume homogeneity across organizations in terms of task and interpersonal processes that are in reality unique and highly contingent (Salas & Stagl, 2009). To address these concerns, we added a component to our intervention that attempts to mold itself to the context by engaging organization members in designing the intervention to fit their unique context by using a modified large group AI framework (Cummings & Worley, 2015).

Then again, the adage of "if it ain't broke, don't fix it" comes to mind. This intervention will most likely produce greater effects with the condition of preestablished overall dissatisfaction with the current performance review process. Member acceptance and energy toward a planned change effort often requires a negative view of current conditions to stimulate readiness to change. If management and employees are satisfied with the current review process, then there exists little to no reason to implement our intervention. Management can stimulate an impetus for change by disseminating the results of a needs assessment with organization members or other related negative implications from maintaining an ineffective review process. Furthermore, disruptions to normative operations such as performance appraisals even if they are entirely ineffective are often met with resistance and definitely pose as a limitation. These disruptions represent a change in the way things are done and bring with them new expectations requiring a combination of different tasks and skills. With this in mind, those intending to implement planned change should be ready to address organization members' fears and concerns.

Future Directions

As noted above, commonly applied human resource performance management processes more often than not are characterized by poor implementation and suboptimal, even harmful, outcomes. To address these inadequacies, we are proposing research with the hope that it can be incorporated into structured, pragmatic training interventions. The intervention's design is intended to apply insight into what motivates performance, where researchers and practitioners can further develop this connection on related factors through extrapolation to facilitate both learning and application of the principles of SBGS through AD to produce optimally motivated performance and well-being. Based on the available research, it is highly probable that training interventions for managers that are rich in goal setting and positive psychological theory will most likely lead to such gains. This would ultimately result in an ROI and increase the organization's competitive advantage within the respective industries. Creating positive alternative solutions that not only work in PRMs but can be transferred across other contexts would be the ultimate goal for enriched, multipurposed integration. Thus, further investigation of SBGS as more than just a tool to develop and deploy, but as a starting point to cultivate lasting change, could be useful across organizational boundaries into other domains that transcend beyond this specific industry.

One possible route to explore is manager BNS and how it affects employees. It would be a simple extra mediating measure within this intervention's frame. As previously mentioned, there is numerous research on the effects of different leadership styles, feedback types, procedural justice, and providing autonomy support. There is less research on managerial BNS through a similar perspective of how BNS mediates employees' performance. Perhaps if managers can gauge their own BNS levels, it could increase self-awareness of their impact on employees. It might even increase relatability to help find commonalities or connections and improve overall communication. Thus, studying BNS effects on employees through the mediational effects of managers' impact on this interaction may be an interesting route to research.

Another interesting route to take would be how SDT can be utilized as a function of well-being. Specifically, evaluating the relationship between BNS in SDT and the multidimensional components of Seligman's conceptualization of well-being in his PERMA model (Seligman, 2011, 2018). Given that autonomy is already included as one of the facets of PERMA, looking at the underlying mechanisms for this need, as well as the others, might be useful to our understanding of drivers and determinants of well-being. Furthermore, looking at the links between increased well-being specifically as a result of increasing BNS on retention and burnout outcomes might be another promising avenue to pursue.

Other directions that would be interesting to study SBGS linkages include best-self activation, incorporating the possible self into goal setting, and NeoFreudian perspectives on self-inhibitions and limiting one's sense of self. Research applying SBGS principles into other areas of life may also have important implications, such as areas looking at personal goals and achievement, especially concerning difficult goals or tasks that require the aid of others (a collective accomplishment that is community oriented).

Conclusion

The proposed intervention in this chapter presents a unique, "intergr-AI-tive" compendium of goal setting within PRMs, conflating both traditional and new perspectives on increasing performance in a way that benefits both employers and employees. The approach uses a positive method to address PRMs that implement goal setting to focus on shortcomings or weaknesses. These traditional PRMs often structure these interactions around organization-wide issues and finances rather than individual growth from building employee well-being, knowledge, skills, motivation, engagement, and commitment to tasks as well as the organization. We hope that by focusing on a specific dimension of an intervention that can be initiated at almost any level of leadership, this small change within the organization can create a ripple or chain reaction for horizontal and vertical transfer of knowledge and application. By applying "the practical legacy of positive psychology" (Seligman et al., 2005, p. 410) that stems from the solid foundation of social psychology, we hope to contribute to the growing body of research on strengths within the organizational context. Particularly, by examining the mediating relationship between BNS from SBGS on performance, we hope to gain insight into the related dimensions of motivation, engagement, commitment, and well-being.

References

Aguinis, H., Gottfredson, R. K., & Joo, H. (2012). Delivering effective performance feedback: The strengths-based approach. *Business Horizons*, 55(2), 105–111.

Allport, F. H., & Allport, G. W. (1921). Personality traits: Their classification and measurement. *The Journal of Abnormal Psychology and Social Psychology*, *16*(1), 6.

Allport, G. (1935). Attitudes. In C. Murchison (Ed.), *A handbook of social psychology* (pp. 789–844). Worcester, MA: Clark University Press.

Armor, D. A., & Taylor, S. E. (1998). Situated optimism: Specific outcome expectancies and self regulation. In M. P. Zanna (Ed.), *Advances in experimental social psychology* (Vol. *30*, pp. 309–379). New York: Academic Press.

Asplund, J., & Blacksmith, N. (2011). Productivity through strengths. In K. Cameron & G. Spreitzer (Eds.), *The Oxford handbook of positive organizational scholarship* (Oxford Library of Psychology) (pp. 353–365). Oxford: Oxford University Press, USA.

Aureli, S. (2010). The introduction of innovative performance measurement and management control systems: The role of financial investors and their acquired companies. In M. J. Epstein, J. F. Manzoni, & A. Daviala (Eds.), *Performance measurement and management control: Innovative concepts and practices.* Bingley: Emerald Group Publishing.

Baard, P. P. (2002). Intrinsic need satisfaction in organizations: A motivational basis of success in for-profit and not-for-profit settings. In E. L. Deci & R. M. Ryan (Eds.), *Handbook of self-determination research* (pp. 255–275). Rochester, NY: University of Rochester Press.

Baard, P. P., Deci, E. L., & Ryan, R. M. (2004). Intrinsic need satisfaction: A motivational basis of performance and well-being in two work settings. *Journal of Applied Social Psychology, 34*, 2045–2068.

Bakker, A. B., Albrecht, S. L., & Leiter, M. P. (2011). Key questions regarding work engagement. *European Journal of Work and Organizational Psychology, 20*(1), 4–28.

Bandura, A. (1982). Self-efficacy mechanism in human agency. *American Psychologist, 37*(2), 122.

Bandura, A. (1997). *Self-efficacy: The exercise of control.* New York, NY: W. H. Freeman/Times Books/Henry Holt & Co.

Baumeister, R., & Leary, M. R. (1995). The need to belong: Desire for interpersonal attachments as a fundamental human motivation. *Psychological Bulletin, 117*, 497–529.

Baumeister, R. F., Bratslavsky, E., Finkenauer, C., & Vohs, K. D. (2001). Bad is stronger than good. *Review of General Psychology, 5*, 323–370.

Beal, D. J., Weiss, H. M., Barros, E., & MacDermid, S. M. (2005). An episodic process model of affective influences on performance. *Journal of Applied Psychology, 90*, 1054–1068.

Bouskila-Yam, O., & Kluger, A. N. (2011). Strength-based performance appraisal and goal setting. *Human Resource Management Review, 21*(2), 137–147.

Bowers, K. M., & Lopez, S. J. (2010). Capitalizing on personal strengths in college. *Journal of College and Character, 11*, 1–11.

Bowman, J. S. (1999). Performance appraisal: Verisimilitude trumps veracity. *Public Personnel Management, 28*(4), 557–576.

Brien, M., Boudrias, J. S., Lapointe, D., & Savoie, A. (2010). Promoting psychological health and performance in educational work context: How the satisfaction of three basic psychological needs can help achieve both. In M. Cortina & G. Tanucci (Eds.), *Boundaryless careers and occupational wellbeing* (pp. 279–288). Basingstoke: Macmillan.

Brien, M., Forest, J., Mageau, G., Boudrias, J., Desrumaux, P., Brunet, L., & Morin, E. (2012). The basic psychological needs at work scale: Measurement invariance between Canada and France. *Applied Psychology: Health and Well-being, 4*(2), 167–187.

Bright, D. S., Powley, E. H., Fry, R. E., & Barrett, F. J. (2011). The generative potential of cynical conversations. In D. Zandee, D. L. Cooperrider, & M. Avital (Eds.), in press. *Generative organization: Advances in appreciative inquiry* (Vol. 4). Bingley, England: Emerald Publishing.

Buehler, R., Griffin, D., & Ross, M. (1994). Exploring the "planning fallacy": Why people underestimate their task completion times. *Journal of Personality and Social Psychology, 67*, 366–381.

Bushe, G. R. (2010). A comparative case study of appreciative inquiries in one organization: Implications for practice. *Revista de Cercetare si Interventie Sociala, 29*, 7–24.

Bushe, G. R. (2013). The appreciative inquiry model. In E. H. Kessler (Ed.), *Encyclopedia of management theory* (Vol. 1, pp. 41–44). Thousand Oaks, CA: Sage Publications.

Cameron, K., Mora, C., Leutscher, T., & Calarco, M. (2011). Effects of positive practices on organizational effectiveness. *The Journal of Applied Behavioral Science, 47*(3), 266–308.

Campbell, D. T. (1958). Common fate, similarity, and other indices of the status of aggregates of persons as social entities. *Behavioural Science, 3*, 14–25.

Choong, K. K. (2013). Are PMS meeting the measurement needs of BPM? A literature review. *Business Process Management Journal, 19*(3), 535–574.

Choong, K. K. (2014). The fundamentals of performance measurement systems. *International Journal of Productivity and Performance Management, 63*(7), 879–922.

Cialdini, R. B., & Trost, M. R. (1998). Social influence: Social norms, conformity, and compliance. In D. T. Gilbert, S. T. Fiske, & G. Lindzey (Eds.), *The handbook of social psychology* (Vol. 1, 4th ed., pp. 151–192). New York, NY, US: McGraw-Hill.

Clifton, D., Ryan, R. M., & Deci, E. L. (2002). Overview of self-determination theory: An organismic dialectical perspective. In E. L. Deci & R. M. Ryan (Eds.), *Handbook of self-determination research* (pp. 3–33). Rochester, NY: University of Rochester Press.

Clifton, D. O., & Harter, J. K. (2003). Investing in strengths. In K. S. Cameron, J. E. Dutton, & R. E. Quinn (Eds.), *Positive organizational scholarship* (pp. 111–121). San Francisco: Berrett-Koehler.

Coens, T., & Jenkins, M. (2000). *Abolishing performance appraisals: Why they backfire and what to do instead.* San Francisco: Berrett-Koehler Publishers.

Connelly, J. (2002). All together now. *Gallup Management Journal, 2*(1), 13–18.

Cooperrider, D. (1990). Positive image, positive action: The affirmative basis for organizing. In S. Srivastva & D. Cooperrider (Eds.), *Appreciative management and leadership.* San Francisco: Jossey-Bass.

Cooperrider, D., & Sekerka, L. E. (2006). Toward a theory of positive organizational change. In J. V. Gallos (Ed.), *Organization development.* San Francisco: Jossey-Bass.

Cooperrider, D. L., & Srivastva, S. (1987). Appreciative inquiry in organizational life. In R. W. Woodman & W. A. Pasmore (Eds.), *Research in organizational change and development* (Vol. *1*). Stamford, CT: JAI Press.

Couturier, J., & Sklavounos, N. (2019). Performance dialogue: A framework to enhance the effectiveness of performance measurement systems. *International Journal of Productivity and Performance Management, 10*, 1–22.

Crano, W. D. (1995). Attitude strength and vested interest. In R. E. Petty & J. A. Krosnick (Eds.), *Attitude strength: Antecedents and consequences* (pp. 131–157). Mahwah, NJ: Erlbaum.

Cummings, T. G., & Molloy, E. S. (1977). *Improving productivity and the quality of work life.* Oxford, England: Praeger.

Cummings, T. G., & Worley, C. G. (2015). *Organization development & change* (10th ed.). Stamford, CT: Cengage Learning.

Damasio, A. R., Damasio, H., & Christen, Y. (Eds.). (1996). *Neurobiology of decision making: Research and perspectives in neurosciences.* Berlin, Germany: Springer.

DeCharms, R. (1968). *Personal causation.* New York: Academic Press.

Deci, E. L. (1975). *Intrinsic motivation.* New York: Plenum.

Deci, E. L., Connell, J. P., & Ryan, R. M. (1989). Self-determination in a work organization. *Journal of Applied Psychology, 74*, 580–590.

Deci, E. L., & Ryan, R. M. (1980). The empirical exploration of intrinsic motivational processes. In L. Berkowitz (Ed.), *Advances in experimental social psychology* (Vol. *13*, pp. 39–80). New York: Academic.

Deci, E. L., & Ryan, R. M. (2000). The "what" and "why" of goal pursuits: Human needs and the self-determination of behavior. *Psychological Inquiry, 11*(4), 227–268.

Deci, E. L., & Ryan, R. M. (2008). Facilitating optimal motivation and psychological well-being across life's domains. *Canadian Psychology/ Psychologie Canadienne, 49*(1), 14.

Deci, E. L., & Ryan, R. M. (2014). The importance of universal psychological needs for understanding motivation in the workplace. In M. Gagné (Ed.), *The Oxford handbook of work engagement, motivation, and self-determination theory.* (Oxford Library of Psychology) Oxford: Oxford University Press.

Deci, E. L., Ryan, R. M., Gagné, M., Leone, D. R., Usunov, J., & Kornazheva, B. P. (2001). Need satisfaction, motivation, and well-being in the work organizations of a former Eastern bloc country. *Personality and Social Psychology Bulletin, 27*, 930–942.

Dewar, B., & Nolan, M. (2013). Caring about caring: Developing a model to implement compassionate relationship centred care in an older people care setting. *International Journal of Nursing Studies, 50*(9), 1247–1258.

Donaldson, S. I., Gooler, L. E., & Scriven, M. (2002). Strategies for managing evaluation anxiety: Toward a psychology of program evaluation. *American Journal of Evaluation, 23*(3), 261–273.

Durham, C. C., & Bartol, K. M. (2009). Pay for performance. In E. A. Locke, *Handbook of principles of organizational behavior: Indispensable knowledge for evidence-based management* (2nd ed.). Chichester: West Sussex: John Wiley & Sons, Ltd.

Dworkin, G. (1988). *The theory and practice of autonomy.* New York: Cambridge University Press.

Earley, P. C., & Lee, C. (1992). Comparative peer evaluations of organizational behavior theories. *Organizational Development Journal, 10,* 37–42.

Eberly, M. B., Holtom, B. C., Lee, T. W., & Mitchell, T. R. (2009). Control voluntary turnover by understanding its causes. In E. A. Locke, *Handbook of principles of organizational behavior: Indispensable knowledge for evidence-based management* (2nd ed.). Chichester: West Sussex: John Wiley & Sons, Ltd.

Edel, R., & Belinda, D. (2016). A reflective account on becoming reflexive: The 7 Cs of caring conversations as a framework for reflexive questioning. *International Practice Development Journal, 6*(1), 1–8.

Eden, D. (1988). Creating expectation effects in OD: Applying self-fulfilling prophecy. In W. Pasmore & R. Woodman (Eds.), *Organizational change and development* (Vol. 2). Greenwich, CT: JAI Press.

Egan, T. M., & Lancaster, C. M. (2005). Comparing appreciative inquiry to action research: OD practitioner perspectives. *Organization Development Journal, 23*(2), 29–49.

Ekman, P. (1984). Expression and then nature of emotion. In K. R. Scherer & P. Ekman (Eds.), *Approaches to emotion*. Hillsdale, NK: Erlbaum.

Fernet, C., Guay, F., Senécal, C., & Austin, S. (2012). Predicting intraindividual changes in teacher burnout: The role of perceived school environment and motivational factors. *Teaching and Teacher Education, 28*(4), 514–525.

Ferris, G. R., Perrewé, P. L., Daniels, S. R., Lawong, D., & Holmes, J. J. (2017). Social influence and politics in organizational research: What we know and what we need to know. *Journal of Leadership & Organizational Studies, 24*(1), 5–19.

Festinger, L. (1954). A theory of social comparison processes. *Human Relations, 7,* 117–140.

Fineman, S. (1996). Emotion and organizing. In S. R. Clegg, C. Hardy, & T. B. Lawrence (Eds.), *The SAGE handbook of organization studies* (pp. 675–700). London, England: SAGE Publications Ltd.

Fineman, S. (2006). On being positive: Concerns and counterpoints. *Academy of Management Review, 31*(2), 270–291.

Fleming, J. H., & Asplund, J. (2007). *Human sigma: Managing the employee-customer encounter*. New York: Gallup Press.

Ford, C., & Sullivan, D. M. (2004). A time for everything: How timing of novel contributions influences project team outcomes. *Journal of Organizational Behavior for Evidence-Based Management, 25*(2), 163–183.

Forrester, J. P., & Adams, G. B. (1997). Budgetary reform through organizational learning: Toward an organizational theory of budgeting. *Administration and Society, 28*(4), 466–488.

Fritz, M. S., & MacKinnon, D. P. (2007). Required sample size to detect the mediated effect. *Psychological Science, 18,* 233–239.

Fritz, M. S., & MacKinnon, D. P. (2008). A graphical representation of the mediated effect. *Behavior Research Methods, 40*(1), 55–60.

Gabris, G. T., & Ihrke, D. M. (2001). Does performance appraisal contribute to heightened levels of employee burnout? The results of one study. *Public Personnel Management, 30*(2), 157–172.

Gagné, M. (Ed.). (2014). *The Oxford handbook of work engagement, motivation, and self-determination theory*. New York, NY: Oxford University Press.

Gagné, M., & Deci, E. (2005). Self-determination theory and work motivation. *Journal of Organizational Behavior, 26*(4), 331–362.

Gagné, M., Forest, J., Gilbert, M. E., Aubé, C., Morin, E., & Marloni, A. (2009). The Motivation at Work Scale: Validation evidence in two languages. *Educational and Psychological Measurement, 70*(4), 628–646.

Garcea, N., & Linley, P. A. (2011). Creating positive social change through building positive organizations: Four levels of intervention. In R. Biswas-Diener (Ed.), *Positive psychology as social change* (pp. 159–174). Dordrecht, The Netherlands: Springer.

Gauggel, S. (1999). Goal-setting and its influence on the performance of brain-damaged patients. Unpublished doctoral dissertation. Germany: Philipps University of Marburg.

Gellatly, I. R., Meyer, J. P., & Luchak, A. A. (2006). Combined effects of the three commitment components on focal and discretionary behaviors: A test of Meyer and Herscovitch's propositions. *Journal of Vocational Behavior, 69*, 331–345.

Gergen, K., McNamee, S., & Barrett, F. (2001). Toward transformative dialogue. *International Journal of Public Administration, 24*(7–8), 679–707.

Geurts, S. A. E., & Demerouti, E. (2003). Work/non-work interface: A review of theories and Findings. In M. Schabracq, J. Winnubst, & C. L. Cooper (Eds.), *The handbook of work and health psychology* (2nd ed., pp. 279–312). Chichester, UK: Wiley.

Ghalayini, A. M., & Noble, J. S. (1996). The changing basis of performance measurement. *International Journal of Operations & Production Management, 16*(8), 63–80.

Govindji, R., & Linley, P. A. (2007). Strengths use, self-concordance and well-being: Implications for strengths coaching and coaching psychologists. *International Coaching Psychology Review, 2*(2), 143–153.

Graen, G. B., Novak, M. A., & Sommerkamp, P. (1982). The effects of leader-member exchange and job design on productivity and satisfaction: Testing a dual attachment model. *Organizational Behavior and Human Performance, 30*(1), 109–131.

Greguras, G. J., & Diefendorff, J. M. (2009). Different fits satisfy different needs: Linking person-environment fit to employee commitment and performance using self-determination theory. *Journal of Applied Psychology, 94*(2), 465.

Guay, F., Ratelle, C. F., & Chanal, J. (2008). Optimal learning in optimal contexts: The role of self-determination in education. *Canadian Psychology, 49*, 233–240.

Halbesleben, J. R. B., Harvey, J., & Bolino, M. C. (2009). Too engaged? A conservation of resources view of the relationship between work engagement and work interference with family. *Journal of Applied Psychology, 94*, 1452–1465.

Harter, J. K., Schmidt, F. L., & Hayes, T. L. (2002). Business-unit-level relationship between employee satisfaction, employee engagement, and business outcomes: A meta-analysis. *Journal of Applied Psychology, 87*, 268–279.

Harter, S. (1978). Effectance motivation reconsidered: Toward a developmental model. *Human Development, 1*, 661–669.

Hiemstra, D., & Van Yperen, N. (2015). The effects of strength-based versus deficit-based self-regulated learning strategies on students' effort intentions. *Motivation and Emotion, 39*(5), 656–668.

Hodges, T. D., & Asplund, J. (2010). Strengths development in the workplace. In P. A. Linley, S. Harrington, & N. Garcea (Eds.), *Oxford handbook of positive psychology* (pp. 21–22). New York: Oxford University Press.

Hogg, M. A. (2010). Human groups, social categories, and collective self: Social identity and the management of self-uncertainty. In R. M. Arkin, K. C. Oleson, & P. J. Carroll (Eds.), *Handbook of the uncertain self* (pp. 401–420). New York, NY: Psychology Press.

Hull, C. L. (1943). *Principles of behavior: An introduction to behavior theory*. New York: Appleton-Century-Crofts.

Ikramullah, M., Van Prooijen, J., Iqbal, M., & Ul-Hassan, F. (2016). Effectiveness of performance appraisal. *Personnel Review, 45*(2), 334–352.

Jawahar, I. (2010). The mediating role of appraisal feedback reactions on the relationship between rater feedback-related behaviors and ratee performance. *Group & Organization Management, 35*(4), 494–526.

Johnson, H. T., & Kaplan, R. S. (1987). *Relevance lost: The rise and fall of management accounting*. Boston, MA: Harvard Business School Press.

Judge, T. A., Thoresen, C. J., Bono, J. E., & Patton, G. K. (2001). The job satisfaction-job performance relationship: A qualitative and quantitative review. *Psychological Bulletin, 127*, 376–407.

Kaplan, R. S. & Norton, D. P. (1992). The balanced scorecard – Measures that drive performance. *Harvard Business Review, 70*(1), 71–79.

Kaplan, R. S., & Norton, D. P. (1996). Linking the balanced scorecard to strategy. *California Management Review, 39*(1), 53–79.

Kelley, H. H. (1967). Attribution theory in social psychology. In D. Levine (Ed.), *Nebraska symposium on motivation, 1967* (pp. 192–240). Lincoln: University of Nebraska Press.

Kennerley, M., & Neely, A. (2003). Measuring performance in a changing business environment. *International Journal of Operations & Production Management, 23*(2), 213–229.

Lakoff, G., & Johnson, M. (1980). *Metaphors we live by*. Chicago, IL: University of Chicago Press.

La Guardia, J. G., & Patrick, H. (2008). Self-determination theory as a fundamental theory of close relationships. *Canadian Psychology/Psychologie Canadienne, 49*(3), 201.

Latham, G. P. (2009a). Appraise and coach your employees to be high performers. In T. L. Giluk (Ed.), *Becoming the evidence-based manager: Making the science of management work for you*. Boston, MA: Davies-Black.

Latham, G. P. (2009b). Motivate employee performance through goal setting. In E. A. Locke, *Handbook of principles of organizational behavior: Indispensable knowledge for evidence-based management* (2nd ed.). Chichester, West Sussex: John Wiley & Sons, Ltd.

Latham, G. P., & Locke, E. A. (1991). Self regulation through goal setting. *Organizational Behavior and Human Decision Process, 50*, 212–247.

Latham, G. P., & Locke, E. A. (2007). New developments in and directions for goal-setting research. *European Psychologist, 12*(4), 290–300.

Latham, G. P., & Wexley, K. N. (1994). *Increasing productivity through performance appraisal* (2nd ed.). New York: Addison-Wesley.

Le, H., Schmidt, F. L., Harter, J. K., & Lauver, K. J. (2010). The problem of empirical redundancy of constructs in organizational research: An empirical investigation. *Organizational Behavior and Human Decision Processes, 112*(2), 112–125.

Lemaire, J., & Wallace, J. (2017). Burnout among doctors. *BMJ, 358*, 358.

Levine, M., & Spreitzer, G. M. (2012). Positive deviance: A metaphor and method for learning from the uncommon. In K. S. Cameron (Ed.), *The Oxford handbook of positive organizational scholarship*. New York, NY: Oxford University Press.

Limb, M. (2015). NHS must show that staff engagement work is effective, researchers say. *BMJ: British Medical Journal (Online), 351*, 1.

Linley, P., Nielsen, K. M., Gillett, R., & Biswas-Diener, R. (2010). Using signature strengths in pursuit of goals: Effects on goal progress, need satisfaction, and well-being, and implications for coaching psychologists. *International Coaching Psychology Review, 5*, 6–15.

Locke, E. (1968). Toward a theory of task motivation and incentives. *Organizational Behavior and Human Performance, 3*(2), 157–189.

Locke, E. A. (1976). The nature and causes of job satisfaction. In M. D. Dunnette's (Ed.), *Handbook of industrial and organizational psychology* (pp. 1300). Chicago: Rand McNally.

Locke, E. A. (Ed.). (2009). *Handbook of principles of organizational behavior: Indispensable knowledge for evidence-based management* (2nd ed.). Chichester, West Sussex: John Wiley & Sons, Ltd.

Locke, E. A., & Latham, G. P. (1990). *A theory of goal setting and task performance*. Englewood Cliffs, NJ: Prentice Hall.

Locke, E. A., & Latham, G. P. (2002). Building a practically useful theory of goal setting and task motivation: A 35-year odyssey. *American Psychologist, 57*, 705–717.

Macey, W. H., & Schneider, B. (2008). The meaning of employee engagement. *Industrial and Organizational Psychology, 1*, 3–30.

Manz, C. C., & Sims, H. P., Jr. (1987). Leading workers to lead themselves: The external leadership of self-managing work teams. *Administrative Science Quarterly, 32*(1), 106–129.

Marchand, M., & Raymond, L. (2008). Researching performance measurement systems: An information systems perspective. *International Journal of Operations & Production Management, 28*(7), 663–686.

Markle, G. L. (2000). *Catalytic coaching: The end of the performance review*. Westport, Conn.: Quorum Books.

Martin, L. L., & Clore, G. L. (Eds.). (2001). *Theories of mood and cognition*: A user's handbook. Mason, Ohio: Thompson South-Western. Mahwah, NJ: Lawrence Erlbaum Associates, Inc.

Maslow, A. H. (1943). A theory of human motivation. *Psychological Review, 50*, 370–396.

McClelland, D. C. (1965). Achievement and entrepreneurship: A longitudinal study. *Journal of Personality and Social Psychology, 14*, 389–392.

McCunn, P. (1998). The balanced scorecard: The eleventh commandment. *Management Accounting, 76*(11), 34–36.

Mengis, J., & Eppler, M. J. (2008). Understanding and managing conversations from a knowledge perspective: An analysis of the roles and rules of face-to-face conversations in organizations. *Organization Studies, 29*(10), 1287–1313.

Merton, R. K. (1968). *Social theory and social structure.* New York: The Free Press.

Meyer, J. P. (2014). Employee commitment, motivation, and engagement. In M. Gagné (Ed.), *The Oxford handbook of work engagement, motivation, and self-determination theory.* New York, NY: Oxford University Press.

Meyer, J. P., & Gagné, M. (2008). Employee engagement from a self-determination theory perspective. *Industrial and Organizational Psychology, 1*(1), 60–62.

Meyer, J. P., & Herscovitch, L. (2001). Commitment in the workplace: Toward the general model. *Human Resource Management Review, 11,* 299–326.

Meyer, J. P., & Maltin, E. R. (2010). Employee commitment and well-being: A critical review, theoretical framework, and research agenda. *Journal of Vocational Behavior, 77,* 323–337.

Meyer, J. P., & Parfyonova, N. M. (2010). Normative commitment in the workplace: A theoretical analysis and re-conceptualization. *Human Resource Management Review, 20,* 283–294.

Meyer, J. P., Stanley, D. J., Herscovitch, L., & Topolnytsky, L. (2002). Affective, continuance, and normative commitment to the organization: A meta-analysis of antecedents, correlates, and consequences. *Journal of Vocational Behavior, 61,* 20–52.

Meyers, M. C., Van Woerkom, M., de Reuver, R., Bakk, Z., & Oberski, D. L. (2015). Enhancing psychological capital and personal growth initiative: Working on strengths or deficiencies? *Journal of Counseling Psychology, 62*(1), 50–62.

Miller, M. G., Fitzgerald, S. P., Murrell, K. L., Preston, J., & Ambekar, R. (2005). Appreciative inquiry in building a transcultural strategic alliance. *Journal of Applied Behavioral Science, 41*(1), 91–110.

Miner, J. B. (1984). The validity and usefulness of theories in an emerging organizational science. *Academy of Management Review, 9,* 296–306.

Minhas, G. (2010). Developing realised and unrealised strengths: Implications for engagement, self-esteem, life satisfaction and well-being. *Assessment and Development Matters, 2*(1), 12–16.

Mintzberg, H. (1975). *The nature of managerial work.* New York, NY: Harper & Row.

Mitchell, T. R., & Daniels, D. (2003). Motivation. In W. C. Borman, D. R. Ilgen, & R. J. Klimoski (Eds.), *Handbook of psychology: Industrial organizational psychology* (Vol. *12,* pp. 225–254). New York: Wiley.

Mouratidis, A., Vansteenkiste, M., Lens, W., & Sideridis, G. (2008). The motivating role of positive feedback in sport and physical education: Evidence for a motivational model. *Journal of Sport and Exercise Psychology, 30,* 240–268.

Moynihan, D. (2005). Goal-based learning and the future of performance management. *Public Administration Review, 65*(2), 203–216.

Najmi, M., Rigas, J., & Fan, I. (2005). A framework to review performance measurement systems. *Business Process Management Journal, 11*(2), 109–122.

Neely, A., Gregory, M., & Platts, K. (1995). Performance measurement system design. A literature review and research agenda. *International Journal of Operations and Production Management, 15*(4), 80–116.

Niemiec, C. P., Ryan, R. M., & Deci, E. L. (2009). The path taken: Consequences of attaining intrinsic and extrinsic aspirations in post-college life. *Journal of Research in Personality, 43,* 291–306.

Nisbett, R. E., & Wilson, T. D. (1977). Telling more than we can know: Verbal reports on mental processes. *Psychological Review, 84,* 231–259.

Nix, G., Ryan, R. M., Manly, J. B., & Deci, E. L. (1999). Revitalization through self-regulation: The effects of autonomous and controlled motivation on happiness and vitality. *Journal of Experimental Social Psychology, 35,* 266–284.

Olivero, G., Bane, K. D., & Kopelman, R. E. (1997). Executive coaching as a transfer of training tool: Effects on productivity in a public agency. *Public Personnel Management, 26*(4), 461–469.

Pádua, S. I. D., & Jabbour, C. J. C. (2015). Promotion and evolution of sustainability performance measurement systems from a perspective of business process management: From a literature review to a pentagonal proposal. *Business Process Management Journal, 21*(2), 403–418.

Pavlov, A., & Bourne, M. (2011). Explaining the effects of performance measurement on performance. *International Journal of Operations & Production Management, 31*(1), 101–122.

Peterson, C., & Seligman, M. E. P. (2004). *Character strengths and virtues: A handbook and classification.* Washington, D.C.: American Psychological Association.

Pezzo, M., Litman, J., & Pezzo, S. (2006). On the distinction between yuppies and hippies: Individual differences in prediction biases for planning future tasks. *Personality and Individual Differences, 41*(7), 1359–1371.

Pinder, C. C. (1998). *Work motivation in organizational behavior* (p. 11). Saddle River, NJ: Prentice Hall.

Pratt, C. (2002). Creating unity from competing integrities: A case study in appreciative inquiry methodology. In R. Fry, F. Barrett, J. Seiling, & D. Whitney (Eds.), *Appreciative inquiry and organizational transformation: Reports from the field* (pp. 99–120). Westport, CT: Quorum Books.

Prigatano, G. P., Wong, J. L., Williams, C., & Plenge, K. L. (1997). Prescribed versus actual length of stay and impatient neurorehabilitation outcome for brain dysfunctional patients. *Archives of Physical Medicine and Rehabilitation, 78,* 621–629.

Proctor, C., Maltby, J., & Linley, P. (2011). Strengths use as a predictor of well-being and health-related quality of life. *Journal of Happiness Studies, 12,* 153–169.

Putnam, L., & Mumby, D. K. (1993). Organizations, emotion and myth of rationality. In S. Fineman (Ed.), *Emotion in organizations.* London: Sage.

Rechter, E. (2010). *Emotional and cognitive reaction to feedforward intervention.* Paper presented at the 11th annual meeting of the Society for Personality and Social Psychology, Las Vegas, NV.

Reis, H. T. (1994). Domains of experience: Investigating relationship processes from three perspectives. In R. Erber & R. Gilmour (Eds.), *Theoretical frameworks for personal relationships* (pp. 87–110). Hillsdale, NJ: Erlbaum.

Reis, H. T., Sheldon, K. M., Gable, S. L., Roscoe, J., & Ryan, R. M. (2000). Daily well-being: The role of autonomy, competence, and relatedness. *Personality and Social Psychology Bulletin, 26,* 419–435.

Rhoades, L., & Eisenberger, R. (2002). Perceived organizational support: A review of the literature. *Journal of Applied Psychology, 87*, 698–714.

Robison, J. (2003). How GlaxoSmithKline builds employee strengths. *Gallup Management Journal, 3*. Retrieved from http://gmj.gallup.com/content/1015/How-GlaxoSmithKline-Builds-Employee-Strengths.aspx.

Rosenthal, R., & Jacobson, L. (1968). *Pygmalion in the classroom: Teacher expectation and pupils' intellectual development.* New York: Holt, Rinehart and Winston.

Rotundo, M. (2009). Conduct performance appraisals to improve individual and firm performance. In E. A. Locke, *Handbook of principles of organizational behavior: Indispensable knowledge for evidence-based management* (2nd ed.). Chichester: West Sussex: John Wiley & Sons, Ltd.

Rozin, P., & Royzman, E. B. (2001). Negativity bias, negativity dominance, and contagion. *Personality and Social Psychology Review, 5*(4), 296–320.

Ryan, R. M. (1995). Psychological needs and the facilitation of integrative processes. *Journal of Personality, 63*, 397–427.

Ryan, R. M., Connell, J. P., & Deci, E. L. (1985). A motivational analysis of self-determination and self-regulation in education. In C. Ames & R. E. Ames (Eds.), *Research on motivation in education: The classroom milieu* (pp. 13–51). New York: Academic.

Ryan, R. M., & Deci, E. L. (2000). Self-determination theory and the facilitation of intrinsic motivation, social development, and well-being. *American Psychologist, 55*(1), 68.

Ryan, R. M., & Deci, E. L. (2009). Promoting self-determined school engagement: Motivation, learning, and well-being. In K. R. Wenzel & A. Wigfield (Eds.), *Educational psychology handbook series. Handbook of motivation at school* (pp. 171–195). Routledge/Taylor & Francis Group.

Ryan, R. M., Patrick, H., Deci, E. L., & Williams, G. C. (2008). Facilitating health behaviour change and its maintenance: Interventions based on self-determination theory. *The European Health Psychologist, 10*(1), 2–5.

Ryan, M., Rigby, C. S., & Przybylski, A. (2006). The motivational pull of video games: A self-determination theory approach. *Motivation and Emotion, 30*(4), 344–360.

Ryan, R. M., Sheldon, K. M., Kasser, T., & Deci, E. L. (1996). All goals are not created equal: An organismic perspective on the nature of goals and their regulation. In P. M. Gollwitzer & J. A. Bargh (Eds.), *The psychology of action: Linking cognition and motivation to behavior* (pp. 7–26). The Guilford Press.

Salas, E., & Stagl, K. C. (2009). Design training systematically and follow the science of training. In E. A. Locke, *Handbook of principles of organizational behavior: Indispensable knowledge for evidence-based management* (2nd ed.). Chichester, West Sussex: John Wiley & Sons, Ltd.

Sayles, L. R. (1964). *Managerial behavior; administration in complex organizations.* New York, NY: McGraw-Hill.

Seligman, M. (2018). PERMA and the building blocks of well-being. *The Journal of Positive Psychology, 13*(4), 333–335.

Seligman, M. E. P. (2011). *Flourish: A visionary new understanding of happiness and well-being.* New York, NY, US: Free Press.

Seligman, M. E. P., Steen, T. A., Park, N., & Peterson, C. (2005). Positive psychology progress: Empirical validation of interventions. *American Psychologist, 60*, 410–421.

Sheldon, K. M., & Elliot, A. J. (1999). Goal striving, need satisfaction, and longitudinal well-being: The self-concordance model. *Journal of Personality and Social Psychology, 76*(3), 482.

Sheldon, K. M., Elliot, A. J., Kim, Y., & Kasser, T. (2001). What is satisfying about satisfying events? Testing 10 candidate psychological needs. *Journal of Personality and Social Psychology, 80*, 325–339.

Sherif, M. (1958). Superordinate goals in the reduction of intergroup conflicts. *American Journal of Sociology, 63*, 349–356.

Sivacek, J., & Crano, W. D. (1982). Vested interest as a moderator of attitude-behavior consistency. *Journal of Personality and Social Psychology, 43*, 210–221.

Skinner, W. (1986). The productivity paradox. *Harvard Business Review, 64*, 5–9.

Smith, B., & Rutigliano, T. (2003). *Discover your sales strengths: How the world's greatest salespeople develop winning careers.* New York: Warner Books.

Soenens, B., & Vansteenkiste, M. (2010). A theoretical upgrade of the concept of parental psychological control: Proposing new insights on the basis of self-determination theory. *Developmental Review, 30*(1), 74–99.

Stipek, D. (2002). *Motivation to learn: Integrating theory and practice* (4th ed.). Boston, MA: Allyn & Bacon.

Sugrue, N. (1982). Emotions as property and context for negotiation. *Urban Life, 11*(3), 225–244.

Tafvelin, S., & Stenling, A. (2018). Development and initial validation of the need satisfaction and need support at work scales: A validity-focused approach. *Scandinavian Journal of Work and Organizational Psychology, 3*(1), 1–1.

Tajfel, H., & Turner, J. C. (1986). The social identity theory of intergroup behavior. In S. Worchel & W. G. Austin (Eds.), *Psychology of intergroup relations* (2nd ed., pp. 7–24). Chicago, IL: Nelson-Hall.

Tett, R. P., & Meyer, J. P. (1993). Job satisfaction, organizational commitment, turnover intention, and turnover: Path analyses based on meta-analytic findings. *Personnel Psychology, 47*, 259–293.

Trice, H., Mowday, R., Porter, L., & Steers, R. (1984). Employee-organization linkages: The psychology of commitment, absenteeism, and turnover. *Contemporary Sociology, 13*(1), 90–90.

Tubre, T. C., & Collins, J. M. (2000). Jackson and Schuler (1985) revisited: A meta-analysis of the relationships between role ambiguity, role conflict, and job performance. *Journal of Management, 26*(1), 155–169.

Tziner, A., & Murphy, K. R. (1999). Additional evidence of attitudinal influences in performance appraisal. *Journal of Business and Psychology, 13*(3), 407–419.

Upadhaya, B., Munir, R., & Blount, Y. (2014). Association between performance measurement systems and organisational effectiveness. *International Journal of Operations & Production Management, 34*(7), 853–875.

Van den Broeck, A., Vansteenkiste, M., & De Witte, H. (2008). Self-determination theory: A theoretical and empirical overview in occupational health psychology. In J. Houdmont & S. Leka (Eds.), *Occupational health psychology: European perspectives on research, education, and practice* (pp. 63–88). Nottingham: Nottingham University Press.

Van den Broeck, A., Vansteenkiste, M., De Witte, H., Soenens, B., & Lens, W. (2010). Capturing autonomy, competence, and relatedness at work: Construction and initial validation of the Work-related Basic Need Satisfaction scale. *Journal of Occupational and Organizational Psychology, 83*(4), 981–1002.

Van Woerkom, M., & De Bruijn, M. (2016). Why performance appraisal does not lead to performance improvement: Excellent performance as a function of uniqueness instead of uniformity. *Industrial and Organizational Psychology, 9*(2), 275–281.

Van Woerkom, M., & Meyers, M. C. (2015). My strengths count! Effects of a strengths-based psychological climate on positive affect and job performance. *Human Resource Management, 54*(1), 81–103.

Van Woerkom, M., Oerlemans, W. G. A., & Bakker, A. B. (2015). Strengths use and work engagement: A weekly diary study. *European Journal of Work and Organizational Psychology, 25*(3), 384–397.

Vancouver, J. B., Thompson, C. M., Tischner, E. C., & Putka, D. J. (2002). Two studies examining the negative effect of self-efficacy on performance. *Journal of Applied Psychology, 87*, 506–516.

Vancouver, J. B., Thompson, C. M., & Williams, A. A. (2001). The changing signs in the relationships between self-efficacy, personal goals and performance. *Journal of Applied Psychology, 86*, 605–620.

Walton, R. E., & Schlesinger, L. A. (1979). Do supervisors thrive in participative work systems? *Organizational Dynamics, 7*(3), 25–38.

Weinberg, R. S. (1994). Goal setting and performance in sport and exercise settings: A synthesis and critique. *Medicine and Science in Sports and Exercise, 26*, 469–477.

Weinberg, R. S., & Gould, D. (2007). *Foundations of sport and exercise psychology.* Champaign, IL: Human Kinetics.

Weisbord, M. R. (1985). Participative work design: A personal odyssey. *Organizational Dynamics, 13*(4), 5–20.

White, R. W. (1963). *Ego and reality in psychoanalytic theory.* New York: International Universities Press.

Wieland, U., Fischer, M., Pfitzner, M., & Hilbert, A. (2015). Process performance measurement system—Towards a customer-oriented solution. *Business Process Management Journal, 21*(2), 312–331.

5

Positive Capacity Building for Social Impact Organizations

Victoria Cabrera

The positive psychology movement has raised a new awareness of the potential for organizations to be vehicles for human flourishing, both for the people who work for them and society. This vision of organizations promotes positive institutions that "serve to elevate and develop our highest human strengths, combine and magnify those strengths, and refract our highest strengths outward in world benefiting ways leading, ultimately, to a world of full-spectrum flourishing" (Cooperrider & Godwin, 2012, p. 744). While different types of organizations can be positive institutions, there is one type in particular that has enormous potential to embody this vision: social impact organizations.

Social impact organizations are mission-based organizations that can take a variety of forms such as non-profit organizations, non-governmental organizations (NGOs), charities, and social enterprises. What these organizations have in common is their primary reason for the organization's existence: to address social problems and create social impact that benefits society (Applegate, 2002). Similar to traditional businesses, social impact organizations face an array of challenges due to operating in an ever-changing environment, driving the need to build organizational capacities, innovate, increase productivity, leverage technology, and ensure sustainability (Wirtenberg et al., 2007). On top of these challenges, social impact organizations tend to be resource constrained while having the added complexity of pursuing a dual mission of both social purpose and financial sustainability, while meeting the demands of diverse stakeholders. Work at these organizations can be highly demanding due to heavy workloads and the emotional labor of helping beneficiaries (Doherty et al., 2014; Morris et al., 2007).

Therefore, capacity building is an essential activity for social impact organizations to continually improve their effectiveness so that they can achieve and grow their social impact (Wagner, 2003). Many of these organizations have turned to traditional organizational development approaches for capacity building (Sawhill & Williamson, 2001; Wirtenberg et al., 2007). These traditional approaches tend to be deficit-focused with an emphasis on fixing problems (Cairns et al., 2005; Cummings & Worley, 2015). However, the fields of positive organizational devel-

Positive Organizational Psychology Interventions: Design and Evaluation, First Edition.
Stewart I. Donaldson and Christopher Chen.
© 2021 John Wiley & Sons Ltd. Published 2021 by John Wiley & Sons Ltd.

opment and positive psychology have brought to light the benefits of focusing on strengths as a way to help organizations and people reach their full potential. Using a strengths-based approach aligns well with capacity building, which aims to bring out the full potential of the organization and its people to increase social impact. Based on theory and research in positive organizational development and positive psychology, this chapter will propose a framework for positive capacity building. Positive capacity building is a strengths-based approach to organizational development that social impact organizations can use to improve their effectiveness and sustainability and build the social and psychological resources of their people in order to maximize social impact.

Prior Theory and Research

The positive capacity building framework is based on theory and research in positive organizational development and positive psychology; two fields focused on bringing out the best in people and organizations. This comprehensive and integrated framework combines two well-established models that have been demonstrated to be effective for organizational development: appreciative inquiry and action research (Cummings & Worley, 2015). It also incorporates training and development, based on positive psychology, to build the social and psychological resources of people to support their well-being and fuel work performance that will help the capacity building effort.

A Positive Organizational Development Approach for Capacity Building

Appreciative inquiry is a collaborative, strengths-based approach to change that focuses on looking for the best in an organization to determine what it is doing well and how to build on that success (Whitney et al., 2010). The approach leverages the power of asking appreciatively-framed questions to learn from success stories and what has gone well as a way to move organizations toward achieving their full potential, rather than narrowly focus on just fixing what is wrong (Cooperrider & Sekerka, 2003). It is based on the principles that language creates reality, inquiry creates change, what we choose to focus on grows, positive images of the future inspire action, and positive questions lead to positive change (Cooperrider & Whitney, 2011). This approach to change encourages innovation to bring out the best in organizations (Cooperrider & Godwin, 2012). A strengths-based approach to change is a good fit for capacity building, which aims to elevate an organization to the next level of effectiveness to maximize its social impact. It is also a good fit with the aspirations of social impact organizations to develop and maximize the potential of people. Through asking appreciative questions and sharing stories focused on success, the appreciative inquiry process creates inspiration, relational energy, and positive emotions (Cooperrider & Sekerka, 2003) that can fuel people through the capacity building process.

However, the appreciative inquiry model alone is not sufficient for capacity building because it is missing one critical element, evaluation. Evaluation is essential for social impact organizations because they need to be able to measure their impact and are often held accountable by funders and the public to do so

(Connolly & York, 2002). To incorporate evaluation, the positive capacity building framework also includes elements from the action research model for organizational development inspired by Kurt Lewin. This model is a popular framework for organizational development that involves data collection and analysis to determine the effectiveness of the intervention and to inform a continuous cycle of ongoing improvement (Cummings & Worley, 2015). Since the goal of capacity building is to increase social impact, data collection and evaluation to measure that impact is an essential part of the capacity building process (Wagner, 2003).

In addition, positive capacity building is also informed by general systems theory to ensure that it is comprehensive in addressing all aspects of the organization. Effective organizational development initiatives recognize organizations as systems and their relationship with their environment as part of larger ecosystems (Cummings & Worley, 2015). Positive capacity building takes a systems view of organizations to address capacity building across systems and at multiple levels (individual, teams, organization) while engaging internal and external stakeholders to collaborate and contribute to the capacity building process.

Building Social and Psychological Resources for Capacity Building

In addition to taking a positive approach to organizational improvement, positive capacity building has an additional focus that is missing from most capacity building and organizational development models: the building of social and psychological resources to fuel staff motivation, well-being and work performance. Positive capacity building provides knowledge, skills and work practices based on positive psychology to help staff at social impact organizations (both employees and volunteers) manage their well-being, build supportive work relationships and build psychological resources that will help them perform at their best.

Research has found that higher levels of employee well-being are associated with higher levels of work performance (Judge et al., 2001; Lyubomirsky et al., 2005; Zelenski et al., 2008). Martin Seligman's well-being theory describes five building blocks that enable well-being: positive emotions, engagement, positive relationships, meaning, and accomplishment. The theory asserts that people can improve their well-being through interventions that target each building block (Seligman, 2018). Psychological capital (PsyCap) has also been found to be established as an important psychological resource that positively impacts work performance and is linked with many positive organizational outcomes (Luthans & Youssef-Morgan, 2017). PsyCap is a positive psychological state characterized by hope, self-efficacy, resilience and optimism and has been linked to higher levels of well-being, engagement and work performance (Luthans, 2002; Luthans et al., 2007). A meta-analysis found that higher levels of PsyCap predict a number of other positive outcomes at work, including higher job satisfaction, more organizational commitment, desirable employee attitudes and more organizational citizenship behaviors. The meta-analysis also found that PsyCap was negatively related to negative work outcomes such as work stress and anxiety, worker cynicism, turnover intentions and negative deviance (Avey et al., 2011). The positive capacity building framework includes training to provide evidence-based skills that people can use to support their well-being and build PsyCap to enable them to perform at their best.

Positive capacity building also aims to empower staff through increased awareness and use of their strengths to bring out their full potential. The use of strengths in organizations is associated with many positive outcomes, including work satisfaction, employee engagement, and improved performance (Biswas-Diener et al., 2011). The use of strengths-based practices and interventions have also been found to increase performance and drive social change (Linley & Garcea, 2011). Positive capacity building places a focus on leveraging the strengths of individuals, teams, and the organization for effective capacity building.

Finally, positive capacity building also builds social resources by providing staff with skills that can help them build supportive work relationships. Research in positive organizational psychology has demonstrated that building high-quality relationships at work can be empowering and energizing for performance (Dutton, 2003). Building positive relationships is also an element of supporting well-being (Seligman, 2011), while having supportive work relationships can also help build resilience (Luthans & Youssef-Morgan, 2017) and motivation (Ryan & Deci, 2000). These relationships can be developed through interpersonal skills that people can use in daily work life, such as expressing appreciation (Grant & Gino, 2010) and recognition (Nelson, 2016). Therefore, the positive capacity building framework includes providing interpersonal skills, based on positive psychology, to build positive and supportive work relationships to facilitate capacity building efforts.

Creating Positive Conditions for Capacity Building

While providing skills that help staff build social and psychological resources is important for capacity building, it is not enough to fully empower people and energize their work performance. It is also important to create a positive work environment and supportive conditions that enable people to build these resources and empower them to be able to perform at their best. According to field theory, human behavior is influenced by a combination of both individual factors and environmental factors (Lewin, 1951). Since leadership plays a crucial role in shaping work environments, the positive capacity building framework also includes leadership capacity building to provide leaders with positive leadership skills. These skills are needed to create supportive work conditions for building the social and psychological resources of staff and supporting capacity building efforts. Positive leadership skills, based on leadership theory and positive psychology, help leaders build work environments that promote staff engagement, self-efficacy, and empowerment to fuel their motivation and work performance.

First, leaders need to understand how to create work conditions that support staff motivation and self-efficacy that will fuel people's work performance through any change initiative. According to self-determination theory, autonomous motivation, a type of motivation characterized by willingness, propensity, and choice, is critical for better, sustained performance (Ryan & Deci, 2017). Autonomous motivation is fueled by the satisfaction of three psychological needs: the need for autonomy, the need for competence, and the need for relatedness. Autonomy refers to an individual's ability to engage in work with a full sense of willingness, choice, and volition. Competence is based on individuals' perceptions of their work being important and leading to significant outcomes.

Relatedness is the desire to have a sense of belonging and meaningful relationships with others (Deci & Ryan, 2000). Research has demonstrated that managers play a key role in fueling their employees' autonomous motivation by creating work conditions that help them meet their needs for autonomy, competence, and relatedness (Ryan & Deci 2017). In addition, leaders can also encourage employees to perform at their best during times of uncertainty or change by creating conditions that promote self-efficacy, the belief in oneself to succeed in a specific situation or task. Leaders can build employees' self-efficacy by clarifying goals, role modeling, and recognizing small wins (Bandura, 1997).

Another important aspect of creating positive conditions for capacity building is leadership style. Positive capacity building provides leaders with positive leadership skills based on leadership theories that will help them motivate and empower the work performance of staff. Strengths-based leadership places a primary focus on managing the strengths of people and helping them to leverage those strengths to perform to their full potential and maximize their contribution to the organization (Rath & Conchie, 2008). Transformational leadership, an inspirational and empowering style of leadership that is effective in leading change, has also been shown to have a positive impact on follower development and performance. (Dvir et al., 2002; Sosik & Jung, 2018). Therefore, these two leadership styles are incorporated into leadership capacity building through positive leadership training.

Finally, leaders also need to understand how to build a positive organizational culture to create a work environment that is supportive of people and capacity building. Organizational culture is an aspect of organizations that needs to be managed by leaders because it influences how people work together through the underlying beliefs, values, and assumptions that drive organizational practices and behavior (Schein, 2010). For a positive capacity building initiative to be successful, leaders need to build a positive work environment that supports people and provides them with the social and psychological resources they need to support well-being and empower work performance. Positive capacity building includes training for leaders to understand organizational culture and how to build a positive work culture to create conditions that support capacity building, well-being, and performance.

Proposed Intervention: Positive Capacity Building for Social Impact Organizations

Positive capacity building is a comprehensive framework designed to be easy to follow and adapt to an organization's specific context and capacity building needs, which can range from a focus on the entire organization to a specific aspect of the organization (such as a specific department, program, or service). Based on the appreciative inquiry and action research models for organizational development, positive capacity building consists of eight phases that build on the "4-D" appreciative inquiry model (Cooperrider & Whitney, 2011) and are tailored to focus on capacity building for social impact organizations: Develop, Desire, Discover, Dream, Design, Deliver, Determine, and Decide. Table 5.1 provides a summary of the positive capacity building phases.

Table 5.1 Positive Capacity Building Phases.

Phase	Description
1. Develop	An orientation and training for capacity building participants to provide them with skills for three levels of positive capacity building: organization, team, and individual.
2. Desire	A reflective visioning session where participants reconnect with the organization's mission, vision, and values and share around their desired social impact.
3. Discover	Participants define the focus of the capacity building, share stories of success, and identify common themes that emerge.
4. Dream	Participants review the themes and envision an ideal future that builds on these themes.
5. Design	Participants identify priority areas and create an action plan for capacity building and evaluation.
6. Deliver	The action plan is implemented.
7. Determine	Data is collected and analyzed to measure the effectiveness and impact of the capacity building.
8. Decide	A session is held to review evaluation findings, discuss insights and learning, and identify priorities and needs for future capacity building.

Phase 1. Develop

This phase initiates the capacity building process with an orientation, team building, and training for capacity building participants to prepare them for later phases and to provide them with skills to build social and psychological resources that will fuel their work performance to drive the capacity building effort. First, an orientation will introduce participants to positive capacity building. It will provide participants with an understanding of a positive approach to capacity building through an introduction to appreciative inquiry. It will also teach participants how to identify and learn from positive deviance, uncommonly positive behaviors or outcomes (Levine, 2012). The goal of the orientation is to introduce participants to a strengths-based approach to capacity building and to shift their focus away from the traditional focus on fixing problems to looking for opportunities to build on their organization's strengths.

Next, the team building component will help participants build positive relationships at work. The goal of team building is to provide skills for participants to build supportive, high-quality relationships that will support their well-being, build relatedness, and promote resilience, as well as the opportunity to practice these skills with their coworkers. Team building will provide positive relationship skills and guide participants through the creation of a plan for using these skills: expressing appreciation (Grant & Gino, 2010) and recognition (Nelson, 2016), strengths-based feedback (Aguinis et al., 2012), non-violent communication as a framework for building empathy through compassionate interpersonal communication (Rosenberg, 2003), and reflected best-self activation where coworkers share times they witnessed each other as their best selves (Cable et al., 2015).

Finally, training will provide participants with positive work skills and practices. The goal of training is to provide skills and work practices, based in positive psychology, that will help participants perform at best by building psychological resources that will support their well-being and work Participants will learn how to manage well-being and how to build psychological resources to support work performance. Training will provide an overview of positive psychology theories, introduce them to evidence-based skills and work practices, and have them create a plan to use their newfound knowledge and skills at work. Training topics include understanding and supporting building blocks of well-being (Seligman, 2018), building psychological capital (Luthans et al., 2007), identifying and using strengths (Peterson & Seligman, 2004), practicing mindfulness to help manage emotions and build resilience (Joyce et al., 2019), and how to cultivate positive emotions (Fredrickson, 2001).

Leaders and managers will receive additional positive leadership training focused on developing positive leadership skills. The goal of positive leadership training is to help leaders bring out the best in the people they manage and create a positive environment that supports people's social and psychological resources to help them achieve higher levels of performance that will drive capacity building. During this training, participants will learn the following positive leadership skills and will create a plan for applying these skills: strengths-based leadership (Rath & Conchie, 2008), transformational leadership practices (Dvir et al., 2002), how to build a positive culture (Schein, 2010), understanding motivation based on self-determination theory (Deci & Ryan, 2000), and creating conditions for self-efficacy (Bandura, 1997).

The Develop phase consists of a series of workshop sessions, but the scheduling of the sessions can be flexible depending on an organization's needs and availability of the participants. The depth of training can also be tailored to the participants and the specific needs of the organization. Organizations may choose to add additional training topics and skills during this phase that will be relevant to their specific capacity building needs. Table 5.2 provides a summary of the training recommended in the Develop phase.

Phase 2. Desire

The goal of this phase is to reconnect participants to the organization's mission, vision, and values to inspire and energize them for the phases that follow. This phase is designed specifically to meet the needs of people who work for social impact organizations. It is based on the assumption that mission-based organizations attract people with shared values who choose to work there because they are passionate about the organization's mission and aspire to help the organization achieve its vision of social impact. However, day-to-day work tasks and challenges can sometimes disconnect people from the bigger picture of why they are doing the work in the first place. This can be especially challenging in social impact organizations that are resource constrained where staff carry heavy workloads and the emotional labor of providing services to beneficiaries. During this session, participants are given the opportunity to pause and reconnect with why they are doing the work: the

Table 5.2 The Develop Phase: Workshop Session Summary.

Session	Goal	Topics and Skills
Positive capacity building orientation	Understand the positive approach to capacity building	Appreciative inquiry, positive deviance
Positive relationships	Team building that provides skills for building supportive, high-quality work relationships	Appreciation, recognition, strengths-based feedback, non-violent communication, reflected best-self activation
Positive work skills and practices	Provide skills and practices for supporting well-being and building psychological capital that will help work performance	Building blocks of well-being, psychological capital, strengths, mindfulness broaden-and-build theory
Positive leadership	Leaders learn how to bring out the best in people and create a positive environment that promotes higher levels of performance	Strengths-based leadership, transformational leadership, building a positive culture, fueling autonomous motivation, nurturing self-efficacy

organization's mission, vision, and values. They will also reflect to reconnect with their own values, sense of meaning, life purpose, and their personal connection with the values and purpose of the organization. They will then share these reflections with those they work with to connect and build a sense of shared values, meaning, and purpose. The session consists of the following exercises:

1) **Individual reflection and visualization.** The goal of this exercise is for participants to identify and connect with what gives their life meaning, their life purpose, their personal values, and the positive impact they want to have on the world. During this exercise, participants write a personal mission, vision, and values statement. Next, they write a story about a time they lived this statement at work. Lastly, they draw a visual representation of the desired impact they want to have in the world.

2) **Sharing in pairs, small groups, or teams.** The goal of this exercise is to help participants understand what drives their colleagues and to develop a shared sense of purpose among participants. During this exercise, participants share their personal mission, vision, and values statements. Next, they share one story about a time they lived this statement. Lastly, they share their visual representation and describe the desired impact they want to have in the world.

3) **Large group sharing as a department, program, or organization.** The goal of this exercise is to further develop a sense of shared purpose among participants by connecting their life purpose to the values and purpose of the organization. During this exercise, participants review the organization's

mission, vision, and values statements and write an individual reflection on what the statements mean to them and what desired impact they would like the organization to have. Next, participants share their reflections during a large group discussion. In the case that an organization does not have articulated mission, vision, and values statements or if the organization would like to improve the statements, this exercise can be adjusted to focus participants on crafting or rewriting these statements together. Lastly, the group creates a summary or visual representation that represents their shared vision of the desired social impact they would like the organization to have.

Like the previous phase, the Desire phase can also be adjusted based on the specific needs of an organization or the availability of participants. In terms of scheduling, it can take place during one long session or over the course of three shorter sessions.

Phase 3. Discover

This phase and the next three phases are taken directly from the 4-D appreciative inquiry model (Cooperrider & Whitney, 2011) with a focus on capacity building for social impact organizations. The goal of the Discover phase is to define the focus of the capacity building and identify the strengths of the organization and what is already working well that the organization can build upon to improve. First, an area of focus for capacity building is determined. In some cases, an organization may want to look at the capacity building of the entire organization. In other cases, an organization may identify a specific focus for capacity building such as a specific department, function, or program to achieve specific goals. Next, during a discovery session, participants write individual reflections in response to a series of appreciatively framed questions to help them identify and share stories about the strengths, best practices, and successes they have experienced or observed. The focus of questions asked can be tailored to the specific capacity building focus of the organization. Participants then share their stories in pairs or small groups. Lastly, the stories are shared with the entire group. As stories are shared, common themes are identified and used to create a visual representation of the themes.

Phase 4. Dream

This phase is also taken from the 4-D appreciative inquiry model. The goal of this phase is to create an aspirational vision of the future based on the themes that emerged from the Discover phase. This phase focuses on creating a shared dream to generate positive emotions and inspiration that will energize the capacity building process, unleash creativity, and help people think big about what is possible for the organization to achieve in the future. This phase focuses on how to maximize the organization's potential and impact, rather than a limited focus on fixing problems that will not necessarily help an organization to grow and achieve its full potential. During this phase, a working session is held where participants review the themes from the Discover session and envision an ideal future that builds on these themes. First, participants reflect on the themes individually, write a statement about an ideal future for the organization based on these themes, and then brainstorm how they can use their strengths to help the organization achieve this vision. Next, participants share their reflections in pairs or small groups. After that, the entire group shares their ideal futures, and they are recorded and organized by common themes to create a shared vision statement for the future. Lastly, the group identifies the priority areas where they want to focus on working toward in the short term and the longer term. The short-term priority areas will become the focus of the capacity building initiative that takes place in the next phases, while the longer-term priorities can be revisited at a later time for future capacity building initiatives. Like the Discovery phase, the Dream phase can be tailored to the specific capacity building needs and focus of the organization.

Phase 5. Design

This Design phase is the action planning phase, also taken from the 4-D appreciative inquiry model (Cooperrider & Whitney, 2011) and similar to the action planning phase of the action research model for organizational development (Cummings & Worley, 2015). The goal of this phase is to create an action plan for the capacity building initiative. During this phase, key stakeholders are brought together, based on the priority areas that were identified in the previous phase, for an action planning session. During this session, SMART (specific, measurable, achievable, realistic, and timely) goals for the capacity initiative are created (Doran, 1981). An action plan is created to achieve the goals, roles and responsibilities that are assigned, and a schedule is created. A specific framework or process for action planning will not be prescribed here as there are many to choose from and some organizations may have a preference for a framework that works for them. However, a good action plan is specific, feasible, and actionable to help ensure successful implementation (Cummings & Worley, 2015). The participants in the process can determine the appropriate framework or process for action planning. However, it is recommended that leveraging the strengths of individuals or teams involved be factored into the action plan. A communications plan should also be created to keep all key stakeholders updated and informed of the progress and outcomes of the positive capacity building initiative.

The action plan should also include a plan for evaluation. Evaluation is critical for social impact organizations to measure their social impact (Connolly & York, 2002). Evaluation is also considered to be an important step to determine if an organizational development initiative was successful (Cummings & Worley, 2015). A comprehensive evaluation plan is needed to measure the effectiveness of the capacity building initiative. Ideally, formative evaluation should be conducted at interim milestones to monitor and adjust implementation as needed. Summative evaluation should also be conducted after the implementation to determine if the capacity building was effective and to inform future capacity building initiatives. Organizations can measure the social and psychological resources addressed during the Develop phase as well as desired outcomes like performance and social impact. Organizations may choose to conduct the evaluation on their own if they have the internal resources and expertise to do so or they may need to seek the help of an external evaluation consultant while setting a longer-term goal of building the evaluation capacity of the organization.

Phase 6. Deliver

The Deliver phase, also known as the "Destiny" phase of the 4-D model of appreciative inquiry (Cooperrider & Whitney, 2011), is where implementation takes place. During this phase, the action plan is implemented. While the scope and timeline for this phase will depend on the action plan, it is recommended that implementation be monitored along the way to address any challenges or changes that arise and to make adjustments to the plan as needed.

Phase 7. Determine

This phase and the phase that follows focus on the evaluation of the capacity building initiative, drawing from the action research model for organizational development (Cummings & Worley, 2015). The goal of this phase is the summative evaluation of the capacity building initiative to determine whether the initiative was successful in achieving its goals. During this phase, data is collected according to the evaluation plan and is analyzed to determine the effectiveness and impact of the capacity building. The timing and specifics of this phase will depend on the evaluation plan.

Phase 8. Decide

This phase also draws from the action research model and is focused on reflecting on the capacity building experience and reviewing the results of the evaluation to understand the impact and decide how to move forward. The goal of the Decide phase is to learn from the capacity building initiative and make decisions about how to approach future capacity building efforts. During this phase, a session is held with relevant stakeholders "to reflect on the process" and review the findings from the the Determine phase. During this session, participants reflect on and participate in discussions based on the following questions: What was the impact of the capacity building? Did we achieve our goals? What worked? What didn't work? What did we learn? Based on the discussion, priorities and needs are identified for the next steps and future capacity building efforts.

Ongoing Positive Capacity Building

Capacity building should not be viewed as a one-time initiative; it should be an ongoing process to be successful (Wagner, 2003). This proposed framework for positive capacity building can be used by an organization for their first capacity building initiative, but it can also serve as a framework for ongoing capacity building and should be viewed as an ongoing cycle, as depicted in Figure 5.1. However, after the first cycle, subsequent cycles of ongoing capacity building can be adjusted and tailored to the organization's needs depending on the outcomes of the first cycle. The first cycle will most likely be the most time intensive, but subsequent cycles may involve shorter phases or even skip certain phases. For example, an organization may decide that it may not need to repeat the Develop phase. Alternatively, it may be decided to provide a refresher training during the Develop phase to focus on building particular skills. An organization may also decide that it may not need to repeat the Desire phase. Alternatively, the Desire phase can consist of a shorter session or exercise people can do on their own or with their teams during their work meetings. In addition to providing a process for ongoing capacity building, the positive capacity building framework is intended to help an organization assess its needs on a regular basis by thinking through each step of the cycle. This framework can be a helpful guide to help organizations think through questions such as: Do we need additional training in a particular area? Would it be helpful and energizing for the team to reconnect to the organization's mission and vision?

Participants in Positive Capacity Building

Positive capacity building is a collaborative, participatory approach to organizational development. Organizations that engage in positive capacity building should carefully consider who should participate in the process to ensure all key stakeholders are represented. Who should participate will depend on the organization and the focus of the capacity building. In some cases, it may be possible for everyone in the organization to participate or in a specific team or department

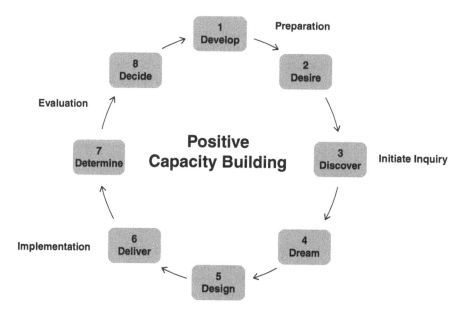

Figure 5.1 The Positive Capacity Building Cycle.

to participate if they can find a time that would not disrupt their normal operations. In other cases, the organization may decide to assemble a group made up of key representative stakeholders.

In deciding who should participate in the process, organizations should be inspired by general systems theory to ensure that all internal and external stakeholders from all related systems are represented in the process (Von Bertalanffy, 1968). In the case of a social impact organization, this can include not only employees, but also volunteers who may serve important roles such as board members, administrative support, fundraising, and direct service for beneficiaries. It can also include external stakeholder representatives from local communities served, governments, partner organizations, and program participants or beneficiaries of the organization. Having all key stakeholders represented in the process will ensure that both a wide range of perspectives and needs are accounted for in the capacity building initiative and the necessary buy-in, support, and cooperation from stakeholders.

Ideal Conditions for Implementation

Positive capacity building is expected to be most effective when implemented as an ongoing cycle. Each phase of the cycle can also be tailored to the specific capacity building needs and focus of the organization, ranging from the entire organization to a specific aspect of the organization like one department, program, or service. Both formative and summative evaluation are also essential to monitor and adjust implementation as needed as well as to measure the effectiveness of the capacity building initiative. All key stakeholders should be represented and engaged in the process, whether they participate in sessions or receive communications to stay informed of the initiative and provide feedback as needed.

In addition, positive capacity building is best suited for organizations with adequate resources that are operationally stable and ready to take the organization to the next level of effectiveness to scale up to grow its impact. It may not be appropriate for organizations in a start-up phase or organizations experiencing a crisis. In addition, the leader of the organization will need to buy into a positive approach to organizational development and see the value of applying positive psychology to the workplace to support employee well-being and performance. This leader will also need to serve as a key advocate and driver of positive capacity building throughout the process to motivate and guide staff and ensure buy-in and commitment from internal and external stakeholders.

Strengths and Limitations

Positive capacity building is an evidence-based framework based on positive organizational development and positive psychology that was designed to be easy for organizations to follow and adapt to their unique contexts and needs. It leverages the power of Switch order and relationships to unleash creativity and maximize the potential of an organization. It is also a comprehensive approach that builds on the appreciative inquiry model of organizational development with additional phases. The preparation phases of Develop and Desire build individual capacity and prepare participants with knowledge and skills for the appreciative inquiry and capacity building process. The incorporation of evaluation "adds" rigor through the collection and analysis of data for learning to inform the process and to measure success.

Additionally, positive capacity building incorporates the application of positive psychology to build the social and psychological resources of the people involved, an aspect of organizational development that is usually neglected. By providing skills and practices that support well-being and work performance, build psychological resources, and build positive relationships, the positive capacity building approach aims to empower those involved to become their best selves at work, and in turn contribute their best selves to the organization to drive capacity building and ensure success of the initiative. However, there are some limitations to this approach. First, positive capacity building is a proposed framework based on theory and research that has not yet been tested with an organization. In addition, a positive approach to capacity building may require a shift in mindsets and behavior for those used to traditional approaches as well as an openness to new ways of working and collaborating, which should be recognized and addressed throughout the process. Finally, the implementation of this approach may also require expert assistance from an outside consultant to facilitate the initial positive capacity building initiative, with the longer-term goal of setting up the organization to continue the process for ongoing positive capacity building on its own.

Conclusion

Social impact organizations can benefit from the fields of positive organizational development and positive psychology to become positive institutions that promote human flourishing and change lives for the better. The goal of this chapter was to propose an innovative new framework for capacity building that social impact organizations can use to build on their strengths and improve their capacities to maximize their social impact. Positive capacity building uses a strengths-based approach to bring out the best in social impact organizations while building the social and psychological resources needed for people to perform at their best to make their best contribution to the capacity building effort. Future research is recommended to test the positive capacity building framework with social impact organizations to determine its feasibility of implementation and its effectiveness.

References

Aguinis, H., Gottfredson, R. K., & Joo, H. (2012). Delivering effective performance feedback: The strengths-based approach. *Business Horizons, 55*(2), 105–111.

Applegate, B. (2002). Allies for democracy. *OD Practitioner, 34*(4), 25–27.

Avey, J. B., Reichard, R. J., Luthans, F., & Mhatre, K. H. (2011). Meta-analysis of the impact of positive psychological capital on employee attitudes, behaviors, and performance. *Human Resource Development Quarterly, 22,* 127–152.

Bandura, A. (1997). *Self-efficacy: The exercise of control.* New York, NY, US: W H Freeman/Times Books/Henry Holt & Co.

Biswas-Diener, R., Kashdan, T. B., & Minhas, G. (2011). A dynamic approach to psychological strength development and intervention. *Journal of Positive Psychology, 6*(2), 106–118.

Cable, D., Lee, J. J., Gino, F., & Staats, B. R. (2015). How best-self activation influences emotions, physiology and employment relationships. Harvard Business School NOM Unit Working Paper, 16-029.

Cairns, B., Harris, M., & Young, P. (2005). Building the capacity of the voluntary nonprofit sector: Challenges of theory and practice. *International Journal of Public Administration, 28*(9/10), 869–885. doi:10.1081/PAD-200067377

Connolly, P., & York, P. (2002). Evaluating capacity-building efforts for nonprofit organizations. *OD Practitioner, 34,* 33–39.

Cooperrider, D. L., & Godwin, L. N. (2012). Positive organizational development: Innovation- inspired change in an economy and ecology of strengths. In K. S. Cameron & G. M. Spreitzer (Eds.), *The Oxford handbook of positive organizational scholarship.* New York, NY, US: Oxford University Press.

Cooperrider, D. L. & Sekerka, L. E. (2003). Toward a theory of positive organizational change. In K. S. Cameron & J. E. Dutton (Eds.), *Positive organizational scholarship: Foundations of a new discipline* (pp. 225–240). San Francisco, CA: Berrett-Koehler.

Cooperrider, D. L. & Whitney, D. (2011). Appreciative inquiry: A positive revolution in change. In P. Holman & T. Devane (Eds.), *The change handbook* (pp. 245–263). Oakland, CA: Berrett-Koehler Publishers.

Cummings, T. G., & Worley, C. G. (2015). *Organization development and change* (10th ed.). Mason, Ohio: Thompson South-Western.

Doherty, B., Haugh, H., & Lyon, F. (2014). Social enterprises as hybrid organizations: A review and research agenda. *International Journal of Management Reviews, 16*(4), 417–436.

Doran, G. T. (1981). There's a S.M.A.R.T. way to write management's goals and objectives. *Management Review, 70,* 35–36.

Dutton, J. E. (2003). *Energize your workplace: How to create and sustain high quality connections at work* (Vol. 50). San Francisco, CA, US: Jossey-Bass.

Dvir, T., Eden, D., Avolio, B. J., & Shamir, B. (2002). Impact of transformational leadership on follower development and performance: A field experiment. *Academy of Management Journal, 45,* 735–744.

Fredrickson, B. (2001). The role of positive emotions in positive psychology: The broaden-and-build theory of positive emotions. *American Psychologist, 56,* 218–226.

Grant, A. M., & Gino, F. (2010). A little thanks goes a long way: Explaining why gratitude expressions motivate prosocial behavior. *Journal of Personality and Social Psychology, 98*(6), 946.

Joyce, S., Shand, F., Lal, T. J., Mott, B., Bryant, R. A., & Harvey, S. B. (2019). Resilience@Work Mindfulness Program: Results from a cluster randomized controlled trial with first responders. *Journal of Medical Internet Research, 21*(2), e12894.

Judge, T. A., Thoresen, C. J., Bono, J. E., & Patten, G. K. (2001). The job satisfaction–job performance relationship: A qualitative and quantitative review. *Psychological Bulletin, 127*(3), 376–407.

Lavine, M. (2012). Positive deviance. In K. S. Cameron & G. M. Spreitzer (Eds.), *The Oxford handbook of positive organizational scholarship* (pp. 1014–1026). New York, NY, US: Oxford University Press.

Lewin, K. Research Center for Group Dynamics. (1951). *Field theory in social science: Selected theoretical papers* First. D. Cartwright Ed. New York, NY, US: Harper & Brothers.

Linley, P. A., & Garcea, N. (2011). Creating positive social change through building positive organizations: Four levels of intervention. In R. Biswas-Diener (Ed.), *Positive psychology as a mechanism for social change*. Utrecht, The Netherlands: Springer.

Luthans, F. (2002). Positive organizational behavior: Developing and managing psychological strengths. *Academy of Management Journal, 16*, 57–72.

Luthans, F., & Youssef-Morgan, C. M. (2017). Psychological capital: An evidence-based positive approach. *Annual Review of Organizational Psychology and Organizational Behavior, 4*, 339–366. doi:10.1146/annurev-orgpsych-032516-1 13324

Luthans, F., Avolio, B. J., Avey, J. B., & Norman, S. M. (2007). Positive psychological capital: Measurement and relationship with performance and satisfaction. *Personnel Psychology, 60*(3), 541–572.

Lyubomirsky, S., King, L., & Diener, E. (2005). The benefits of frequent positive affect: Does happiness lead to success? *Psychological Bulletin, 131*(6), 803–855.

Morris, M. H., Coombes, S. M. T., Allen, J., & Schindehutte, M. (2007). Antecedents and outcomes of entrepreneurial and market orientations in a non-profit context: Theoretical and empirical insights. *Journal of Leadership and Organizational Studies, 13*, 12–39.

Nelson, B. (2016). You get what you reward: A research-based approach to employee recognition. In M. J. Grawitch & D. W. Ballard (Eds.), *The psychologically healthy workplace: Building a win-win environment for organizations and employees*. Washington, DC, US: American Psychological Association.

Peterson, C., and Seligman, M. E. P. (2004). *Character strengths and virtues: A handbook and classification*. New York, NY: Oxford University Press.

Rath, T., & Conchie, B. (2008). *Strengths-based leadership: Great leaders, teams, and why people follow*. New York, NY, US: Gallup Press.

Rosenberg, M. (2003). *Nonviolent communication: A language of life* (2nd ed.). Encinitas, CA, US: PuddleDancer Press.

Ryan, R. M., & Deci, E. L. (2000). Self-determination theory and the facilitation of intrinsic motivation, social development, and well-being. *American Psychologist, 55*(1), 68–78. doi:10.1037/0003-066X.55.1.68

Ryan, R. M., & Deci, E. L. (2017). *Self-determination theory: Basic psychological needs in motivation, development, and wellness*. New York, NY: Guilford.

Sawhill, J. C., & Williamson, D. (2001). Mission impossible?: Measuring success in nonprofit organizations. *Nonprofit Management and Leadership, 11*(3), 371–386. doi:10.1002/nml.11309

Schein, E. (2010). *Organizational culture and leadership* (4th ed). The Jossey-Bass Business & Management Series. San Francisco, CA, US: Jossey-Bass.

Seligman, M. (2011). *Flourish: A visionary new understanding of happiness and well-being*. New York, NY, US: Simon & Schuster.

Seligman, M. (2018). PERMA and the building blocks of well-being. *The Journal of Positive Psychology, 13*(4), 333–335.

Sosik, J. J., & Jung, D. I. (2018). *Full range leadership development: Pathways for people, profit, and planet* (2nd ed.). New York, NY, US: Routledge Taylor & Francis Group.

Von Bertalanffy, L. (1968). *General system theory: Foundations, development*. New York, NY, US: George Braziller.

Wagner, L. D. (2003). Why capacity building matters and why nonprofits ignore it. *New Directions for Philanthropic Fundraising, 2003*(40), 103–111.

Whitney, D., Trosten-Bloom, A., & Cooperrider, D. (2010). *The power of appreciative inquiry: A practical guide to positive change*. San Francisco CA, US: Berrett-Koehler.

Wirtenberg, J., Backer, T. E., Chang, W., Lannan, T., Applegate, B., Conway, M., & Slepian, J. (2007). The future of organization development in the nonprofit sector. *Organization Development Journal, Chesterland, 25*(4), 179–195.

Zelenksi, J., Murphy, S., & Jenkins, D. (2008). The happy-productive worker thesis revisited. *Journal of Happiness Studies, 9*, 521–537.

6

Positive Cultural Humility in Organizations

Improving Relationships in the Workplace

Lawrence Chan & Adrian Reece

Learning and retaining knowledge about cultures and different identities, particularly in the context of the workplace environment, tends to lodge individuals in their own mental models. Our worldviews are constructed by our own learned predispositions regarding how things should occur, which we develop from childhood, and put into practice during adulthood. These psychological underpinnings about the ways in which the world operates inform our ability to think, communicate, and perceive occurrences throughout our daily lives. Moreover, these mental models, known as psychosocial habits, are constantly reinforced by our own assumptions, given that the way we experience life is largely informed by these existing beliefs. When our own assumptions are reinforced, we are often unable to discern objective truths from subjective interpretations.

Engrained assumptions regarding our perceptions of cultural differences tend to restrict us from learning, as our familiarity provides a safety net from knowledge that may challenge our presumptions about the way things are. In the context of diversity of inclusion within organizations, this poses an innate problem as the workforce becomes increasingly diverse and complex.

For example, multiracial Americans, otherwise known as individuals who identify as mixed race with more than one racial identity, are one of the fastest-growing racial demographics in the United States (Masuoka, 2008). This poses a unique and adaptive cultural environment where individuals may draw upon lived experiences that are vastly different and unique from their peers. Moreover, individuals who identify as multiracial may outwardly be perceived to belong to a certain demographic or culture; however, they may hold multiple cultural identities at the same time with vastly different morals, values, and religions. In public health, for example, consideration of cultural differences becomes particularly salient for diverse medical facilities that serve different types of patient populations, as the relational aspects of cultural humility increase respect, trust, and overall effectiveness of the care programs (Foster, 2009).

Positive Organizational Psychology Interventions: Design and Evaluation, First Edition.
Stewart I. Donaldson and Christopher Chen.
© 2021 John Wiley & Sons Ltd. Published 2021 by John Wiley & Sons Ltd.

Cultural Reflection

When people view the world through their vantage points, they generate countless interpretations of activities in attempts to assign meaning. From these vantage points, our perceptions may be objective, but there often exists a paradox in how we perceive our actions. How can one who acts objectively report on their behaviors? This question thus becomes the central point of cultural reflexivity. Cultural reflexivity represents the bidirectional relationship between a subject and another person, where the actions of one directly impact the future state of the other and vice versa, creating a cyclical relationship where cause and effect become entangled and manifest as one of the same (Flanagan, 1981). Cultural reflexivity thus occurs optimally when we attempt to perceive our actions objectively through our perception. Our perceptions create filters that provide us with heuristics to operate within the world. When making sense of the world, our filters become both the subjects and the objects of investigation, as our conscious experiences influence our actions and our actions influence our conscious experiences. When we intentionally make sense of the world, we become both the actors and the ones acted upon.

Positive Relationships

Professionals exhibiting this self-reliance and attentiveness to the cultural experience of individuals lay the groundwork toward creating a positive relationship, or high-quality relationships, with their cultural others. Through positive relationships, professionals and those from other cultural backgrounds, including coworkers and clients, can build resilience into their relationship, therefore positively influencing their relational outlook over time (Wagnild & Young, 1993).

Positive relationships traditionally refer to the abundance of interpersonal connections an individual possesses, and thus positive social behaviors and traits that tend to help individuals create meaningful partnerships in their lives (Seligman, 2002). In the context of work, positive relationships help to buffer a person against the negative effects of stress and promote adaptive behaviors such as help-seeking behaviors and meaningful networking (Dutton & Ragins, 2017). Within the context of nurturing positive relationships at work, we adopt Walsh's (2003) definition of positive relational resilience that captures the interpersonal bond between people as they collaboratively problem solve, connect, have open emotional expression, and make sense of adversity. Walsh's definition of relational resilience differs from others, such as DeMichelis (2016), who defines relational resilience as a process that occurs within complex interpersonal, institutional, and political interactions, and Jordan's (2013) definition that highlights an individual's capacity to make connections. Walsh's definition focuses exclusively on the promotion of high-quality, meaningful relationships that develop between people through positive feedback loops.

We hypothesize that our positive cultural humility intervention will impact the degree to which positive relationships between people of culturally diverse backgrounds develop. Our cultural humility intervention encourages professionals and clients to engage one another in a manner that builds resilience within their work relationships, such that the positive feedback generated by engaging in our cultural humility intervention is the catalyst that drives those positive relationships. Our cultural humility intervention framework enhances relationships by providing a platform for culturally diverse others to connect, learn from one another, and continuously collaborate, in turn helping individuals to build a greater understanding of how other cultures may positively impact experiences and environments at work.

Prior Theory and Research

Cultural Awareness

In the process of applying positive cultural humility in organizations, it is important to incorporate the framework of cultural awareness, otherwise known as an individual's ability to regulate self-awareness and intercultural communication channels, such that learned differences and values are thoughtfully incorporated into the workplace environment. Cultural awareness is defined as the self-awareness that enables individuals to learn and understand people who are different from themselves (Kumpfer et al., 2002). Moreover, this includes acknowledging the notion that individuals from diverse backgrounds possess different modalities with which they view the world. Bhawuk et al. (2008) highlight the importance of shifting from a solely ethnocentric attitude, or individualistic point of view, to integrate an ethnorelativist view, also known as other orientation when becoming more culturally sensitive. This process occurs when a person consciously recognizes values and behaviors beyond the existing framework of what they may believe to be true parameters on culture.

This introspective consideration of others thus includes acceptance of differing cultures, adaptation to cultural outlooks or behaviors, and integration of these concepts, values, and behaviors that are important to those multicultural situations (Pope-Davis et al., 2001). The notion of developing cultural awareness, therefore, reflects changes in our mental models that become malleable over time, in turn re-evaluating our sensitivity according to our learned experiences. Additionally, cultural awareness considers both individualistic and collectivistic cultures, which reduce the barriers that inhibit person–environment fit (Edwards et al., 1998; Hofstede, 2011).

Cultural Awareness in Practice

In the public health sector, cultural awareness has been defined as a framework that comprises helping healthcare professionals understand patients on both a surface and deep level (Resnicow et al., 1999). The surface level pertains to the receptivity or acceptance of the message, such as willingness to receive treatment implementation. The deep level pertains to the understanding of deeply rooted and engrained cultural differences that may come into conflict with messages, such as willingness to receive treatment implementation that may interfere with a patient's cultural beliefs for end-of-life care and terminal disease progression. Using this model of understanding cultural sensitivity and awareness in this organizational environment, applying the framework of positive cultural humility may be particularly salient in addressing the psychological, social, and cultural influences that may create tension between healthcare providers and care recipients in administering suggested health interventions.

Cultural Competency

Cultural competency refers to the attitudes, knowledge, and skills necessary for service providers to provide quality care to diverse populations (Inouye et al., 2005). Within organizations, cultural competency manifests as a variety of interventions that focus on improving the accessibility and effectiveness of services for racial and ethnic minorities (Truong et al., 2014). Cultural competency interventions focus on enhancing provider-related outcomes, such as altering attitudes and levels of cultural awareness, client-related outcomes such as increased satisfaction, and outcomes related to service access and utilization such as client health-related outcomes and cost-effectiveness through linguistic and informative means.

For many interventions, cultural competency interventions had a positive impact on the future provider-, client-, and outcome-related metrics further legitimizing a cultural competency interventions' ability to positively impact the organization (Truong et al., 2014). For example, Gallagher and Polanin's (2015) meta-analysis of interventions designed to enhance cultural competency in professionals and students noted that out of the 25 studies assessed, only four studies found a decrease in cultural competency as a result of participating in an educational intervention. Interestingly, Gallagher and Polanin found that professional nurses benefited more from the cultural competency interventions relative to nursing students. The authors posit that the availability of information by virtue of experience gave professional nurses incentive to see a greater benefit in the intervention.

Current Issues in Cultural Competency Interventions

Cultural competency interventions are designed to alter our naturally forming filters by philosophically challenging the assumptions and beliefs that form the structure of a filter by opening the participant to new possibilities. Cultural competency inventions seek to align and orientate the perspectives of professionals toward their client and promote openness and advocacy when their client comes from a culture that is distinct from the professionals' (Tervalon & García-Murray, 1998). To alter the filters of professionals, interventions focus on providing professionals with knowledge and resources related to the culturally diverse other, aggregating the other into distinct categories and ultimately ignoring the roles culture plays in the life of individuals who identify with that distinct culture. When a cultural competency program taxonomizes the culturally diverse other, it teaches cultural sensitivity while inadvertently creating alternative, general paradigms (Manson, 2001) susceptible to stereotyping.

In theory, cultural competency would involve an ongoing process of learning and relearning as one gains a growing appreciation of the diverse variations in human experiences as they relate to culture. In practice, cultural competency becomes a diversity and inclusion initiative hosted by human resources to reduce the number of culturally related infractions (malpractice) that may occur within an organization (Khazai, 2018). The positive business incentives related to reducing the number of potentially damaging culturally related infractions creates a strong incentive to circulate the knowledge, skills, and attitudes learned in cultural competency programs as quickly as possible.

Unfortunately, cultural competency interventions fail to account for humans' inability to completely discern objective truths from subjective interpretations of their environment. When interacting with a client from a different culture, the person will generally rely on previous knowledge and experience to make sense of their situation (Koriat & Levy-Sadot, 2001). When the professional believes they have all known variables to form a judgment, they bias their judgment on what they believe is known, limiting their ability to recognize what is unknown. The overconfidence of the professional obfuscates their Achilles' heel, their inability to recognize how their client experiences their own culture. This vulnerability cannot be addressed by a traditional cultural competency and requires that the professional humble themself and becomes a life-long learner. Similar to Achilles' mother failing to remove all of Achilles' humanity while placing him in the River Styx, so too do traditional cultural competency interventions fail to account for human filters that produce overconfident perspectives. Small vulnerabilities such as low humility can produce major challenges when working with clients from cultures distinct from the professional, similar to Achilles' humanity in his heel, which was his eventual downfall.

The feelings of confidence experienced by professionals will not always translate seamlessly into effective interpersonal interactions with culturally diverse clients (Allwood & Granhag, 1999). Confidence judgments are determined by the features the professional attends to and the professional going through a cultural competency training may attend to trivial features. These professionals fail to recognize the diverse experiences characteristic of their client's reality. The information the professional acquires through cultural competency training is more representative of the overall culture of clients rather than how the clients' experience of their culture shapes their worldviews. If the cultural competency program hopes to maximize its return on investment, we strongly recommend the cultural competency program attends to the individual experiences of those they represent and challenge the assumptions of professionals who believe they can deduce objective truth regarding the experience of a culturally diverse client through lecture-style instruction alone.

Ongoing Learning in Cultural Competency

While strong efforts have been cultivated to enhance cultural competency at a macro level within organizations, the current educational model is largely insufficient in the context of the continually developing workforce population, particularly amid multinational global markets. Cultural competency, defined as the

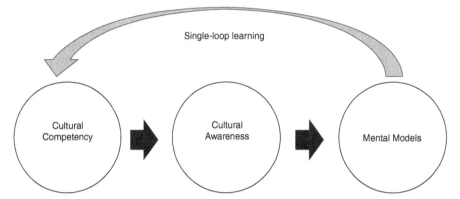

Figure 6.1 Theoretical Model Depicting the Single-Loop Learning Cycle of Cultural Competency, Cultural Awareness, and Mental Models.

ability to understand and communicate effectively with individuals from other cultures (Inouye et al., 2005), does not adequately inform the iterative or ongoing nature of the evolving cultural landscape. The assumption is that once cultural awareness is learned, this competency model suggests that once this knowledge is obtained, positive attitudes and prosocial outcomes occur organically (Figure 6.1). However, without a continuous directed effort to increase cultural sensitivity, mental models are unlikely to continue to evolve without this targeted consideration of double-loop learning.

Therefore, this chapter proposes a positive human process intervention that will enhance an individual's innate abilities to learn, and more importantly, apply a recursive model of positive cultural humility to enhance meaningful relationships at work. A recursive model of positive cultural humility, also known as ongoing learning, is defined as an individual's ability to maintain an interpersonal stance that is other oriented, particularly concerning aspects of cultural identity that are most important to the values of the culturally diverse other (Hook et al., 2013).

Drawing on Argyris' double-loop learning theory (2002), our cultural humility intervention suggests a novel framework (Figure 6.2) to help professionals diagnose and increase their propensity to be more self-reliant and attentive to the dissemination of cultural competency.

Cultural Humility

Cultural humility captures a person's ability to assume and maintain an interpersonal stance where they are open to the other with respect to aspects related to cultural identities the other holds as most important (Hook et al., 2013). With such a stance, a person is better able to understand the unique beliefs, values, and worldviews held by those whose cultures differ from their own. In a diversifying workplace, practicing cultural humility offers professionals a competitive advantage as they integrate the unique perspectives of their followers and better attend to their needs. The competitive advantage gained is an outcome of the diverse,

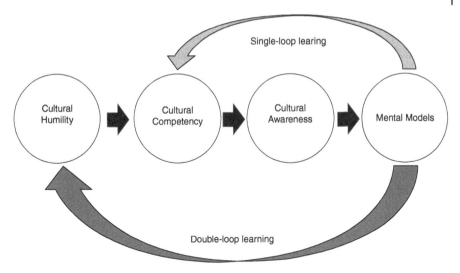

Figure 6.2 Theoretical Model Depicting the Double-Loop Learning Cycle of Cultural Humility, Cultural Awareness, and Mental Models.

functional configurations professionals maintain by integrating the cultural beliefs, values, and worldviews of others.

Cultural humility builds on the concept of humility where a person has an accurate self-view, appreciation of others, and is generally teachable (Owens et al., 2013). When the person is a leader and expresses their humility, it fosters a supportive climate among their followers and empowers them to perform prosocial activities, such as sharing information and generating psychological safety among their team (Hu et al., 2018). Humble leaders seek critical feedback, are open to the advice of others, and take notice of others' strengths. Under a culturally humble leader, followers become more inclined to express themselves through voice behaviors, increase the quality and quantity of their creative outputs, and utilize their strengths (Tangney, 2000).

Professionals who practice cultural humility allot themselves the capacity to transform their organizations by the fortune of becoming more attentive to the diverse cultural realities experienced by those within their organization. These culturally humble professionals attend to the diverse challenges and imbalances impacting others with distinct cultural identities from their own and integrate these distinct realities into their decision-making schema (Tervalon & García-Murray, 1998). Culturally humble professionals see themselves as lifelong learners, practice critical reflection, recognize and challenge power imbalances, and instill consistent institutional accountability. They see others as complex, multidimensional beings who bring more than their bodies to work and use their power to advocate for the welfare of others.

McElroy-Heltzel et al. (2018) explore how cultural humility explains the relationship between culturally based ineffective arguing and relationship quality, measured through relationship satisfaction and commitment. The authors use the social bond hypothesis to explain how culturally based ineffective arguing leads to a person viewing the other as being less humble, lowering the relational bonds between them. Results showed cultural humility's positive relationship with relationship quality and negative relationship with culturally based ineffective arguing. These results suggest that taking an egocentric view of cultural conflict results in lower relational satisfaction and commitment.

Cultural Humility in Practice

We advocate cultural competency training programs that make cultural humility a focus of their interventions to promote openness and non-judgment (Tervalon & García-Murray, 1998) among healthcare workers. Cultural humility places healthcare workers in the mindset to better attend to the needs of their patients and their communities by granting them access to how culture and potential structural barriers may impact their ability to best serve them. In Johnston and Herzig (2006), the researchers noted discrepancies between Mexican agricultural workers and their healthcare providers in determining the drivers of patient–provider interactions. The authors interviewed rural Montana Mexican agricultural workers who cited low wages, long work hours, distances from home, and cumbersome medical tests as determinants influencing their patient–provider interactions. Providers focused on culture-centric dimensions of the agricultural workers, citing cultural beliefs such as superstitions and a lack of trust in the healthcare system as the primary drivers shaping their patient–provider relationship. The incongruency between the patients and their providers makes it impossible for providers to accurately attend to the real needs of their patients as they focus on static cultural generalizations learned through cultural competency programs, failing to recognize the lived experiences of others. We need to move away from rigid conceptualizations of culture and pay attention to the material obstacles that influence the differences we see in outcomes.

Research shows cultural humility shares a positive association with higher ratings of the hospital's safety culture (Hook et al., 2016). A hospital's safety culture captures the shared understanding among management and staff of what is important in patient safety. With a hospital safety culture, management and staff share values, beliefs, and norms about what is important in the hospital, how to behave, what attitudes and actions are appropriate and inappropriate, and what should and should not be rewarded and punished. Researchers found that cultural humility at the organizational level predicted 15%–21% of the variance in hospital safety culture even when controlling for mean differences between hospitals, which questions the power of cultural humility in healthcare. The researchers hypothesized that the cultural humility of management and staff played a role in the communication styles adopted, the levels of cooperation performed, the beliefs created and shared around health, and ultimately the better identification and treatment of psychosocial factors related to healthcare (i.e., pain, anxiety, depression).

Cultural Reflection in Healthcare Organizations

Cultural reflection is an ideology within cultural humility that refers to both organizations' and individuals' ability to incorporate positive cultural patterns and values into conscious thoughts and feelings (Hofstede, 2011). Hofstede (2011) asserts that cultural reflection is a process that cultivates an aggregate of perceptions, beliefs, and thoughts about the social norms and behaviors that illustrate cultural materials, espoused and implicit beliefs, and symbolic cultural customs.

In the organizational context, cultural materials, or artifacts, give substantial information about certain elements of an organization (Schein, 2010). For example, some of Kaiser Permanente's artifacts for employees include generous compensation benefits, including flexible retirement accounts, comprehensive healthcare plans, and Paid Time Off benefits for supporting work–life balance (Porter & Kellogg, 2008). Artifacts such as these suggest several implications. Reflecting on the incorporation of these cultural artifacts into the organization relays transient information to both internal and external stakeholders, as the care that is offered for employees provides a clear depiction of the organization's inherent values. When these implicit priorities of the organization, in this case, employee well-being, are embedded into the fabric of the organization, a supportive, nurturing environment is created and translated into the organizational culture and management framework (Drucker, 2012).

In applying the framework of cultural reflection to patient-centered care at the individual level, it is the responsibility of healthcare employees to learn about cultural differences among their patient populations. Espoused beliefs, or declared sets of norms and customs, directly affect how the patient sees, interacts with, and incorporates the care implementation protocol into their lives (Argyris & Schön, 1996). However, the culturally reflective healthcare professional seeks to identify the patient's implicit beliefs, otherwise known as the embedded beliefs, behaviors, and practices that are covert, and brings them to the surface. This process helps uncover nuanced information that can help healthcare professionals deliver more effective and informed care protocols that incorporate the patient's espoused and implicit belief systems. This custom-iterative process thus provides a layer of attentiveness and personability to the healthcare environment, which has shown to increase return on investment in the form of patient retention and decreased error rates over time (Oates et al., 2000).

Limitations and Ideal Conditions

There are several limitations in which the positive cultural humility intervention may not work optimally. The most salient limitation, which also largely affects other established forms of diversity and inclusion training, pertains to language barriers that pose innate dialogue and communication issues between individuals (Fassinger, 2008). Additionally, limited language interpretation may also negatively moderate the relationship between dialogue and positive cultural humility (Tange & Lauring, 2009). Future research on the efficacy of positive cultural humility interventions should seek to build in consideration of these language effects to achieve more favorable outcomes, particularly in multinational organizations. Additionally, providing diversity and inclusion training in an employee's native language, in addition to the language utilized at work, may help in ensuring effective communication in minimizing language abstraction (Roberson & Stevens, 2006).

Another ideal condition where this intervention would work optimally is if the employees within the organization already value diversity. Adopting a strengths-based approach, the positive cultural humility perspective fits well with how consideration of culture is already working within the organization (Cooperrider & Srivasta, 2017). Additionally, this suggests that positive cultural humility would work best if the organization is already invested and finds value in diversity initiatives as something important to the overall mission and vision of the firm (see Stevens et al., 2008). If not, then the continuing diversity education that will ensue with the intervention will not provide additional training as it intends to.

Conclusion

Cultural competency programs are effective at introducing professionals to cultures distinct from their own, but often fail to implement recursive or ongoing learning approaches that would help their participants operate and learn at an optimal level across cultures. Cultural humility can build on the foundations of cultural competency by highlighting the ways culture impacts culturally diverse others' worldviews and experiences in life. Cultural humility reminds us to look beyond the labels assigned to others and to recognize where personal biases might be adversely impacting your clients. Lastly, cultural humility reminds professionals that culture operates as a dynamic system, impacting each client differently.

References

Allwood, C. M., & Granhag, P. A. (1999). Feelings of confidence and the realism of confidence judgments in everyday life. In P. Juslin & H. Montgomery (Eds.), *Judgment and decision making: Neo-Brunswikian and process-tracing approaches* (pp. 123–146). Mahwah, NJ: Lawrence Erlbaum Associates Publishers.

Argyris, C. (2002). Double-loop learning, teaching, and research. *Academy of Management Learning & Education, 1*(2), 206–218.

Argyris, C., & Schön, D. (1996). *Organizational learning II: Theory, method, and practice.* Reading, MA: Addison-Wesley.

Bhawuk, D. P. S., Sakuda, K. H., & Munusamy, V. P. (2008). Intercultural competence development and triple loop cultural learning. In Soon Ang & Linn Van Dyne (Eds.), *Handbook of cultural intelligence: Theory measurement and application* (pp. 342–345). Armonk, NY: M. E. Shape.

Cooperrider, D. & Srivasta, S. (2017). The gift of new eyes: Personal reflections after 30 years of appreciative inquiry in organizational life. *Research in Organizational Change and Development, 25*, 81–142. doi:https://doi.org/10.1108/ S0897-301620170000025003

DeMichelis, C. (2016). Relational resilience: an interdisciplinary perspective. In *Child and Adolescent Resilience Within Medical Contexts* (pp. 1–10). Springer, Cham.

Drucker, P. (2012). *The practice of management.* London: Routledge.

Dutton, J. E., & Ragins, B. R. (2017). *Exploring positive relationships at work: Building a theoretical and research foundation.* Mahwah, NJ: Lawrence Erlbaum Associates.

Edmondson, A. (1999). Psychological safety and learning behavior in work teams. *Administrative Science Quarterly, 44*(2), 350–383.

Edwards, J. R., Caplan, R. D., & Van Harrison, R. (1998). Person–environment fit theory. *Theories of Organizational Stress, 28*, 67.

Flanagan, O. J. (1981). Psychology, progress, and the problem of reflexivity: A study in the epistemological foundations of psychology. *Journal of the History of the Behavioral Sciences, 7*, 375–386.

Fassinger, R. E. (2008). Workplace diversity and public policy: Challenges and opportunities for psychology. *American Psychologist, 63*(4), 252.

Foster, J. (2009). Cultural humility and the importance of long-term relationships in international partnerships. *Journal of Obstetric, Gynecologic, & Neonatal Nursing, 38*(1), 100–107.

Gallagher, R. W., & Polanin, J. R. (2015). A meta-analysis of educational interventions designed to enhance cultural competence in professional nurses and nursing students. *Nurse Education Today, 35*(2), 333–340.

Hofstede, G. (2011). Dimensionalizing cultures: The Hofstede model in context. *Online Readings in Psychology and Culture, 2*(1), 8.

Hook, J. N., Boan, D., Davis, D. E., Aten, J. D., Ruiz, J. M., & Maryon, T. (2016). Cultural humility and hospital safety culture. *Journal of Clinical Psychology in Medical Settings, 23*(4), 402–409.

Hook, J. N., Davis, D., Owen, J., & DeBlaere, C. (2017). Cultural humility: Engaging diverse identities in therapy. *American Psychological Association.* doi:https://doi. org/10.1037/0000037-000

Hook, J. N., Davis, D. E., Owen, J., Worthington, E. L., Jr., & Utsey, S. O. (2013). Cultural humility: Measuring openness to culturally diverse clients. *Journal of Counseling Psychology, 60*(3), 353–366.

Hu, J., Erdogan, B., Jiang, K., Bauer, T. N., & Liu, S. (2018). Leader humility and team creativity: The role of team information sharing, psychological safety, and power distance. *Journal of Applied Psychology, 103*(3), 313–323.

Inouye, T. E., Yu, H. C., & Adefuin, J.-A. (2005). Commissioning multicultural evaluation: A foundation resource guide. Retrieved from http://www.spra.com/ wordpress2/wp-content/uploads/2015/12/TCE-Commissining-Multicutural- Eva.pdf

Johnston, M. E., & Herzig, R. M. (2006). The interpretation of "culture": Diverging perspectives on medical provision in rural Montana. *Social Science & Medicine, 63*(9), 2500–2511.

Jordan, J. V. (2013). *Relational resilience in girls* (pp. 73–86). New York, NY: Springer.

Khazai, M. N. (2018). Preventing malpractice claims and strengthening the doctor–patient relationship with cultural competence. Retrieved May 1, 2019, from https://www.lexology.com/library/detail.aspx?g=495e25db-5766-4fa3-ab3a-4446d55c9718

Koriat, A., & Levy-Sadot, R. (2001). The combined contributions of the cue-familiarity and accessibility heuristics to feelings of knowing. *Journal for Experimental Psychology, 27*(1), 34–53.

Kumpfer, K. L., Alvarado, R., Smith, P., & Bellamy, N. (2002). Cultural sensitivity and adaptation in family-based prevention interventions. *Prevention Science, 3*(3), 241–246.

Manson, S. M. (2001). Simplifying complexity: A review of complexity theory. *Geoforum, 32*, 405–414.

Masuoka, N. (2008). Political attitudes and ideologies of multiracial Americans: The implications of mixed race in the United States. *Political Research Quarterly, 61*(2), 253–267.

McElroy-Heltzel, S. E., Davis, D. E., DeBlaere, C., Hook, J. N., Massengale, M., Choe, E., & Rice, K. G. (2018). Cultural humility: Pilot study testing the social bonds hypothesis in interethnic couples. *Journal of Counseling Psychology, 65*(4), 531–537.

Oates, J., Weston, W. W., & Jordan, J. (2000). The impact of patient-centered care on outcomes. *Family Practice, 49*(9), 796–804.

Owens, B. P., Johnson, M. D., & Mitchell, T. R. (2013). Expressed humility in organizations: Implications for performance, teams, and leadership. *Organization Science, 24*(5), 1517–1538.

Pope-Davis, D. B., Liu, W. M., Toporek, R. L., & Brittan-Powell, C. S. (2001). What's missing from multicultural competency research: Review, introspection, and recommendations. *Cultural Diversity and Ethnic Minority Psychology, 7*(2), 121.

Porter, M., & Kellogg, M. (2008). Kaiser Permanente: An integrated health care experience. *Revista De Innovación Sanitaria Y Atención Integrada, 1*(1), 5.

Resnicow, K., Baranowski, T., Ahluwalia, J. S., & Braithwaite, R. L. (1999). Cultural sensitivity in public health: Defined and demystified. *Ethnicity & Disease, 9*(1), 10–21.

Roberson, Q. M., & Stevens, C. K. (2006). Making sense of diversity in the workplace: Organizational justice and language abstraction in employees' accounts of diversity-related incidents. *Journal of Applied Psychology, 91*(2), 379.

Schein, E. H. (2010). *Organizational culture and leadership* (Vol. 2). Hoboken, NJ: John Wiley & Sons.

Stevens, F. G., Plaut, V. C., & Sanchez-Burks, J. (2008). Unlocking the benefits of diversity: All-inclusive multiculturalism and positive organizational change. *The Journal of Applied Behavioral Science, 44*(1), 116–133.

Tange, H., & Lauring, J. (2009). Language management and social interaction within the multilingual workplace. *Journal of Communication Management, 13*(3), 218–232.

Tangney, J. P. (2000). Humility: Theoretical perspectives, empirical findings and directions for future research. *Journal of Social and Clinical Psychology, 19*(1), 70–82.

Tervalon, M., & García-Murray, J. (1998). Cultural humility versus cultural competence: A critical distinction in defining physician training outcomes in multicultural education. *Journal of Health Care for the Poor and Underserved, 9*(2), 117–125.

Truong, M., Paradies, Y., & Priest, N. (2014). Interventions to improve cultural competency in healthcare: A systematic review of reviews. *BMC Health Services Research, 14*(1), 1–31.

Wagnild, G. M., & Young, H. M. (1993). Development of psychometric evaluation of the resilience scale. *Journal of Nursing Measurement, 1*(2), 165–178.

Walsh, F. (2003). Crisis, trauma, and challenge: A relational resilience approach for healing, transformation, and growth. *Smith College Studies in Social Work, 74*(1), 49–71.

Appendix

Components of the Positive Cultural Humility Intervention

Title: Positive Cultural Humility Intervention
Unit of Analysis: Individual/dyadic
Target Population: Leadership, management, change agents
Targeted Behaviors for Change: Expressed leader humility, cultural humility scale (Hook et al., 2013), effective communication, self-awareness
Targeted Attitudes for Change: Openness to experience and curiosity
Industry: Any client-facing industry
Duration: One-day workshop
Frequency: Recurring – biannually
Proximal Outcomes: Cultural competence, organizational citizenship behaviors, leader self-awareness
Distal Outcomes: Decreases in turnover and culture-related lawsuits. Increases perceived resources. Increase in organizational virtue and values.

Positive Organizational Development (OD) Intervention

Overview

Table 6.1 presents an overview of the cultural humility intervention process with comparisons to traditional organizational development processes.

Application Stages

Below are the steps to our proposed Positive Cultural Humility Intervention. The intervention operates as a stand-alone intervention or can be embedded into an existing cultural competency program. If embedded into an existing program, please use the prompts from Table 6.2 prior to starting the intervention. Question and flow were designed using the questions presented in Hook et al. (2017).

Table 6.1 Cultural Humility Process Traditional OD Processes.

Positive Cultural Humility Intervention	Microcosm Group	Large Group Meeting	Open Systems Method
(Preliminary) Recognize the cultural composition of your stakeholders	Identify the issue	Compelling meeting theme	–
Identify and convene relevant stakeholders	Convene the group	Appropriate participants	–
Map cultural composition with stakeholders	–	Relevant task to address the conference theme	Map the current environment surrounding the organization
Reflect on cultures identified	–	–	Assess the organization's responses to environmental expectations
Reconvene group and create personal goals	–	–	Identify the core mission of the organization
Connect with first-hand accounts of cultural experience	Provide group training	–	Create a realistic future scenario of environmental expectations and organization responses
Incorporate various identities into the larger organizational identity	–	–	Create an ideal future scenario of environmental expectations and organization responses
Develop new processes and norms	Address the issue	–	Compare the present with the ideal future and prepare an action plan for the discrepancy
Self-directed positive cultural humility conversation and reflection	Dissolve the group	–	–
Ongoing learning	Opportunities to reconvene	Post-meeting follow-through	–

Note: The Positive Cultural Humility Intervention compared to three traditional OD interventions.

Table 6.2 Post-Cultural Competency Module.

Questions presented post-diversity/cultural competency modules and before cultural humility intervention

5. What did you learn about the cultural group?

6. How has your understanding or perspective about this cultural group changed?

7. Was anything that you saw or read surprising?

8. What feelings came up for you as you learned (e.g., sad, angry, scared, excited, happy)?

9. Did this experience motivate you to engage in any further learning for exploration about this cultural group?

1. **Recognize the cultural composition of your stakeholders.** In this initial step, leadership recognizes the cultural diversity of their organization's stakeholders, internal and external. At this stage, leadership may notice their organization is unable to effectively address the needs of a given population.
2. **Identify and convene relevant stakeholders.** In this step, identify and select all leaders, managers, and change agents to take part in this intervention. Non-leadership personnel are strongly encouraged to join as well.
3. **Map cultural composition with stakeholders.** In this step, the participants break into smaller groups to map the cultural taxonomies recognized by leadership, managers, and change agents (for example, list all cultural identities held by stakeholders). The mapping process is done with all participants in attendance.
4. **Reflect on cultures identified.** In this step, reflect on the cultural taxonomies created and identify which cultural groups the participants do not have much experience with/do not know much about (Table 6.3).

Table 6.3 Positive Cultural Humility Intervention – Setting the Stage.

Reflect on a cultural group you do not know much about/do not have much experience with
Level 1
1. Do you feel you have a tendency to make judgments about any of the cultural groups on your list?
2. Do you feel any of the cultural groups from your list are superior or inferior to you?
3. Do you disagree with any of these cultural groups or worldviews?
Level 2
1. What do you know (or think that you know) about these cultures?
2. What do you not know about these cultures?
3. What are your personal experiences with these cultures?
4. What are you curious about regarding these cultures?

Note: Guiding questions for stage 4 of Positive Cultural Humility Intervention.

5. **Reconvene group and create personal goals.** In this step, the attendees join together to share their responses to the guiding questions and develop their own goal for learning more about a specific culture.
6. **Connect with first-hand accounts of cultural experience.** In this step, the OD practitioner and the attendees collaborate to identify people among them whose experiences in the organization are distinct from the dominant group due to culture. These attendees identified are encouraged to share their first-hand experience with the group with the guidance of the OD practitioner. It is imperative that the OD practitioner helps to maintain psychological safety (Edmondson, 1999) among the group as sharing one's cultural experience is the core of cultural humility.
7. **Incorporate various identities into organization identity.** In this step, the OD practitioner and attendees collaborate to form new identities that capture the diversity and experiences of all stakeholders.

8. **Develop new processes and norms.** In this step, a new mission is planned, focusing on diffusing humility and instilling cultural humility into group norms. Processes for evaluating cultural humility via expressed humility become routinized and part of performance management. Communication processes are put in place to allow for richer communication between diverse stakeholders.

9. **Self-directed cultural humility conversation and reflection.** In this step, all attendees are given an assignment of having an in-depth conversation with a friend or colleague from a different cultural background (Table 6.4).

Table 6.4 Positive Cultural Humility Intervention – Exploration and Reflection.

Have an in-depth cultural conversation with a friend or colleague from a culturally different background. Please ensure the conversation is balanced with both you and your friend or colleague responding to each question.

What is your cultural heritage?

10. What is the culture of your parents or primary caregivers?

11. With what cultural groups do you identify?

12. Which of your cultural identities are most salient to your identity?

13. Which of your cultural identities are less salient to your identity?

14. What beliefs, values, and attitudes do you hold that are important to you?

15. What beliefs, values, and attitudes do you hold that are consistent with the dominant culture?

16. Which are inconsistent with the dominant culture?

Reflective questions for self after the conversation.

1. What thoughts, feelings, and reactions came up for you during the conversation?

2. What parts of the conversation were easy or flowed naturally?

3. What parts of the conversation were difficult or awkward?

4. What was it like for your discussion partner to ask you about your cultural identities?

5. What was it like to share your cultural identities?

6. Did the conversation motivate you to talk more about culture and cultural identities?

7. Following the conversation, how do you feel toward your discussion partner?

    • Do you feel more or less connected to them?

    • Would you like to continue the conversation and talk more about anything that came up?

Note: Guiding questions for stage 9 of Positive Cultural Humility Intervention.

10. **Ongoing learning.** This final step involves instilling accountability within the intervention's attendees. All attendees are encouraged to join the next positive cultural humility intervention to share their experiences speaking with a person from a cultural background distinct from their own. The Positive Cultural Humility Intervention is designed to occur in the same venue biannually. Participants should expect individual changes in cultural and expressed humility over time.

7

Bystander Intervention

A Positive Approach to Sexual Harassment Prevention

Eli Kolokowsky & Sharon Hong

Sexual harassment in the workplace is a prevalent issue, with 60% of women reporting that they have experienced workplace sexual harassment (Feldblum & Lipnic, 2016). Sexual harassment has many definitions, and because of this it is often seen as a murky and unclear concept. Farley (1978) defined sexual harassment as persistent sexual attention, repeated requests for dates, or comments, jokes, or materials of a sexual nature. The Sexual Experiences Questionnaire includes forms of gender harassment such as crude comments of a sexual nature (i.e., using gendered slurs in the workplace or sexist comments) (EEOC, 2016). People who experience sexual harassment often do not report it – an estimated 87%–94% of workplace sexual harassment cases go unreported (EEOC, 2016). The silence on sexual harassment, when repeated in this way, can lead to a culture of remaining silent when harassment happens.

The organizational culture and climate hold a heavy influence on how safe and comfortable the organization's members feel, how they are treated, and the manner in which they treat each other. Companies like Vice Media, Bank of America, Papa John's, and Nike have been criticized for promoting a "bro culture." Perhaps unsurprisingly and uncoincidentally, these organizations have also faced recent lawsuits on sexual harassment and discrimination (Creswell & Draper, 2018; Fickenscher, 2018; Merle, 2016; Steel, 2017). Multiple streams of research have identified organizational climate as a significant antecedent and predictor of sexual harassment in the workplace (Fitzgerald et al., 1995; Pryor et al., 1993; Welsh, 1999). Factors that contribute to a toxic organizational climate and "bro culture" include male superiority, cultural symbols of masculinity, and working in male-dominated occupations or industries (Glick, 1991; Stockdale, 1993; Willness et al., 2007). Organizational climates that are tolerant and permissive of sexual harassment behaviors are likely to see greater cases of these actions being present. Although changing something as deep rooted as the culture or climate of an organization takes considerable time and effort, there are still steps that can and should be taken to direct an organization's currently toxic culture toward the right direction in decreasing sexual harassment incidents at work.

Positive Organizational Psychology Interventions: Design and Evaluation, First Edition.
Stewart I. Donaldson and Christopher Chen.
© 2021 John Wiley & Sons Ltd. Published 2021 by John Wiley & Sons Ltd.

The vast majority of organizations (approximately 94%) have some form of anti-harassment policies in place (Taylor, 2018). Clearly, employers see the need to protect their employees from unwanted sexual advances. Yet, the issue still prevails. With the rise of the #MeToo movement and high-profile allegations of sexual harassment at work, it becomes ever more critical to find a solution to dealing with this serious matter. Thus, we offer the bystander intervention as a strategy for preventing and coping with sexual harassment at work.

The Bystander intervention is not necessarily a new resolution. Bystander intervention behavior can include removing a victim from a harassing situation, speaking up to a harasser, or reporting the harasser on behalf of the victim (McDonald et al., 2016). Many business-oriented publications, such as the *Harvard Business Review*, advocate using this method above others. However, case studies showing these interventions in action are few and far between.

Unfortunately, empirical research on sexual harassment interventions and bystander intervention is also sparse. However, we propose several areas of research to help guide our thinking in our endeavor – specifically, research on prohibitive voice behavior, acquiescent silence, and positive deviance. Speaking up against sexual harassment falls under the umbrella of prohibitive voice behavior, or the act of speaking up against harmful practices or behaviors in an organization (Liang et al., 2012). Speaking up against sexual harassment is also an example of positive deviance or a behavior that deviates from a norm in a successful and honorable way (Lavine, 2012). Alternatively, remaining silent when one witnesses sexual harassment could be considered a form of acquiescent silence, or staying silent on an issue to conform to the culture of the organization due to fear of repercussion (Van Dyne et al., 2003).

Incorporating these three streams of research into a bystander intervention training would involve taking a preventive approach and increasing a psychological safety climate, a known predictor of prohibitive voice (Liang et al., 2012). Though changing climate is challenging, several experimental studies show climate change is indeed possible (e.g., Zohar & Polachek, 2014). By incorporating well-established theories on voice, silence, and positive deviance into our training, we hope to create a bystander intervention training that is based on theory and applicable to practice.

The Consequences of Sexual Harassment

Sexual harassment has a wealth of detrimental outcomes for individuals, teams, and organizations at large. Targets of sexual harassment are disproportionately female, and often work alone as opposed to in groups (Ollo-Lopez & Nunez, 2018). Additionally, those in contracted positions are at higher risk for sexual harassment, as well as those who have lower employee status in the organization (Ollo-Lopez & Nunez, 2018). Organizations with a structure that promotes isolated work may experience increased negative consequences of sexual harassment. Additionally, organizations that contract employees or give limited attention to their lower status employees run the risk of experiencing these negative consequences, along with the individuals experiencing harassment.

The Effect on Individuals

The effects of sexual harassment vary from individual to individual and can have a significant negative impact. Regardless of the type of sexual harassment, the pervasiveness of harassment behavior impacts the outcomes for receivers of harassment (Langhout et al., 2005). Whether the harassment is in the form of inappropriate jokes at the water cooler, or comments on one's appearance, a negative appraisal by the recipient is likely to lead to negative outcomes (Langhout et al., 2005).

Another outcome of workplace sexual harassment is decreased psychological well-being (Dionisi et al., 2012). This decreased psychological well-being could be the result of self-blame, fear of repeated harassment, or stress of working alongside their harasser (Millegan et al., 2015). Those who experience sexual harassment may see an increase in depression and anxiety, and overall decreased mental health (Millegan et al., 2015). These outcomes are not only detrimental in the workplace but can pervade all areas of one's life.

Women who work in male-dominated fields such as engineering, construction, and automotive services are especially at risk for negative outcomes of sexual harassment. When women in male-dominated fields interact with sexist men at work, they can experience social identity threat on top of the negative outcomes already described (Logel et al., 2009). Social identity threat, or the devaluation of a person's social identity in a specific context (Steele et al., 2002), can decrease female employees' work performance (Logel et al., 2009).

Women in male-dominated fields also tend to suppress their concerns about gender inequality when exposed to sex-based harassment (Logel et al., 2009). Since sexual harassment is already an isolating event, it is worrisome that female targets of sexual harassment in male-dominated fields are pushed to silence themselves on this issue. This type of silence, conceptualized by Van Dyne and colleagues (2003) as defensive silence, is self-protective in nature. Receivers of sexual harassment may be motivated to use this type of silence due to the high percentage of people who face retaliation from speaking up against sexual harassment (Cortina & Magley, 2003). This type of quiescent silence is associated with higher depersonalization and emotional exhaustion – two of the main components in employee burnout (Knoll et al., 2018).

The Effect on Teams

Sexual harassment not only impacts the individual victim, teams and workgroups suffer as a consequence as well. Research evidence (O'Leary-Kelly et al., 2009; Willness et al., 2007) shows that as a result of sexual harassment in the workplace, workgroup productivity and performance (i.e., the ability for the workgroup to perform quality work together; Bergman & Drasgow, 2003) experience significant losses. Furthermore, sexual harassment is positively associated with task conflict and interpersonal conflict and negatively related to team cohesion, impacting everyday team processes in addition to a team's functioning and performance in the long run (Baillien et al., 2008; Raver & Gelfand, 2005).

The Effect on Organizations

One common outcome of workplace sexual harassment is workplace withdrawal (Dionisi et al., 2012). Examples of this behavior include absenteeism, failure to complete work, and avoiding other people at work (Dionisi et al., 2012). Workplace withdrawal behavior is detrimental not only to the individual, who may fall behind, but to the coworkers, teams, and managers that rely on this individual. Not attending meetings, inability to meet deadlines that others rely upon, and skipping work altogether can detriment the relationships a person has in their workplace. Additionally, those experiencing sexual harassment may change their routines surrounding work such as where they travel within the physical workspace, who they interact with, or what projects they choose to take on due to a desire to avoid their harasser (Dionisi et al., 2012). Others may decide to leave their job altogether, causing strain on the self and the organization they are leaving.

Why Bystander Intervention?

Traditional sexual harassment trainings have often proven to be ineffective in reducing incidents and changing attitudes on sexual harassment at work (Antecol & Cobb-Clark, 2003). This may be because traditional sexual harassment trainings often feel punitive, and employees may feel as though the trainings are not relevant to them. Bystander intervention training, on the other hand, involves employees in a participative and positive manner. Bystander intervention trainings are sexual harassment trainings in which employees are taught strategies to intervene when they see sexual harassment (Katz & Moore, 2013).

Encouraging bystanders in the workplace to step in when they witness cases of sexual harassment is useful for a number of reasons. First, third parties are often more effective than those directly involved in resolving different types of problems among people (Ury, 2000). In addition, sexual violence interventions that involve community-focused solutions have been shown to produce greater results in increasing receptivity to messages around preventing sexual violence and increasing the likelihood of members taking active roles in prevention and intervention (Banyard et al., 2004). Furthermore, recent studies on bystander interventions suggest that implementation of these interventions not only decreases sexual violence but also other varieties of interpersonal violence and victimization, thus having broader positive effects on the environment (Coker et al., 2017). Finally, this type of intervention encourages prohibitive voice and normalizing positive deviant behavior, theoretically giving employees a greater sense of influence and agency. Although the empirical evidence and evaluations around bystander interventions are relatively limited and young, we propose that a bystander intervention training will produce more desirable results than traditional approaches for reducing sexual harassment at work.

State of the Research

General Bystander Intervention Research

Bystander intervention research is largely done on college populations. This focus is likely due to the contextual factors of young adults, newly found freedom, and alcohol. In college populations, bystander intervention trainings are shown to increase an individual's intention to intervene when they see a sexual harassment incident, as well as bystander efficacy and actual helping behaviors (Katz & Moore, 2013; Kettery & Marx, 2019). Bystander intervention trainings are also shown to positively change perceptions on issues of gender equity and sexual harassment (Kettery & Marx, 2019).

Bystander Interventions in the Workplace

There is a significant body of work on the effectiveness of bystander interventions in response to dating and domestic violence, especially in the university context (Chamberlain, 2008; Coker et al., 2016; Cornelius & Resseguie, 2007). There is much less research done on bystander interventions in the workplace, but the college and working populations are shown to be comparable on the subject of bystander action (Jacobson & Eaton, 2018). Bowes-Sperry and O'Leary-Kelly (2005) wrote in their theory paper on bystander intervention that bystander action is a complex process with many determining factors. For example, people are more likely to intervene if they are close to the subject of the harassment behavior, and are less likely to intervene if they believe they will lose social capital from doing so. Those who perceive they will lose social capital but still want to help might approach the target later and offer advice, or console them. However, in high-stakes situations where there is a high risk of social punishment, people will rarely choose to intervene in the moment. Organizational policy also affects bystander action – those in organizations with salient zero-tolerance sexual harassment policies are more inclined to report on behalf of a target of sexual harassment, especially when they perceive the harassment to be severe (Jacobson & Eaton, 2018).

Prohibitive Voice Behavior

Voice behavior is well studied in organizational contexts and has many benefits, as well as boundary conditions. The primary predictor of prohibitive voice is psychological safety, or the feeling that one can state opinions or ideas without consequence in a team (Liang et al., 2012). Prohibitive voice is also higher, on average, with people who have a supportive relationship with their leader (i.e., high leader–member exchange; Kong et al., 2017). Kong and colleagues found in their study on need for affiliation and voice behavior that need for affiliation is positively related to prohibitive voice behavior by the means of leader–member exchange, but that groups high in cohesion also experience high levels of prohibitive voice behavior. Considering one aim of bystander interventions is to create a sense of community and collective responsibility in preventing sexual harassment, it seems reasonable to expect that prohibitive voice would increase as a product of this. Peer support at work is also shown to be a predictor of psychological safety (Frazier et al., 2017), an essential component in both bystander intervention trainings and prohibitive voice. From a research standpoint, prohibitive voice and bystander intervention trainings go hand in hand in their antecedents and outcomes.

Positive Deviance

Positive deviance can be a large factor in bystander interventions. In organizations where it is the norm to stay silent when witnessing sexual harassment, speaking up to protect another deviates from the norm in a positive way. Once this deviant behavior is employed enough, it is no longer deviant, and becomes the new norm (Spreitzer & Sonenshein, 2004). Spreitzer and Sonenshein (2003) theorize that positive deviance likely strengthens the relationships between the deviant and those helped by the deviant behavior, and that positive deviance overall increases organizational effectiveness. In the context of sexual harassment, this likely holds true as the deviant behavior is directly benefiting another person, and creating a safer culture for employees to operate in.

According to Lavine (2012), positive deviance is effectively implemented when people are already exhibiting the solution behavior (i.e., intervening in harassment situations), other solutions have not worked (i.e., traditional sexual harassment training), and when there is leadership buy-in. We acknowledge that leadership buy-in is a large factor in the effectiveness of our intervention, and hope that the benefits we provide are clear to those leaders who are uncertain about implementing this intervention.

Bystander Intervention Training

Measurement and Preparation

Before the training, several preliminary performance indicators of the training must be measured as a comparison point. These performance indicators will also be measured after employees have completed the bystander intervention training to assess its effectiveness. If scores are not significantly different, we recommend that the training is evaluated by stakeholders and those implementing the training to identify potential gaps and areas for improvement.

Measures

Climate Survey
We recommend that organizations conduct a general climate survey before implementing the trainings. The results of the climate survey will give insight into issues specific to the organization, which can then be addressed in training. For example, organizations with a large population of LGBT individuals may need to consider harassment based on sexual orientations and harassment situations unique to this community.

Bystander Efficacy

Measuring bystander efficacy before the bystander training will give stakeholders insight into employees' current beliefs that they can effectively intervene in a sexual harassment situation. One goal of the training is to see an increase in bystander efficacy following implementation.

Psychological Climate

Psychological climate of sexual harassment refers to perceptions of the psychological climate in a workplace in terms of how much the workplace accepts or enables sexual harassment. While this may not change immediately after the first training, repeated implementations of the training should be associated with improved psychological climate.

Intention to Intervene

One's intention to intervene in a sexual harassment situation is a key measurement point in this training. Comparing the pre- and post-intervention scores of intention to intervene will give stakeholders and training experts a view into the extent of training transfer and information retention.

Collective Responsibility

We recommend measuring collective responsibility specifically in relation to sexual harassment to assess employee perceptions that they share influence in preventing sexual harassment. Depending on the current culture of the organization, this may stay the same or increase after the training.

Social Desirability

We recommend controlling for social desirability in the post-test due to its possible interaction with intentions to intervene following the training.

Training

The first activity in our interactive workshop will be a facilitated discussion about related attitudes, behaviors, and processes around sexual harassment at work. The process begins with a trained facilitator posing the question of what participants think is considered sexual harassment. After the initial discussion, the facilitator will provide a clear, definitive explanation of sexual harassment as there are many interpretations of "sexual harassment," thus causing uncertainty around what and when people should report. The facilitator will then direct the participants in a conversation to share examples of bystander interventions they have seen or done (e.g., "When has someone stood up for you?" to reframe the "victim" perspective in a more psychologically safe way). In addition, the facilitator will highlight positive deviance examples of bystander action by providing case studies of individuals who took a stand and resulted in an effective outcome in hopes of making the positive possibilities salient.

The second phase of our interactive workshop will be a roleplay activity. This activity will involve two actors roleplaying a sexual harassment situation, while employees will have the opportunity to intervene. The employees will be taught four types of intervention techniques based on Bowes-Sperry and O'Leary-Kelly's (2005) theory paper on bystander action and a later bystander action study by McDonald et al. (2016). The first type of intervention is low immediacy, low involvement. This happens after the harassment event and is focused on an attempt to prevent future harassment without public connection to the incident. The second action type is low immediacy, high involvement, in which an individual responds retroactively to a harassment event with a public connection to the incident (i.e., confronting the harasser later). The third strategy is high immediacy, low involvement, where a person intervenes while the harassment is happening without direct confrontation of the harasser (i.e., removing the target from the situation). The last type of action is high immediacy, high involvement, in which a person directly confronts the harassment while it is happening. The goal of this roleplay activity is first to provide practice to employees and to increase training transfer of these intervention techniques.

The last part of the workshop will be focused on victim strategies in sexual harassment situations. When a victim is alone in a sexual harassment situation or is not able to safely leave the situation, immediate bystander action may not be feasible. Though there is not always a safe or ready-made strategy for a victim to stop harassment, they can rely on others in the organization for low-immediacy strategies and support. Participants in the workshop will be encouraged to identify an ally in their workplace who they can go to for support if sexual harassment occurs. This could be a friend at work or a trusted human resources (HR) representative.

Employee Involvement

To be effective, we recommend that employers have all employees go through this intervention by the department or team. However, if this is not feasible, we recommend having managers or other types of leads go through the intervention, as these are the individuals in the organization who have the potential to influence organizational culture. In the case that all employees are trained, we recommend that managers go through separate training from their employees so that the intervention can be focused on the needs of specific groups. Those with power over others in organizations are more likely to sexually harass due to gendered power imbalances (Rospenda et al., 1998), thus a separate training for those in power is ideal. The goal of a separate training is to push managers to use their power to help and support their employees, and remind managers that they do not have to be a part of this statistic.

Timeline

We offer several recommendations to maximize the effectiveness of the program. Researchers state that the most effective training is at least four hours, interactive, and tailored specifically to the organization in focus (Miller, 2017). Thus, we advise, so much as an organization's resources allow, that our bystander intervention lasts a duration of four hours and be implemented twice a year. Although the various formats and components of our intervention already can encourage greater training transfer for participants, implementing the intervention at multiple points of the year provides more chances for the information to stick and for employees to feel comfortable and confident in getting involved.

Desired Outcomes

Our hopes for the outcomes of this intervention are manyfold. First, we hope that it will increase the efficacy of bystanders to make a difference. Those who may have witnessed sexual harassment in the past will now have tools to intervene if they see it again. Rewarding prohibitive voice in the case of sexual harassment is likely to create a feedback loop where intervention and reporting behavior become more and more common. We believe that implementing this intervention would decrease sexual harassment behavior, both because potential harassers will be educated on harassment and because potential harassers who still have the intention to harass will expect their coworkers to intervene. By creating a punitive environment for harassers and an empowering one for victims and bystanders, we hope to see a shift in culture that places added value on collective responsibility and helping behaviors.

We also hope that this intervention will increase perceptions of safety in the workplace, in that individuals know that their coworkers will be looking out for them. Victims of sexual harassment will now have others to look to when they need support or help in reporting their harassers. Coworker support is shown to be a predictor of psychological safety (Frazier et al., 2017), so it stands to reason that a supportive coworker climate stemming from this intervention could have a similar effect.

Ideal Conditions

We offer our bystander intervention as one method for addressing the issue of sexual harassment at work. However, at the end of the day, it is not only a matter of implementing the right intervention. It is also a concern for organizational culture. For the bystander intervention to produce ideal results, an organization needs to foster a culture of mutual respect, equality, diversity, and inclusion, and collective responsibility (Fischer et al., 2011; Janove, 2018; Johnson et al., 2018; Miller, 2017). Oftentimes what interferes with witnesses' abilities to follow through and speak out on injustices they observe at work is the diffusion of responsibility. Diffusion of responsibility (Fischer et al., 2011; Latané & Darley, 1970) suggests that when more bystanders are present, any individual bystander is likely to feel less personal responsibility to help. One way to address this assumption is by fostering a shared sense of collective responsibility. Engaging people at work and offering realistic tools for intervening can help employers and employees see these incidents as a shared problem that is within their control to resolve.

The culture of an organization cannot be changed in a day. According to Edgar Schein, an organization's culture can only evolve if mutual experience and shared learning are involved (Ashkanasy et al., 2011; Schein, 2004). The process is long and strenuous, which becomes even more salient the larger the organization. But our intervention, let alone any intervention regarding sexual harassment, will not be truly effective if the organization's culture and climate are not aligned with these change efforts. Hence, organizations must also simultaneously prioritize addressing the systemic cultural issues of sexual violence at work for the intervention to produce desirable results.

One factor of the organization that may support quicker changes in culture and effect better results for intervening against sexual harassment is the organization's size. For better or for worse, individual employees can have a greater impact on the overall culture of a smaller organization than a large-sized corporation with multiple, complex subcultures. Because employees in small to medium-sized organizations tend to play greater roles in impacting culture, our bystander intervention may see greater and quicker results in smaller organizations if accepted by the members.

The success of the bystander intervention is also contingent upon the role that HR plays in the organization. The human resources department has become a feared, political, negative entity within organizations in the eyes of many employees. HR tends to be perceived as a brutal, nitpicky force whose main purpose of existence is to save the face of the organization and to get its people in trouble for even the smallest infractions (Ryan, 2016). When organizations encourage their members to see HR as a protector of the people instead, sexual harassment prevention practices such as the bystander intervention may be more positively received. To achieve this goal, proper changes to behavior and priorities need to be made within HR. For one, HR must ensure that there are policies in place to protect those who choose to get involved directly or indirectly in addition to the victims of harassment.

Furthermore, we recommend that HR communicates overtly and covertly to its employees that sexual harassment is not tolerated in the workplace. HR can carry out this message in various ways, such as by not dismissing reports or delaying appropriate and necessary action. Concerns often fall around ineffective voice systems such as the deaf-ear syndrome, in which sexual harassment reporting falls on deaf ears and results in organizational inaction (Peirce et al., 1998). Studies show that when sexual harassment complaints and reporting go ignored, this negligence results in perceived injustice, decreased productivity, and increased turnover (O'Hara, 1998; Peirce et al., 1998). Thus, it is important for the well-being of individual employees, teams, and the organization as a whole for human resource personnel to exhibit due diligence when handling sexual harassment cases. This means that those in HR need also to serve as active, sensitive, and sympathetic listeners when victims and bystanders of sexual harassment incidents approach HR for support (Conner & Ulrich, 1996).

In addition, organizations implementing the bystander intervention should have the leadership support necessary for greater impact. Organization-wide changes oftentimes begin with those at the top. When the organization's top leaders communicate the message, demonstrate a commitment to the cause through their actions, and are held at the same level of accountability as those in lower levels of the organization, employees will have greater trust in the leader and the initiative (Offermann & Malamut, 2002). Employees' trust in their leaders, in turn, will lead to acceptance of organizational decisions (Ilgen et al., 1979). Additionally, leader buy-in allows for greater devotion of resources to the cause to maintain the momentum of the change movement (Gilley, 2005).

Although the size of the organization can influence the effectiveness of the bystander intervention, small size is not necessary for the successful implementation of the intervention. Rather, we argue that it is the combination of leadership support, proper HR involvement, and a culture of mutual respect, collective responsibility, and equality that is essential to catalyzing the movement toward reduced sexual harassment and increased reporting behavior at work. Without these three conditions, in particular, it is extremely difficult to see lasting positive results. Therefore, organizations should assess if they satisfy these criteria not only to address sexual harassment but also to improve the overall state of their organization.

Strengths

This intervention is different from many sexual harassment trainings in that it goes above and beyond a simple statement of policies and punishments. Traditional sexual harassment trainings that simply go over policies can actually reinforce gender stereotypes (Tinkler, 2013), and it is not clear that they change attitudes or behavior surrounding sexual harassment (Antecol & Cobb-Clark, 2003). Bystander intervention trainings, on the other hand, are shown to be effective in changing attitudes on sexual assault and harassment (Kettery & Marx, 2019).

Bystander intervention trainings also have the ability to give men the perception of psychological standing in the issue of sexual harassment. Oftentimes, men feel as though they should not speak up on gender equity issues or initiatives because it often does not directly involve them (Sherf et al., 2018). This is especially relevant in traditional sexual harassment trainings, where men who do not intend to harass cannot see the point of their inclusion in the training. Though women indeed have a higher chance of being victims of sexual harassment (Ollo-Lopez & Nunez, 2018), it is far from true that men do not experience sexual harassment in the workplace. Through this intervention, we hope that male targets of harassment can find community and allies to support them. Bystander intervention training allows both men and women to see the important role they can play in preventing sexual harassment by giving them tools and promoting prohibitive voice to intervene in harassment situations.

Limitations

Although several practices for preventing sexual harassment in the workplace (e.g., in-person classroom sessions, online modules) have been implemented and evaluated, the effectiveness of bystander interventions is uncertain as it is a relatively new approach to the field, particularly in the corporate world. Thus, we acknowledge the limitation of not knowing the longitudinal impact of such an intervention. However, the intervention has been shown to produce desirable results in college campuses, in the military, and even in non-profits (Miller, 2017). With further research, we are hopeful that we can continue to see these positive outcomes in the workplace as well.

A second limitation of the intervention is the buy-in needed not only from leadership but from the employees themselves who are encouraged to intervene. The purpose of bystander interventions is to galvanize all members of the organization to take action when they see injustice. However, if organization members do not feel a sense of responsibility, comfort, or confidence to address such issues, many sexual harassment incidents may continue to go unreported.

Third, employee acceptance and organizational impact of the bystander intervention depend on the organizational culture. As mentioned previously, organizations that possess more communal, equal, and respectful cultures are more likely to see better results than organizations that do not bear such qualities. If organizations do not have such cultures and instead promote a "bro culture," they may face difficulty in implementing bystander interventions and reducing sexual harassment effectively. However, culture is not easily changed. Our intervention's reliance on a slow-changing and durable factor such as organizational culture is a considerable limitation to our proposal.

Conclusion

This intervention is perfect for forward-looking companies who want to stay ahead of the curve in terms of organizational culture. Laws requiring sexual harassment training for organizations statewide are starting to gain traction and will likely be widespread in the future. Maine, for example, has a law that any employer with 15 or more employees that is doing business in the state must provide sexual harassment training within employees' first year. As these laws become more and more common, it is imperative that we implement the best possible sexual harassment trainings to reduce harassment behavior and increase reporting behavior in harassment situations.

Our hope is that bystander intervention trainings become a common method of sexual harassment prevention in the workplace. We also hope to see this method adapted to other contexts such as the prevention of microaggressions or workplace bullying. Finally, we aspire toward a general culture of organizational positive deviance. By implementing innovative and positively deviant processes, future oriented organizations can be drivers of significant positive social change.

References

Antecol, H., & Cobb-Clark, D. (2003). Does sexual harassment training change attitudes? A view from the federal level. *Social Science Quarterly, 84*, 826–842. doi:10.1046/j.00384941.2003.08404001.x

Ashkanasy, N., Wilderom, C., & Peterson, M. (2011). *Handbook of organizational culture and climate.* Thousand Oaks, CA: Sage.

Baillien, E., Neyens, I., & De Witte, H. (2008). Organizational, team related and job related risk factors for bullying, violence and sexual harassment in the workplace: A qualitative study. *International Journal of Organisational Behavior, 13,* 132–146.

Banyard, V. L., Plante, E. G., & Moynihan, M. M. (2004). Bystander education: Bringing a broader community perspective to sexual violence prevention. *Journal of Community Psychology, 32,* 61–79. doi:10.1002/jcop.10078

Bergman, M. E., & Drasgow, F. (2003). Race as a moderator in a model of sexual harassment: An empirical test. *Journal of Occupational Health Psychology, 8,* 131–145. doi:10.1037/1076-8998.8.2.131

Bowes-Sperry, L., & O'Leary-Kelly, A. M. (2005). To act or not to act: The dilemma faced by sexual harassment observers. *The Academy of Management Review, 30,* 288–306. https://doi-org.ccl.idm.oclc.org/10.2307/20159120

Chamberlain, L. (2008). *A prevention primer for domestic violence: Terminology, tools, and the public health approach.* Harrisburg, PA: The National Online Resource Center on Violence Against Women (VAWnet).

Coker, A. L., Bush, H. M., Cook-Craig, P. G., DeGue, S. A., Clear, E. R., Brancato, C. J., Fisher, B. S., & Recktenwald, E. A. (2017). RCT testing bystander effectiveness to reduce violence. *American Journal of Preventive Medicine, 52,* 566–578. doi:10.1016/j.amepre.2017.01.020

Coker, A. L., Bush, H. M., Fisher, B. S., Swan, S. C., Williams, C. M., Clear, E. R., & DeGue, S. (2016). Multi-college bystander intervention evaluation for violence prevention. *American Journal of Preventive Medicine, 50,* 295–302. doi:10.1016/j.amepre.2015.08.034

Conner, J., & Ulrich, D. (1996). Human resource roles: Creating value, not rhetoric. *Human Resource Planning, 19,* 38.

Cornelius, T., & Resseguie, N. (2007). Primary and secondary prevention programs for dating violence: A review of the literature. *Aggression and Violent Behavior, 12,* 364–375. doi:10.1016/j.avb.2006.09.006

Cortina, L. M. & Magley, V. J. (2003). Raising voice, risking retaliation: Events following interpersonal mistreatment in the workplace. *Journal of Occupational Health Psychology, 8,* 247–255. doi:10.1037/1076-8998.8.4.247

Creswell, J., & Draper, K. (2018, May 8). 5 more Nike executives are out amid inquiry into harassment allegations. The New York Times. Retrieved from https://www.nytimes.com/2018/05/08/business/nike-harassment.html

Dionisi, A. M., Barling, J., & Dupré, K. E. (2012). Revisiting the comparative outcomes of workplace aggression and sexual harassment. *Journal of Occupational Health Psychology, 17,* 398–408. https://doi.org/10.1037/a0029883

Farley, L. (1978). *Sexual shakedown.* New York City, NY: McGraw Hill.

Feldblum, C. R., & Lipnic, V. A. (2016). Select task force on the study of harassment in the workplace. Report prepared for U.S. Equal Employment Opportunity Commission.

Fickenscher, L. (2018, October 1). Papa John's founder admits to deal with woman accusing him of sexual harassment. New York Post. Retrieved from https://nypost.com/2018/10/01/

papa-johns-founder-admits-to-deals-with-women-accusing-him-of-sexual-harassment/

Fischer, P., Krueger, J. I., Greitemeyer, T., Vogrincic, C., Kastenmüller, A., Frey, D.,... Kainbacher, M. (2011). The bystander-effect: A meta-analytic review on bystander intervention in dangerous and non-dangerous emergencies. *Psychological Bulletin, 137*, 517–537. doi:10.1037/a0023304

Fitzgerald, L. F., Gelfand, M. J., & Drasgow, F. (1995). Measuring sexual harassment: Theoretical and psychometric advances. *Basic & Applied Social Psychology, 17*, 425–445. doi:10.1207/s15324834basp1704_2

Frazier, M. L., Fainshmidt, S., Klinger, R. L., Pezeshkan, A., & Vracheva, V. (2017). Psychological safety: A meta analytic review and extension. *Personnel Psychology, 70*, 113–165. doi:10.1111/peps.12183

Gilley, A. M. (2005). *The manager as change leader*. Westport, CT: Greenwood Publishing Group.

Glick, P. (1991). Trait-based and sex-based discrimination in occupational prestige, occupational salary, and hiring. *Sex Roles, 25*, 351–378. doi:10.1007/BF00289761

Ilgen, D. R., Fisher, C. D., & Taylor, M. S. (1979). Consequences of individual feedback on behavior in organizations. *Journal of Applied Psychology, 64*, 349–371. doi:10.1037/0021-9010.64.4.349

Jacobson, R. K., & Eaton, A. A. (2018). How organizational policies influence bystander likelihood of reporting moderate and severe sexual harassment at work. *Employee Responsibilities and Rights Journal, 30*, 37–62. https://doi-org.ccl.idm.oclc.org/10.1007/s10672-017-9309-1

Janove, J. (2018, January 18). Viewpoint: It's time to take a new approach to sexual harassment prevention. The Society for Human Resource Management. Retrieved from https://www.shrm.org/ResourcesAndTools/hr-topics/employee-relations/Pages/Viewpoint-Its-Time-to-Take-a-New-Approach-to-Sexual-Harassment-Prevention.aspx

Katz, J., & Moore, J. (2013). Bystander education training for campus sexual assault prevention: An initial meta-analysis. *Violence and Victims, 28*, 1054–1067. https://doi-org.ccl.idm.oclc.org/10.1891/0886-6708.VV-D-12-00113

Kettery, H. H., & Marx, R. A. (2019). The effects of bystander programs on the prevention of sexual assault across the college years: A systematic review and meta-analysis. *Journal of Youth and Adolescence, 48*, 212–227. doi:10.1007/s10964-018-0927-1

Knoll, M., Hall, R. J., & Weigelt, O. (2018). A longitudinal study of the relationships between four differentially motivated forms of employee silence and burnout. *Journal of Occupational Health Psychology*. Advance Online Publication. https://doi.org/10.1037/ocp0000143

Kong, F., Huang, Y., Liu, P., & Zhao, X. (2017). Why voice behavior? An integrative model of the need for affiliation, the quality of leader–member exchange, and group cohesion in predicting voice behavior. *Group & Organization Management, 42*, 792–818. https://doi-org.ccl.idm.oclc.org/10.1177/1059601116642084

Johnson, P. A., Widnall, S. E., & Benya, F. F. (2018). *Sexual harassment of women: Climate, culture, and consequences in academic sciences, engineering, and medicine*. Washington, DC: The National Academies Press. doi:10.17226/24994

Langhout, R. D., Bergman, M. E., Cortina, L. M., Fitzgerald, L. F., Drasgow, F., & Williams, J. H. (2005). Sexual harassment severity: Assessing situational and personal determinants and outcomes. *Journal of Applied Social Psychology, 35*, 975–1007. doi:10.1111/j.1559-1816.2005.tb02156.x

Latané, B., & Darley, J. M. (1970). *The unresponsive behavior: Why doesn't he help?* New York, NY: Appleton-Century-Croft.

Lavine, M. (2012). Positive deviance: A metaphor and method for learning from the uncommon. In G. M. Spreitzer & K. S. Cameron (Eds.), *The Oxford handbook of positive organizational scholarship* (pp. 1014–1026). Oxford, UK: Oxford University Press.

Liang, J., Farh, C. I., & Farh, J.-L. (2012). Psychological antecedents of promotive and prohibitive voice: A two-wave examination. Academy of Management Journal, *55*, 71–73. https://doi.org/10.5465/amj.2010.0176

Logel, C., Walton, G. M., Spencer, S. J., Iserman, E. C., von Hippel, W., & Bell, A. E. (2009). Interacting with sexist men triggers social identity threat among female engineers. *Journal of Personality & Social Psychology, 96*, 1089–1103. doi:10.1037/a0015703

McDonald, P., Charlesworth, S., & Graham, T. (2016). Action or inaction: Bystander intervention in workplace sexual harassment. *The International Journal of Human Resource Management, 27*, 548-566. doi:10.1080/09585192.2015.1023331

Merle, R. (2016, May 17). Bank of America accused of running a "bros club" that underpaid female executives. The Washington Post. Retrieved from https://www.washingtonpost.com/news/business/wp/2016/05/17/bank-of-america-accused-of-running-a-bros-club-that-underpaid-female-executives/?noredirect=on&utm_term=.aa31b8c9e9bd

Millegan, J., Milburn, E. K., LeardMann, C. A., Street, A. E., Williams, D., Trone, D. W., & Crum-Cianflone, N. F. (2015). Recent sexual trauma and adverse health and occupational outcomes among US service women. *Journal of Traumatic Stress, 28*, 298–306. doi:https://doi.org/10.1002/jts.22028

Miller, C. C. (2017, December 11). Sexual harassment training doesn't work. But some things do. The New York Times. Retrieved from https://www.nytimes.com/2017/12/11/upshot/sexual-harassment-workplace-prevention-effective.html

Offermann, L. R., & Malamut, A. B. (2002). When leaders harass: The impact of target perceptions on organizational leadership and climate on harassment reporting and outcomes. *Journal of Applied Psychology, 87*, 885-893. doi:10.1037/0021-9010.87.5.885

O'Hara, J. (1998). Of rape and justice. *Maclean's, 111*, 16–21.

O'Leary-Kelly, A. M., Bowes-Sperry, L., Bates, C. A., & Lean, E. R. (2009). Sexual harassment at work: A decade (plus) of progress. *Journal of Management, 35*, 503–536. doi:10.1177/0149206308330555

Ollo-Lopez, A., & Nunez, I. (2018). Exploring the organizational drivers of sexual harassment: Empowered jobs against isolation and tolerant climates. *Employee Relations, 40*, 174–192. doi:10.1108/ER-04-2017-0074

Peirce, E., Smolinski, C., & Rosen, B. (1998). Why sexual harassment complaints fall on deaf ears. *Academy of Management Executive, 12*, 41–54. doi:10.5465/ame.1998.1109049

Pryor, J. B., LaVite, C. M., & Stoller, L. M. (1993). A social psychological analysis of sexual harassment: The person/situation interaction. *Journal of Vocational Behavior, 42,* 68–83. doi:10.1006/jvbe.1993.1005

Raver, J. L., & Gelfand, M. J. (2005). Beyond the individual victim: Linking sexual harassment, team processes, and team performance. *Academy of Management Journal, 48,* 387–400. doi:10.5465/AMJ.2005.17407904

Rospenda, K. M., Richman, J. A., & Nawyn, S. J. (1998). Doing power: The confluence of gender, race, and class in contrapower sexual harassment. *Gender & Society, 12,* 40–60. doi:10.1177/089124398012001003

Ryan, K. (2016, July 27). Ten reasons everybody hates HR. Forbes. Retrieved from https://www.forbes.com/sites/lizryan/2016/07/27/ten-reasons-everybody-hates-hr/#a2a7a7e5af4a

Schein, E. H. (2004). *Organizational culture and leadership* (3rd ed.). San Francisco, CA: Jossey-Bass.

Sherf, E. N., Tangirala, S., & Weber, K. C. (2018). It is not my place! Psychological standing and men's voice and participation in gender-parity initiatives. *Organization Science, 28.* doi:10.1287/orsc.2017.1118

Spreitzer, G., & Sonenshein, S. (2004). Toward a construct definition of PD. *American Behavioral Scientist, 47,* 828–847.

Spreitzer, G. M., & Sonenshein, S. (2003) PD and extraordinary organizing. In K. Cameron, J. Dutton, & R. Quinn (Eds.), *Positive organizational scholarship* (pp. 207–224). San Francisco, CA: Berrett-Koehler.

Steel, E. (2017, December 23). At Vice, cutting-edge media and allegations of old-school sexual harassment. The New York Times. Retrieved from https://www.nytimes.com/2017/12/23/business/media/vice-sexual-harassment.html?hp&action=click&pgtype=Homepage&clickSource=story-heading&module=photo-spot-region&region=top-news&WT.nav=top-news

Steele, C. M., Spencer, S. J., & Aronson, J. (2002). Contending with group image: The psychology of stereotype and social identity threat. In M. P. Zanna (Ed.), *Advances in experimental social psychology* (Vol. 34, pp. 379–440). San Diego, CA: Academic Press.

Stockdale, M. S. (1993). The role of sexual misperceptions of women's friendliness in an emerging theory of sexual harassment. *Journal of Vocational Behavior, 42,* 84–101. doi:10.1006/jvbe.1993.1006

Taylor, J. C. (2018, October 9). Ask HR: Some insights on the #MeToo movement and harassment in the workplace. USA Today. Retrieved from https://www.usatoday.com/story/money/careers/work-relationships/2018/10/09/ask-hr-insights-metoo-movement-harassment-workplace/1536433002/

Tinkler, J. E. (2013). How do sexual harassment policies shape gender beliefs? An exploration of the moderating effects of norm adherence and gender. *Social Science Research, 42,* 1269–1283. doi:10.1016/j.ssresearch.2013.05.002

Ury, W. L. (2000). *The third side: Why we fight and how we can stop.* New York, NY: Penguin.

Van Dyne, L., Ang, S., & Botero, I. C. (2003). Conceptualizing employee silence and employee voice as multidimensional constructs. *Journal of Management Studies, 40,* 1359–1392. https://doi.org/10.1111/1467-6486.00384

Welsh, S. (1999). Gender and sexual harassment. *Annual Review of Sociology, 25,* 169–190. doi:10.1146/annurev.soc.25.1.169

Willness, C. R., Steel, P., & Lee, K. (2007). A meta-analysis of the antecedents and consequences of workplace sexual harassment. *Personnel Psychology, 60,* 127– 162. doi:10.1111/j.1744-6570.2007.00067.x

Zohar, D., & Polachek, T. (2014). Discourse-based intervention for modifying supervisory communication as leverage for safety climate and performance improvement: A randomized field study. *Journal of Applied Psychology, 99,* 113–124. https://doi-org.ccl.idm.oclc.org/10.1037/a0034096

8

Promoting Optimal Well-Being Among Law Enforcement Employees

Emily Zavala & Lawrence Chan

The Los Angeles Police Department is comprised of 13,091 employees with 3,077 of those identified as civilians (Los Angeles Police Department, 2019). These civilian employees are not sworn personnel, but they serve as part of an integral support system for the officers, detectives, sergeants, lieutenants, captains, deputy chiefs, and even the Chief of Police. Among the civilian employees, 609 are classified as Police Service Representatives (PSRs) within the Communications Division (Los Angeles Police Department, 2019), the central entity for communications and support for the entire Los Angeles Police Department. This division is also responsible for the city's two public-safety answering points (PSAP's), the Metropolitan and Valley Communications Dispatch Centers (Los Angeles Police Department, 2019a).

As call-takers and dispatchers, PSR's serve as the primary point of contact at the PSAP for processing incoming emergency calls, coordinating the response of police, and acting as a link to fire and medical resources. Even though police officers, firefighters, emergency medical technicians, and paramedics are typically recognized as first responders because they come face to face with emergency situations (Sewell & Crew, 1984), in reality, the PSR's (i.e., police and emergency responders) are the "true" first responders because they are the initial point of contact between the public and emergency resources (Anshel et al., 2013; Blankenship, 1990; Gurevich et al., 2007).

As first responders, police and emergency dispatchers are exposed to situations involving violence, loss of life, and other tragic events (Davis, 2005; Jenkins, 1997; Turner, 2015) similar to their counterparts in the field. However, initial studies surrounding the effects of traumatic events on law enforcement personnel were primarily focused on police officers (Kroes et al., 1974; Territo & Vetter, 1981; Volanti & Marshall, 1983), until Doerner (1987) conducted a study with 21 police dispatchers identifying that, although these particular employees were generally satisfied with their jobs, they felt that barriers within the organization prevented them from doing their job of assisting the public.

Positive Organizational Psychology Interventions: Design and Evaluation, First Edition.
Stewart I. Donaldson and Christopher Chen.
© 2021 John Wiley & Sons Ltd. Published 2021 by John Wiley & Sons Ltd.

Doerner's (1987) study only focused on the impact of the organizational structure on police dispatcher stress, but it didn't address how the nature of the job impacts the psychological well-being of these dispatchers. Today, several studies have started to examine the development of stress and burnout in relation to job satisfaction among police dispatchers (Burke, 1995; Jenkins, 1997; Troxell, 2008), the difficulties in balancing the demands of work and home life (Turner, 2015), and the propensity for them to develop serious psychological stress, including posttraumatic stress (Pierce & Lily, 2012). Based on current research, this chapter will address the concerns regarding the mental health of Los Angeles police dispatchers and propose a strategy to provide mindfulness-based training to enhance their overall health.

Burnout, Stress and Job Satisfaction

Since the early 1980s, concerns regarding insufficient training, inadequate equipment, perceptions that police dispatchers were seen as second-class citizens, and issues involving stress associated with the job had only been addressed in law enforcement bulletins (Sewell & Crew, 1984) until studies began to surface further examining these variables. Early studies involving dispatcher stress observed how job satisfaction, measured by the nature of the work, availability of promotional opportunities, training, supervisory, and coworker support impacted the degree of stress and burnout employees experienced (Burke, 1995). Studies discovered that dispatchers were satisfied with their occupation when they felt a sense of accomplishment in their work and believed they received enough support from their coworkers, but this was not the norm (Burke, 1995). Dispatchers were not satisfied with their occupation and the contributing factors for dissatisfaction included feeling unaccomplished with their daily tasks, their perceptions that they earned low salaries, the lack of training and promotional opportunities available, and insufficient supervisor support (Burke, 1995). In general, dispatchers were unhappy because the work was emotionally and psychologically taxing causing them to act uncaringly toward the community that they served and, ultimately, becoming stressed, strained, and burnt out (Burke, 1995).

Diving deeper into the nature of the work, future studies began to examine the type of emergency calls encountered and radio transmissions received from officers in the field to determine the effects of exposure to those high-stress conditions (Troxell, 2008). Emergency dispatchers encounter myriad situations, including suicides, shootings, stabbings, robberies, violence against children, officer emergencies, and even sometimes the death of an officer in the field (Davis, 2005; Pierce & Lily, 2012; Troxell, 2008). They attached personal emotions to their calls and have identified feeling gratification, satisfaction, and a sense of pride when the outcome of their calls is positive (Troxell, 2008). But on the opposite spectrum, emergency dispatchers will attach negative emotions of guilt, sadness, frustration, anger, and shame when the outcome of calls did not go well or as planned (Troxell, 2008). This type of labeling can be stressful and cause a great deal of emotional demand especially if there is no closure or follow-up after stressful situations (Troxell, 2008). Ultimately, the type of calls was not the source of trauma but rather the way they categorized them by the tone and emotions of the caller, the background noises, the words being used, and the thoughts and emotions felt by the dispatcher (Troxell, 2008).

Troxell (2008) found that 14.7% of emergency dispatchers were at risk for burnout due to exposure to traumatic calls, and 16.3% were at risk for developing secondary traumatic stress, which surfaces in the course of helping others who are experiencing trauma. The implications are that even though the emergency dispatchers were not physically present during the situations surrounding their calls they still experienced the emotional trauma and the consequences associated with them (Pierce & Lily, 2012; Troxell, 2008; Turner, 2015).

Work–Life Balance and Coping

The work of an emergency dispatcher is demanding, and often dispatchers can feel slightly pulled between their work and home life (Turner, 2015). According to Turner (2015), emergency dispatchers who experienced high stress levels felt that they were not able to manage work–life balance, more likely to suffer from psychological and physiological problems, believed that they could not find time to enjoy life outside of work, and experienced a decrease in life satisfaction. Dispatchers rely on support from their family, friends, spouses, and other loved ones outside of the workplace to assist in improving the work–life balance and ultimately increasing their satisfaction in life (Turner, 2015). Therefore, it is essential for emergency dispatchers to foster those relationships at home to buffer the stress they experience at work. The repeated exposure to other people's trauma, being engrossed in their problems, and constantly helping affect the dispatcher's perception of stress, physiological and psychological issues (Turner, 2015).

To cope with exposure to an array of stressful calls, emergency dispatchers will often use humor, venting, and attempt to harden themselves emotionally (Turner, 2015). But despite their attempts to balance their psychological distress with the realities of their job, often dispatchers will experience intrusion and avoidance symptoms (Jenkins, 1997). Intrusion symptoms occur when the individual relives or re-experiences a traumatic event and avoidance symptoms are when the individual avoids anything that reminds them of a traumatic event, including people, places, and things (Warner et al., 2013).

In a study concerning police and emergency dispatchers who lived through Category 5 Hurricane Andrew in the Bahamas and Florida in 1992, the effects of their occupational and personal distress were measured in terms of how they coped with intrusion and avoidance symptoms (Jenkins, 1997). The dispatchers that experienced anger distanced themselves from others, became less involved in their social networks, and suffered from avoidance symptoms related to the traumatic event. However, those who coped by seeking support from their social networks seemed to be able to combat intrusion symptoms and process their stress (Jenkins, 1997). The research implies the importance of establishing appropriate coping skills, strengthening support networks, and risking developing serious psychological complications.

Peritraumatic Distress and Posttraumatic Stress Disorder

Over the years, growing concern has centered around the risk of police and emergency dispatchers developing serious psychological problems, including peritraumatic and posttraumatic stress (Pierce & Lily, 2012; Troxell, 2008). "Peritraumatic distress is defined as the emotional and physiological distress experienced during and/or immediately after a traumatic event" (Burnell et al., 2018, p. 8). "Post-traumatic stress disorder (PTSD) is a mental health condition that's triggered by a terrifying event – either experiencing it or witnessing it," where the individual has difficulty recovering from the experience and their symptoms impact social and personal functioning (Mayo Clinic, 2019). Using measures such as the Peritraumatic Distress Inventory and the PTSD Checklist, relationships could be made between both surveys indicating that there is an association with peritraumatic distress and "the development and severity of posttraumatic stress disorder (PTSD)," which could be observed even 30 days after the traumatic event (Burnell et al., 2018, p. 8).

Since emergency dispatchers encounter an array of calls that cause them feelings of fear, helplessness, and horror, they report experiencing peritraumatic distress in reaction to these situations (Pierce & Lily, 2012; Troxell, 2008). Approximately 32% of calls experienced by the dispatchers caused peritraumatic distress, which suggests that even though emergency dispatchers are removed physically from the situation and do not experience a direct threat, they are not shielded from the future development of peritraumatic distress and PTSD (Pierce & Lily, 2012).

The strain of being an emergency dispatcher can affect the development of negative health symptoms, psychological problems, and an inclination for PTSD, with 40% of dispatchers attributing job stress to dealing with a crisis (Steinkopf et al., 2018). In fact, 24% of dispatchers, on average, report experiencing stress related to work. However, psychological problems are a big concern because 31% of emergency dispatchers experience high levels of distress with 14% demonstrating issues with paranoia and 11% with hostility (Steinkopf et al., 2018). These factors lead to greater complications, and between 13% and 15% of dispatchers exhibit symptoms that could qualify them as being diagnosed with PTSD, which are higher levels than those seen in police officers (12.9%; Steinkopf et al., 2018). Police, firefighters, and emergency dispatchers are all at risk not just because of the nature of their work, but also because of the psychological damage exposure causes, which is why it is important to safeguard their mental health.

Positive Organizational Interventions in Law Enforcement

Positive Psychological Capital and Law Enforcement

Positive psychological capital (PsyCap) was developed as a higher-order construct that comprises four positive subfactors: hope (redirecting paths to work goals), resilience (ability to bounce back at work), self-efficacy (confidence in one's ability to succeed at work), and optimism (positive attributions about the future of work) (Luthans et al., 2007). PsyCap has emerged as a focal predictor of human capital performance for employees in diverse organizations, including professional service industries and social service organizations (Luthans et al., 2013; Luthans, 2002). Findings of PsyCap's potency have been constant across findings within broad domains of organizational literature, including positive organizational behavior, positive organizational psychology, positive organizational scholarship, and cross-cultural management (Avey et al., 2008; Cameron et al., 2003; Donaldson & Ko, 2010; Luthans et al., 2007). PsyCap is a human capital, "state-like" construct that is best utilized in human resource management practices due to its adaptability and developable capacity. Recent findings of PsyCap in other work domains have found the construct to be indicative of employee performance while controlling for differences in age, gender, education, and culture (Villalobos et al., in review; Rao & Donaldson, 2015; Warren et al., 2019).

Recent empirical evidence of PsyCap in law enforcement purports that PsyCap is positively related to an increase in positive emotions, job satisfaction, and stress symptoms, in addition to lower rates of turnover intention, especially for police officers. Nathawat and Dadarwal (2014) found in their study of Indian police officers that PsyCap is inversely correlated with job stress, suggesting that law enforcement officers with high PsyCap experience a lower negative emotional stress state. Other PsyCap interventions in law enforcement have found that PsyCap training helps with a reduction in officer stress, and an increase in resilient behavior (Browning, 2013). For higher-ranking police offers, including captains and sergeants, PsyCap has led to an increase in leader responsiveness, authentic leadership, and mitigation of negative impacts associated with traumatic and critical incident stress (Murray, 2019; von Trytek, 2019). Findings are also consistent across demographic variables, including race, gender, and education level. Moreover, at this leader unit of analysis, PsyCap training also positively impacts affective commitment, and the social relationships between leaders and subordinates (leader–member exchange) (Brunetto et al., 2017). Trainings with PsyCap-related curriculum are typically embedded into officer professional development programs, such as Peace Officer Basic Training, or other day- or week-long professional development trainings (Pitts et al., 2007).

Mindfulness-Based Training and Law Enforcement Officers

One program specifically designed to address police officer stress is Mindfulness-Based Resilience Training (MBRT), which integrates traditional Mindfulness-Based Stress Reduction principles grounded in Buddhist meditation practices and beliefs, and creates a framework "to enhance physical and mental resilience in the face of the stressors common in the culture of law enforcement" (Christopher et al., 2016, p. 18). The training includes group discussions, "body scan, sitting meditation, mindful movement, walking meditation, eating meditation and mindful martial arts" (p. 18). As part of addressing interpersonal conflict, MBRT asks participants to imagine mindful tactics during encounters off the job and at home, and for homework, officers are asked to practice mindfully dressing and removing their uniform (Christopher et al., 2016).

MBRT was found to improve mindfulness, resilience, stress, burnout, health outcomes, emotional functioning, and family functioning in police officers" (Christopher et al., 2016, p. 24). Upon completion of the 8-week MBRT course a decline "in sleep disturbance, anger, fatigue, burnout, difficulties with emotional regulation, general stress, organizational police stress, and operational police stress" was observed among officers (Christopher et al., 2016, p. 24). Another benefit of MBRT is that it increases resilience, which "is the process of adapting well in the face of adversity, trauma, tragedy, threats or significant sources of stress" (American Psychological Association, n.d.) and having the ability to bounce back.

Other Mindfulness-Based Training Programs

Previous mindfulness-based trainings specifically targeting emergency medical dispatchers were conducted online and demonstrated reduction of stress post-treatment, as well as at a 3-month follow-up, which continued to show progress in lowering stress levels (Lilly et al., 2019). Although an online-based program could be cost effective, the benefits of in-person training would strengthen the retention of the program and ensure that participants fully engage in the training. Currently, the Los Angeles Police Department does not have a mindfulness-based training in place for dispatchers.

A typical MBRT program is 8 weeks long with 2-hour weekly classes and assignment of homework (Christopher et al., 2016); however, the PSAP is a 24-hour operation and potential scheduling conflicts with days off could impact the ability to attain maximum participation, if the training was held on a voluntary basis. The proposal is to mandate that each employee participates in a one-day 8-hour mindfulness-based training/workshop structured around three primary training goals: (1) introduce the concepts of mindfulness, (2) learn techniques for practicing mindfulness, and (3) create a personal plan to integrate and apply the knowledge acquired into daily work and home life.

Typically, participants' complaints in mindfulness-based trainings have revolved around not having enough time to attend the sessions, being able to keep up with the weekly homework, and fears surrounding the stigma of being involved in a mental health training (Eddy et al., 2019). To address these concerns, all employees will be expected to take the training as part of their primary work duty for the day, therefore giving the department the ability to make the necessary modifications to work schedules to cover the call load on the dispatch floor and eliminate any socially negative implications concerning participation.

The most helpful aspects of mindfulness-based trainings have been identified as the body scan, learning how to mindfully move through hands-on yoga-type exercises, utilizing informal mindfulness practices in simple everyday routines, and having the opportunity for a dedicated space to practice mindfulness (Eddy et al., 2019). The workshop will incorporate these elements into the learning techniques and create a space for employees to remove themselves from the dispatch floor, when needed, to practice mindfulness tactics after encountering difficult calls or situations at work.

Benefits to the Department

As prior research has indicated, stressful factors surrounding emergency call-taking and dispatching police officers comes with a heavy toll on the psychological well-being of the employee and could result in job dissatisfaction, burnout, stress, and possibly a diagnosis of PTSD (Burke, 1995; Jenkins, 1997; Klimley et al., 2018; Pierce & Lily, 2012; Troxell, 2008; Turner, 2015). Mindfulness-based trainings focus on remaining in the moment, slowing reactions, and have been known to improve interpersonal communication at home and work (Eddy et al., 2019).

The Los Angeles Police Department's Strategic Goal 6 for 2019–2020 is to maximize the workforce potential by raising the levels of service provided to the citizen and increasing the productivity of the work environment (Los Angeles Police Department, 2019b). Initiative C of the Strategic Plan primarily focuses on promoting employee wellness specifically to improve job satisfaction (Los Angeles Police Department, 2019b). The benefits of mindfulness-based training to the department would be a possible reduction in conflicts with coworkers, lower complaints from citizens, fewer employees experiencing burnout with the intention to leave the job, and greater job satisfaction. Research has shown that mindfulness-based trainings are the most successful treatments for stress surrounding emergency and first responder occupations (Christopher et al., 2016; Eddy et al., 2019; Kaplan et al., 2017); therefore, possible long-term benefits of a training program could result in a more efficient workforce and engaging employees who can better serve the community.

Conclusion

This chapter highlighted several intervention strategies to combatting law enforcement, namely police dispatcher issues in psychological distress and well-being. Focusing on PsyCap interventions and MBSR, there have been found to be several potential avenues training programs can take when addressing the mental health of law enforcement personnel. The authors have suggested that the most effective programs are customizable, time sensitive, and also mandatory for the department.

In the specific case of the Los Angeles Police Department, the Police Service Representatives (i.e. police and emergency dispatchers) account for approximately 21% of the civilian workforce, and the nature of their work exposes them to high-stress situations on the phones and over the radio that pose many complications (Davis, 2005; Pierce & Lily, 2012; Troxell, 2008; Turner, 2015). Repeated exposure to these situations bring consequences to the emotional, psychological and social well-being of the dispatchers (Burke, 1995; Gurevich, Halpern, Brazeau, Defina, & Schwartz, 2007; Klimley, Hasslt, & Stripling, 2018; Pierce & Lily, 2012; Troxell, 2008; Turner, 2015). Therefore, preservation of these true first responders is integral to the effectiveness of the city's public safety answering point, the ability for law enforcement personnel to keep the citizens safe, and ensures longevity in the city's workforce.

References

Anshel, M. H., Umscheid, D., & Brinthaupt, T. M. (2013). Effect of combined coping skills and wellness program on perceived stress and physical energy among police emergency dispatchers: An exploratory study. *Journal of Police and Criminal Psychology, 28*(1), 1–14. doi:10.1007/s11896-012-9110-x

Avey, J. B., Wernsing, T. S., & Luthans, F. (2008). Can positive employees help positive organizational change? Impact of psychological capital and emotions on relevant attitudes and behaviors. *The Journal of Applied Behavioral Science, 44*(1), 48–70.

Blankenship, B. (1990). Dispatching units: Improvements for the "first line." *FBI Law Enforcement Bulletin, 59*, 12–13.

Browning, S. L. (2013). *Risk and resilience in law enforcement stress: Contributions of the Law Enforcement Officer Stress Survey (LEOSS)* (Order No. 3630819). Available from ProQuest Dissertations & Theses Global (1564233323). Retrieved from http://ccl.idm.oclc.org/login?url=https://search.proquest.com/docview/156 4233323?accountid=1014

Brunetto, Y., Teo, S., Shacklock, K., Farr-Wharton, R., & Shriberg, A. (2017). The impact of supervisor–subordinate relationships and a trainee characteristic upon police officer work outcomes. *Journal of Management & Organization, 23*(3), 423–436.

Burke, T. W. (1995). The relationship between dispatcher stress and social support, job satisfaction and locus-of-control. *FBI Law Enforcement Bulletin, 64*, 1–6.

Burnell, B. E., Davidson, T. M., & Ruggiero, K. J. (2018). The peritraumatic distress inventory: Factor structure and predictive validity in traumatically injured patients admitted through a Level I trauma center. *Journal of Anxiety Disorders, 55*, 8–13.

Cameron, K. S., Dutton, J. E., & Quinn, R. E. (2003). An introduction to positive organizational scholarship. *Positive Organizational Scholarship, 3*(13).

Christopher, M. S., Goerling, R. J., Rogers, B. S., Hunsinger, M., Baron, G., Bergman, A. L., & Zava, D. T. (2016). A pilot study evaluating the effectiveness of mindfulness-based intervention and cortisol awakening response and health outcomes among law enforcement officers. *Journal of Police and Criminal Psychology, 31*, 15–28.

Davis, J. B. (2005). Finding calm after the call. *American Bar Association Journal, 91*(3), 75.

Doerner, W. (1987). Police dispatcher stress. *Journal of Police Science and Administration, 15*(4), 257–261.

Donaldson, S. I., & Ko, I. (2010). Positive organizational psychology, behavior, and scholarship: A review of the emerging literature and evidence base. *The Journal of Positive Psychology, 5*(3), 177–191.

Eddy, A., Bergmen, A. L., Kaplan, J., Goerling, R. J., & Christopher, M. S. (2019). A qualitative investigation of the experience of mindfulness training among police officers. *Journal of Police and Criminal Psychology*, 1–9. doi:https://doi.org/10.1007/s11896-019-09340-7

Gurevich, M., Halpern, J., Brazeau, P., Defina, P. S., & Schwartz, B. (2007). *Frontline stress behind the scenes: Emergency medical dispatchers.* Toronto, ON: Ryerson University, Department of Psychology.

Jenkins, S. R. (1997). Coping and social support among emergency dispatchers: Hurricane Andrew. *Journal of Social Behavior and Personality, 12*(1), 201–216.

Kaplan, J., Bergman, A., Christopher, M. S., & Bowen, S. (2017). Role of resilience in mindfulness training for first responders. *Mindfulness, 8*, 1373–1380. doi:10.1007/s12671-017-0713-2

Klimley, K. E., Hasslt, V. B., & Stripling, A. M. (2018). Posttraumatic stress disorder in police, firefighters, and emergency dispatchers. *Aggression and Violent Behavior, 43*, 33–44.

Kroes, W. H., Margolis, L. L., & Hurrell, J. J. (1974). Job stress in policemen. *Journal of Police Science and Administration, 2*(2), 145–155.

Lilly, M., Calhoun, R., Painter, I., Beaton, R., Stangenes, S., Revere, D., ... Meischke, H. (2019). Destress 9-1-1 – An onine mindfulness-based intervention in reducing stress among emergency medical dispatchers: A randomised controlled trial. *Occupational Environmental Medicine, 76*, 705–711.

Los Angeles Police Department. (2019, October 27). *Sworn and Civilian Report.* Retrieved from Official Site of the Los Angeles Police Department: http://www.lapdonline.org/sworn_and_civilian_report

Los Angeles Police Department. (2019a). *Communications Division.* Retrieved from Official Site of the Los Angeles Police Department: http://www.lapdonline.org/communications_division

Los Angeles Police Department. (2019b). *Historical Documents and Internal Reports: The Los Angeles Police Department Strategic Plan 2019–2020.* Retrieved November 20, 2019, from The Official Site of the Los Angeles Police Department: http://www.lapdonline.org/home/content_basic_view/62284

Luthans, F. (2002). The need for and meaning of positive organizational behavior. *Journal of Organizational Behavior: The International Journal of Industrial, Occupational and Organizational Psychology and Behavior, 23*(6), 695–706.

Luthans, F., Avolio, B. J., Avey, J. B., & Norman, S. M. (2007). Positive psychological capital: Measurement and relationship with performance and satisfaction. *Personnel Psychology, 60*(3), 541–572.

Luthans, F., Youssef, C. M., Sweetman, D. S., & Harms, P. D. (2013). Meeting the leadership challenge of employee well-being through relationship PsyCap and health PsyCap. *Journal of Leadership & Organizational Studies, 20*(1), 118–133.

Mayo Clinic. (2019). *Mayo Clinic.* Retrieved November 20, 2019, from Post-Traumatic Stress Disorder (PTSD): https://www.mayoclinic.org/diseases-conditions/post-traumatic-stress-disorder/symptoms-causes/syc-20355967

Murray, E. (2019). *Psychological capital: Law enforcement leadership strategies to mitigate traumatic incident stress among police officers*(Order No. 13812703). Available from ProQuest Dissertations & Theses Global; Publicly Available Content Database (2246420231). Retrieved from http://ccl.idm.oclc.org/login?url=https://search.proquest.com/docview/2246420231?accountid=10141

Nathawat, S. S., & Dadarwal, M. (2014). A study of job stress and psychological capital in Rajasthan police officers. *Indian Journal of Positive Psychology, 5*(1), 66.

Pierce, H., & Lily, M. M. (2012). Duty-related trauma exposure in 911 telecommunicators: Considering the risk for posttraumatic stress. *Journal of Traumatic Stress, 25*, 211–215.

Pitts, S., Glensot, R. W., & Peak, K. J. (2007). The Police Training Officer (PTO) program: A contemporary approach to postacademy recruit training. *Police Chief, 74*(8), 114.

Rao, M. A., & Donaldson, S. I. (2015). Expanding opportunities for diversity in positive psychology: An examination of gender, race, and ethnicity. *Canadian Psychology/Psychologie Canadienne, 56*(3), 271.

Sewell, J. D., & Crew, L. (1984). The forgotten victim: Stress and the police dispatcher. *FBI Law Enforcement Bulletin, 53*, 7.

Steinkopf, B., Reddin, R. A., Black, R. A., Hasselt, V. B., & Couwels, J. (2018). Assessment of stress and resiliency in emergency dispatchers. *Journal of Police and Criminal Psychology, 33*, 399–411. doi:https://doi.org/10.1007/s11896-018-9255-3

Territo, L., & Vetter, H. (1981). Stress and police personnel. *Journal of Police Science and Administration, 9*(2), 195–207.

Troxell, R. M. (2008). Indirect exposure to the trauma of others: The experiences of 9-1-1 telecommunicators. *Dissertation Abstracts International: Section B: The Sciences and Engineering, 69*, 11-B.

Turner, K. D. (2015). Effects of stress on 9-1-1 call-takers and police dispatchers: A study at the San Jose police department. *Master's Thesis.* doi:https://doi.org/10.31989/etd.3yxn-3pvm

Volanti, J. M., & Marshall, J. R. (1983). The police stress process. *Journal of Police and Science Administration, 11*(4), 389–394.

von Trytek, A. S. (2019). *A study of the relationships between authentic leadership and job satisfaction among women in federal law enforcement* (Doctoral dissertation Our Lady of the Lake University.

Warren, M. A., Donaldson, S. I., Lee, J. Y., & Donaldson, S. I. (2019). Reinvigorating research on gender in the workplace using a positive work and organizations perspective. *International Journal of Management Reviews, 21*(4), 498–518.

Warner, C. H., Warner, C. M., Appenzeller, G. N., & Hoge, C. W. (2013). Identifying and managing posttraumatic stress disorder. *American Family Physician, 88*(12), 827–834.

9

Implementing a Positive Leader Development Program

Jennifer M. Nelson

Organizations today are facing new trends related to globalization, technology, and a shift in emphasis on tangible assets to that of human capital, all while producing more results for less money. Many organizations are recognizing that employees are the company's greatest asset. Employees bring value to the company in a way that technology, data, and physical property cannot. Because of this, organizations want to know how to leverage their best assets to increase performance, productivity, and ultimately the company's bottom line. By the same token, employees want to get the most out of their work life, which comprises at least one-third of their day (Csikszentmihalyi, 1997). They want to be happy and productive as well, ultimately to improve their quality of life. If organizations can be successful without any unnecessary expenses to those that provide the company's services/products, they can play a major role in improving society by allowing their employees to thrive.

The key to organizational success is a structured approach to improving performance and quality of work life through strong and effective leadership through a positive lens (Godbole et al., 2017). Traditional approaches to implementing planned change through systematic analysis and design that are effective yet deficit-based can be strategically paired with methods in positive psychology that take an asset-based approach, bringing benefits from both worlds. This intervention entails a sound theory of change using effective frameworks in leader development and organizational behavior research combined with leadership strategies from positive psychology to not only improve performance in today's volatile marketplace but also improve the well-being of employees.

Organizations can be prosperous, but they can also thrive and flourish to their highest potential by diverting their focus from what goes wrong to what goes right and leverage those opportunities for success. Through positive leader development centered around continuous feedback for growth and leadership that facilitates positive deviant behaviors in followers, building positive relationships within the workplace, and improving individual well-being, organizations can enact extraordinary performance and significantly impact the community.

Positive Organizational Psychology Interventions: Design and Evaluation, First Edition.
Stewart I. Donaldson and Christopher Chen.
© 2021 John Wiley & Sons Ltd. Published 2021 by John Wiley & Sons Ltd.

The following theory and research justify the general framework for this intervention and delineate the guiding principles for implementing and evaluating planned change.

Theory

Leaders have the ability to directly affect organizational success such as excellent employee performance, high-quality services/products, and healthy finances, as well as positive human capital outcomes such as employee engagement and overall well-being (Wallace & Trinka, 2009). A structured approach to improving performance is a human resource intervention that develops leaders using best practices in transdisciplinary literature. These involve planned change through the ADDIE training model (i.e., analyze, design, develop, implement, and evaluate) in organizational behavior (Locke, 2009), positive leadership practices in positive psychology (Cameron, 2012; Dutton, 2003; Lavine, 2012; Warren et al., 2017), and the assessment, challenge, and support (ACS) framework by Van Velsor et al. (2010) in leader development literature.

Perhaps the most salient concepts are the ACS framework and positive leadership practices. The elements of the ACS framework bring increased self-awareness, motivation to perform, and the self-efficacy needed to develop as an effective leader, with a focus on a positive leadership style. Van Velsor et al. (2010) stated that all successful leader development programs (LDPs) have a formal or informal assessment of its leaders, potent developmental experiences that present a challenge to the leaders and stretch their abilities, and support for growth that provides continuous feedback throughout the developmental process. Guided by the ADDIE training model, the ACS framework provides the structure necessary to facilitate planned change in a leader development intervention that will improve organizational performance.

Huang et al. (2018) stated that one of the pillars of positive psychology is positive institutions; institutions that "facilitate the development and display of positive traits, which in turn facilitates positive subjective experiences" (Peterson, 2006, p. 20). The best way to create a positive institution is through positive leadership. Positive leadership works toward enhancing positive traits in individuals through building psychological capital and creating meaningful relationships at work. Paired with traditional approaches to planned change such as the ACS framework, organizations can produce desired organizational and individual outcomes that can better society as a whole.

Beginning with the ACS model, the following research on traditional and positive leader development provides a theoretical justification for this intervention. The key to ACS is continuous feedback that helps leaders leverage their strengths and follow a personal leader development plan (LDP*) to be effective in leading themselves, leading others, and leading the organization. Only through continuous learning, which requires consistent and actionable feedback, will the developmental process be worthwhile.

Note: The abbreviation LDP for leader development plan is differentiated from LDP for leader development program with an asterisk.

Assessment

Assessment is feedback that provides participants with a starting-off point and a benchmark for future success (King & Santana, 2010). It can be formal (e.g., performance appraisals) or informal (e.g., comments from a supervisor after a team meeting) but is best when utilized in a variety of forms. Three hundred and sixty degree assessments are formal assessments that incorporate self-report measures with the viewpoints of others who have witnessed the leader's behavior. "They are particularly powerful because the feedback comes from a variety of sources, as different rater groups have different views of the individual" (King & Santana, 2010, p. 102). These assessments increase the leader's self-awareness of their behavior, reveal gaps in current and desired leadership competencies, aid in motivating the leaders to develop, and measure data for program evaluation.

Assessment is a key feature of feedback-intensive programs or programs that systemically assess an individual's personality and effectiveness on various dimensions from multiple perspectives and present this information as a tool for continuous learning (King & Santana, 2010). The first phase of an effective training program assesses the needs of an organization and the individual juxtaposed to the organization's culture and strategy. It is during this stage that the desired competencies for an effective leader are determined and clearly outlined. Therefore, it is a critical step in the evaluation of an LDP's effectiveness.

Self-Awareness

360° feedback is used frequently in LDP's as they include multiple objective viewpoints that enhance the validity of the data. Interestingly, it is the level of agreement between the individual's perspective and the other raters that provide insight into how self-aware the leader is, and therefore how effective that leader may be. Two key assumptions about 360° assessments are that (1) the awareness between the discrepancy between how we rate ourselves and how others rate our behavior will enhance our self-awareness and self-management abilities, and (2) enhanced self-awareness is a key leadership competency that will lead to more effective behavior (Van Velsor et al., 1993). Stawiski et al. (2016) stated that self-awareness, building relationships, and developing others are three key competencies that coaches of developing leaders strive for when supporting them in achieving challenging goals. These outcomes are important for positive leaders whose goal is to foster flourishing in an organization.

"Self-awareness stems from the individual's ability to assess others' evaluations of the self and to incorporate those assessments into one's self-evaluation" to manage behavior when making positive change (Van Velsor et al., 1993). Therefore, a self-aware individual has the ability to use informative feedback to adjust their effectiveness as a leader. In fact, self-awareness is positively related to performance and is one of the best predictors of behavior, especially when the leader tends to overestimate their performance compared to the perceptions of others (Van Velsor et al., 1993).

More research is needed on the relationship between performance and self-awareness but there is adequate research on the link between feedback and performance. Cummings and Worley concluded that "objective feedback does not usually work, it virtually always works" (2015, p. 452). A recent meta-analysis stated that when feedback is used to improve individual or group-level performance it has a positive effect across studies. In field studies that contained feedback with behavior-specific or less-specific information, there was a median performance improvement of 33%–47% (Cummings & Worley, 2015).

Challenge

The second major component in a successful leader development intervention is challenge through goal setting. "The most potent developmental experiences are ones that force people out of their comfort zone and require them to develop new capacities or ways of understanding to be successful" (Van Velsor et al., 2010, p. 9). McCall (2010) stated that it is these experiences that make up 70% of successful development, while 20% of development comes from interactions from others and just 10% comes from formal education. Therefore, human resource (HR) professionals or organizational development (OD) practitioners should focus a large portion of an LDP on creating opportunities that allow emerging leaders to stretch their skillset while applying lessons learned on the job. These opportunities are unexpected, have high stakes, are complex, novel, or have high-pressure circumstances (McCall, 2010). Locke (2009) stated that goal setting can aid in creating these opportunities and providing the motivation required to attain difficult goals. Goal setting involves developing goals that are challenging as well as SMART: specific, measurable, attainable, relevant, and time bound (Lathum, 2018). Challenging goals are not effective without feedback and feedback is irrelevant unless it is tied to actionable goals.

The crux of challenging experiences revolves around setting goals that create a disequilibrium between a challenging task and the necessary skills needed to complete that task (Csikszentmihalyi, 1997). Goal-setting theory provides a framework for leaders and their coaches to devise an appropriate leader development plan that leverages the leader's strengths revealed in the prior needs assessment. Locke (2009) stated that the simplest reason why some people perform better than others is that they are working toward difficult and specific goals that they are committed to. This is because goal setting creates focus, builds a sense of accomplishment, reduces ambiguity, reduces dysfunctional stress, and sets up a challenge that ultimately improves performance (Lathum, 2018).

Motivation

Motivation and self-efficacy are strong predictors of successful goal adoption, maintenance, and adherence over time (Nowack, 2017). For example, a leader development plan tied to a hospital's strategy of reducing waste to improve quality provides a road map to focus the efforts of the developing leader. Goal-setting theory states that goals are motivating when they are specific, measurable, attainable, realistic, and timely. Furthermore, there should be adequate resources available to the leader to enact these goals, learning goals should be set first to meet performance goals (e.g., acquiring the active-listening skills necessary to create meaningful connections in the workplace and build effective teams), the leader should have the opportunities to deliberately practice, and most importantly the leader should receive continuous feedback for improvement (Locke, 2009). The function of challenging goals is to provide the motivation for development as well as the opportunity to develop (Van Velsor et al., 2010).

There is extensive research on the positive impact of goal setting and aligning management objectives with the organizational strategy to improve performance. Positive results have been shown over a wide range of jobs and industries where performance has increased by 11%–27% (Cummings & Worley, 2015). In a study at the Center for Effective Organizations at USC, there was a strong correlation between perceptions of performance and goals tied to organizational strategy (Cummings & Worley, 2015). At the very least, if goals are difficult and specific and they are set in collaboration with the leader and their supervisor, goal setting achieves positive results across studies with groups and individuals.

Positive Leadership

Structured experiences provide a platform to put these goals into action. The core activities of this intervention that provide challenging experiences are creating an individual leader development plan and putting that plan into action through an action-learning project that is relevant to the leader's department. As positive leadership leads to extraordinary performance and enables positive deviance in the workplace, the action-learning experiences will take a positive psychology approach to meet these objectives (Lavine, 2012).

Positive leadership is an umbrella term that encompasses various leadership styles such as authentic and transformational leadership and theories that align with positive work outcomes such as building psychological capital (PsyCap) and fostering meaningful relationships (Warren et al., 2017). Authentic leaders are self-aware, optimistic, developmentally oriented, and have a high moral character (Avolio & Gardner, 2005). This leadership style is "the root construct that underlies positive forms of leadership" (Gardner & Carlson, 2015) and is therefore the foundational style of any effective leader. Key components of positive leadership that enable extraordinary performance are positive deviance, affirmative bias, and organizational virtuousness (Cameron, 2012). Lavine (2012) defined positive deviance as "uncommon behavior that is norm-defying yet socially desirable" (p. 1014). For example, the new protocol for disposing of gowns and gloves that was piloted in six US hospitals in 2006 drastically reduced the prevalence of the dangerous bacteria MRSA (ACP Hospitalist & American College of Physicians, 2019). Affirmative bias uses strengths to bolster weaknesses to thrive in the workplace and organizational virtuousness nurtures the best of the human condition to better society (Cameron, 2012).

Building PsyCap and creating high-quality connections are two methods in positive leadership that will increase productivity and employee well-being (Dutton, 2003; Warren et al., 2017). Positive leaders can build the phycological capital necessary for improving emotional and mental health through intentional actions that build their follower's hope, efficacy, resilience, and optimism in the workplace (Warren et al., 2017). Positive leaders can also create high-quality connections or meaningful relationships among employees by embedding relationship-building practices into the cultural DNA and organizational systems and structures (Dutton, 2003). Cameron (2012) stated that positive leadership diverts an organization's attention away from what is going wrong to what is going right to harness the power of positivity and create a thriving organization that allows its members to flourish. It emphasizes what elevates and inspires individuals in addition to what is challenging or problematic (Cameron, 2012), circumventing what Cooperrider and Godwin (2012) call the 80/20 trap. Positive psychology helps organizations leverage 20% of their strengths instead of obsessing about 80% of their weaknesses.

Positive psychology approaches have been gaining popularity with organizations in the last few decades and there is considerable research on its benefits. Desired outcomes of authentic leadership are psychological well-being and empowerment for employees, which leads to increased performance for the organization (Gardner & Carlson, 2015). Warren et al. (2017) corroborates this in their recent literature review on positive psychology; employee well-being predicts job performance and psychological well-being is a stronger predictor of job performance than job satisfaction. It was also found that PsyCap is a significant predictor of desired attitudes (such as organizational commitment and psychological well-being), behaviors (such as organizational citizenship), and self-rated and supervisor-rated performance. Finally, high-quality relationships are linked with outcomes that foster individual and team flourishing such as greater psychological safety (Warren et al., 2017). These outcomes are evidence of how positive leaders can enable extraordinary performance and improve the quality of work life.

Support

Lastly, the support from mentors, coaches, supervisors, coworkers, or family members is critical to the developmental success of a strong and effective leader. "Support is a key factor for leaders in maintaining their motivation to learn and grow. It helps engender a sense of self-efficacy about learning, a belief that one can learn, grow, and change" (Van Velsor et al., 2010, p. 13). Van Velsor et al. (2010) stated that support in the form of coaching and mentoring provides an important source of feedback on how to improve behavior and increase competencies through familiar and trusted sources that foster a safe and supportive learning environment. Other benefits of coaching and mentoring are path–goal clarity, values clarity, increased knowledge, skills and abilities, more opportunities to exercise those skills through the coach's or mentor's network, and an understanding of organization-specific politics that may hinder individual or organizational success (Gentry & Walsh, 2015). Planned change for a leader development intervention that includes ACS has a high chance of creating positive and lasting outcomes (Van Velsor et al., 2010).

Self-Efficacy

Creating a leader development plan and then carrying it out in an action-learning project can be a formidable task. A supportive and trusting relationship with a coach or mentor can aid in building the necessary self-efficacy to stay motivated and committed to accomplishing challenging goals (Locke, 2009). Locke (2009) stated that "self-efficacy is the conviction that one can mobilize one's resources to attain a specific level of performance" (p. 165). Figure 9.1 depicts that the role of a coach is to help the leader reveal their strengths through assessment, create disequilibrium through challenging goals, and support the leader by reinforcing changes in their performance while building self-efficacy throughout the relationship (Frankovelgia & Riddle, 2010).

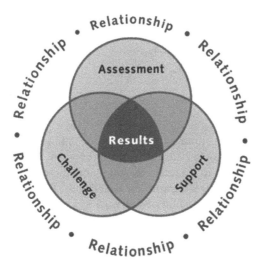

Figure 9.1 Center for Creative Leadership's RASCR Model of the Guiding Principles in Coaching. Source: Based on Assessments Powered by CCL Compass: Benchmarks for Managers. (2019). Center for Creative Leadership.

More than 70% of formal leadership development programs include some amount of coaching or mentoring (Stawiski et al., 2016). Results center around performance (i.e., the behavior of the coachee) and development (i.e., the thinking behind that behavior) (Frankovelgia & Riddle, 2010). Although coaching is not an unfamiliar practice in many organizations, there is a small amount of research confirming its effectiveness (Cummings & Worley, 2015). A few large sample studies found that coaching improved personal productivity, quality, working relationships, and job satisfaction with a return of 5.7 times the initial investment (Cummings & Worley, 2015). A randomized control trial in a public health agency that utilized 360° feedback, one half-day leadership workshop, and four individual coaching sessions over 10 weeks saw improvements on goal attainment, increased resilience and workplace well-being, and reduced depression and stress among its developing leaders (Cummings & Worley, 2015). Although further research is needed, coaching and mentoring is clearly crucial to supporting the personal growth of leaders.

To summarize, the ACS model is a valuable tool when designing an effective LDP and taking a positive approach to planned change is an effective asset-based strategy in improving individual and organizational outcomes. At a minimum, there should be an assessment of the leader's individual training needs concerning the needs of the organization, the leader should experience stretch experiences that challenge them to grow, and they should be supported throughout their journey toward positive leadership. Feedback on strengths that can be leveraged for desired behavior will create a heightened sense of self-awareness, challenging goals relevant to positive leadership practices will aid in motivation for high performance, and coaching/mentoring will boost self-efficacy. This theory and research lays the foundation for the efficacy of a positive LDP. The following framework will provide the guiding principles in this intervention: analyzing, designing, developing, implementing, and evaluating planned changes.

Intervention

Implementation of this program will focus on continuous qualitative and quantitative feedback to enhance decision-making and will place an emphasis on stakeholder collaboration to aid in successful planned change. The participatory action research model is a classic framework used in the field of OD. Collaboration with stakeholders reduces resistance to change and the systematic collection of data is used to make informed decisions throughout each step of the process. Gathering feedback on the process and outcomes of implementation ensures a quality intervention. The steps are iterative and much collaboration between the OD practitioner and stakeholders is necessary to facilitate accuracy as well as feasibility (Cummings & Worley, 2015).

Analyze

Through a positive psychology lens, the action in this intervention will be centered around Locke's (2009) ADDIE training model (i.e., analyze, design, develop, implement, and evaluate); an effective framework for systematically designing and implementing any training program. The ADDIE model begins with analyzing the training needs to "clarify the purposes of training, illuminate the organizational context, define effective performance and its drivers, and begin to cultivate a climate of learning" (Locke, 2009). This includes assessing the organization's systems and structures to determine whether the organization can support a feedback-intensive intervention, assessing the organization's strategy to understand what leadership competencies are needed to align organizational goals with its mission, and assessing the gaps in the individual leader's current and desired behavior. For example, a 360° assessment (such as the Center for Creative Leadership Benchmarks for Managers assessment) coupled with a self-assessment relevant to the essential domains of competency (such as the Healthcare Leadership Alliance Competency Model [HLACM] in healthcare seen in Figure 9.2) would evaluate an existing pool of candidates at a 360° angle and determine the leader's strengths and areas of improvement that leader development activities should focus on (Stefl, 2008).

In addition to the 360° assessment, leaders should take an evaluation centered on their individual strengths such as the Gallup StrengthsFinder. The 360° feedback will illuminate gaps in leadership skills relevant to the competencies needed to deliver quality service/products (such as critically evaluating protocols to improve service delivery), while the strengths assessment will reveal stable leadership characteristics (such as strategy execution or relationship building qualities) that can be utilized when developing specific tactics in their LDP*.

Figure 9.2 Domains of the Healthcare Leadership Alliance Competency Model.
Source: American College of Healthcare Executives 2020 Competencies Assessment Tool.,
Page 1. Healthcare Leadership Alliance and the American College of Healthcare Executives.
© 2020 American College of Healthcare Executives.

Design and Develop

During the design and development steps in the ADDIE model, program outcomes
are clearly outlined when designing the learning architecture, developing training
content, and selecting assessment tools to measure those outcomes. Figure 9.3 cat-
egorizes key leader competencies in an integrated competency framework

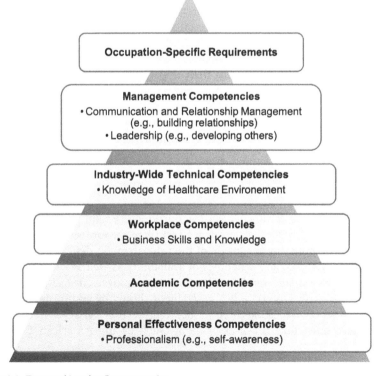

Figure 9.3 Targeted Leader Competencies.

(Godbole et al., 2017) that includes the three targeted competencies for this positive intervention: self-awareness, building relationships, and developing others. Competencies from the HLACM are used as examples for relevant dimensions.

These competencies are relevant to specific behavioral and personal effectiveness changes that define effective leadership, for example, management competencies (such as communication and relationship management) or personal effectiveness competencies (such as the self-awareness that is required for personal and professional accountability). To increase the quality of consumer outcomes the focus for this intervention is performance improvement: tactics that will aid leaders in being effective in their leadership and management roles. Performance improvement is the short-term goal that leads to long-term intangibles – "those measures that cannot be converted to monetary values as they are elements of human dynamics" – such as engagement and well-being (Phillips & Phillips, 2007, p. 145). A positive leader should also be concerned with creating an empowering organizational climate that fosters meaningful connections and encourages positively deviant behaviors. Self-awareness, building relationships, and developing others are key competencies needed for high performance through positive leadership.

A leader development intervention should be designed with the context in mind: the competencies needed for top challenges in relation to the needs of the individual and the organizational strategy. These competencies are different for individual leaders; therefore, activities should be geared toward meeting goals delineated in individual leader development plans. Although activities may vary, five major learning methods reflecting contemporary practices in leader development are action learning, skill-building seminars, individual readings, reflective journaling, and coaching/mentoring (Miller et al., 2007). Lacerenza et al. (2017) stated that moderators of leadership training and its effectiveness include offering multiple methods – especially those with opportunities for repeated practice – multiple, spaced training sessions opposed to a few lengthy sessions delivered in short durations, and on-site, face-to-face training. Therefore, this intervention will include four phases of training (see Figure 9.4) over the course of six months to one year, depending on the feasibility of the organization, and should first be piloted to a preselected cohort in one department of the organization for evaluation purposes.

Assessment Component

• Phase 1: Orientation and assessment

The first phase should commence with an introductory seminar in orientation to the theories behind leader development to set the stage for learning. Leaders are matched with mentors in or outside of their department, depending on similar personalities, interests, and schedules of availability as well as certified coaches from a reputable outside vendor or the trained employees from within, whichever is more practical. Next, a 360° assessment should be administered to their peers and supervisors, asking them to rate their current behavior. In the meantime, leaders must take a self-assessment (such as the American College of

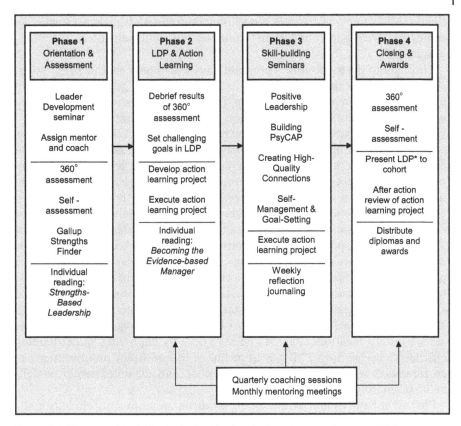

Figure 9.4 Phases and Activities in the Positive Leader Development Program (LDP).

Healthcare Executives 2019 Competencies Assessment Tool) relevant to the selected competency model (such as the HLACM). This self-assessment should be paired with the Gallup StrengthsFinder to aid the leaders in leveraging their top strengths to address areas of improvement.

Evaluation studies of LDPs revealed that self-paced individual readings can further educate the leader on important concepts that pertain to their personal development and spark discussions with their peers (e.g., *Strengths-Based Leadership* by Tom Rath or *Becoming the Evidence-Based Manager* by Gary P. Lathum). Therefore, these readings should be assigned during orientation to be completed throughout the first two phases of the program.

Challenge Component: Positive Leadership

- Phase 2: LDP* and action-learning
- Phase 3: Skill-building seminars

During the second phase, the leaders are debriefed on the assessment results with the support and guidance of their coaches. Their coaches should help them create a personalized LDP* outlining their SMART goals, strategies for achieving those goals, and their strengths that will help them overcome obstacles.

Throughout the 6–12-month program, they will implement this LDP* alongside an action-learning project that puts their challenging goals into action and utilizes methods in positive leadership. For example, Cameron (2012) outlined an effective positive leadership practice. Leaders should initiate a project relevant to their departmental needs such as redesigning and improving new employee orientation. Instead of focusing on new procedures, organizing processes or paperwork, and avoiding errors, the practicing leader can focus on using positivity to enhance their current assets (i.e., their people) by implementing a personal management interview (PMI) before the project launches. This is a one-time interview session where the leader and the project manager discuss responsibilities and accountability, values, and goals, and the dynamics of their relationship followed by regularly scheduled check-ins throughout the duration of the project. During these meetings the leader should nurture a positive relationship (by bolstering the employee's strengths and fostering positive energy), create a positive work climate (by promoting compassion, forgiveness, and gratitude), and foster positive communication through meaningful feedback on the employee's best-self. These regular meetings create a constant feedback channel and save time by improving and sustaining efficiency. Research on PMI has been linked to significant improvements in performance, reduced stress and work overload, and enhanced employee well-being (Cameron, 2012).

Phase 3 comprises four skill-building seminars on positive psychology and a traditional leader development topic incorporated to educate leaders on the major concepts, application, and benefits of these topics: positive leadership, building PsyCap, creating high-quality connections, and self-management and goal setting. These seminars, including activities with their cohort, will assist in executing their action-learning project. Leaders should also be encouraged to reflect on their developmental experiences through weekly reflection journaling.

Support Component

- Phase 4: Closing and awards
- Regular coaching and mentoring

In phase 4, after the leaders are assessed again to detect changes in behavior, they should publicly commit to continuing their growth by presenting their LDP* to their cohort or their peers in their department and partake in a group debriefing experience to reflect on lessons learned in a formal after-action review. To reward their efforts and send a message to other leaders outside of the program, leaders who complete this program are presented with diplomas of completion and awards for their excellence.

Furthermore, in addition to the coaching they receive for their assessments and LDPs*, the leaders should be granted at least four individual coaching sessions and monthly check-ins with their assigned mentors in support of their development throughout the training process (Cummings & Worley, 2015).

Implement

During implementation, it is important to set the stage for learning by preparing the leader for acquiring new knowledge, skills, and abilities, and clearly stating the objectives and desired standards for performance as well as evaluating targeted competencies throughout the training process. It is also important to deliver a blended learning solution through presentation, modeling, and practice, and support the transfer and maintenance of knowledge through reflection, coaching, mentoring, and reward systems within the organization that encourage and recognize new behavior (Locke, 2009).

Evaluate

The final phase of the ADDIE training model is evaluating the LDP to determine whether the training was effective and why and how the intervention was successful (or not). Interventions are effective if (1) they are based on valid information, involve key stakeholders in the process, and have internal commitment, (2) they are based on the organization's capacity to change, and (3) they have a sound theory of change (Cummings & Worley, 2015). The most common issue in LDPs is conceptual fuzziness regarding underlying assumptions and theory of change (Edmonstone, 2013).

The ACS model for best practices in leader development is the evidence-based framework of logic behind this program (see Figure 9.5). Three hundred and sixty degree feedback to assess leadership strengths and enhance self-awareness, challenging, and motivating goals that are relevant to methods in positive psychology, accompanied by the emotional and mental support from coaching and mentoring to increase self-efficacy, is this program's sound theory of change.

This program logic should drive the evaluation questions when determining the fidelity of implementation and whether desired individual and organizational outcomes were reached. When evaluating this program, at least the first three of Kirkpatrick's (1959) four levels of evaluation criteria that are most commonly used in evaluating the return on investment in LDPs should be assessed: reaction, learning, behavior, and results. Specifically, satisfaction surveys and objective tests can assess participant reaction and learning. The cohort's 360°

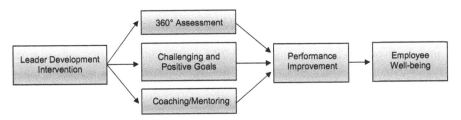

Figure 9.5 Theory of Change for the Positive Leader Development Program.

assessments would serve as pre- and post-intervention measures compared to another wait-listed cohort.

If the particular program is "high profile, especially expensive, and likely to draw scrutiny from top executives" (Phillips & Phillips, 2007, p. 162), then the business impact such as productivity or customer satisfaction can be converted to monetary values and the return on investment can subsequently be calculated. Simultaneously, observation of activities, a post-intervention survey, and focus groups could be conducted to assess the fidelity of implementation as compared to the originally intended program plan. The evaluation should yield preliminary results as soon as 30 days after the participants have completed the core activities and conclude in a few months after the first cohort completes the program.

Ideal Conditions for Implementation

As previously mentioned, leader development activities should be designed with the ACS model in mind for a successful impact. However, Phillips and Phillips (2007) stated that contextual factors such as management and HR systems can moderate the relationship between intervention activities and outcomes. It is necessary for management systems (such as performance appraisal and rewards and recognition systems) to be conducive to activities and support developmental growth. For example, performance appraisals should explicitly rate behaviors that reflect the desired competencies and should provide clear and actionable feedback for improvement. Individual and group-level rewards should recognize and reward new behavior. For example, annual bonuses can be given to supervisors based on the development of their subordinates. HR systems (such as selection and promotion) can also bolster leader development initiatives and avoid obstacles that could hinder succession processes or the transfer of learning (Phillips & Phillips, 2007). Organizational systems that are in line with this planned change cultivate the capacity for effective leadership.

Positive leader development should not only build on strengths to improve targeted competencies, but should also create or sustain an empowering organizational culture that endorses positive communication, optimism, and ultimately positively deviant performance (Cameron, 2012; Godbole et al., 2017). Therefore, the setting should be one that welcomes a culture of collaboration and teamwork. Many organizations achieve success through control, efficiency, and consistency in operations. There may or may not be an emphasis on positivity and relationship building among employees. Positive LDPs such as this should be implemented in a culture that encourages positive deviance, high-quality connections, and healthy psychological capital, parallel with top management that will champion the development of its leaders (Young et al., 2017).

Strengths and Limitations

Strengths of this intervention include a sound theory of change, a flexible framework, and vigorous research and theory behind essential activities considering psychosocial phenomena, including sufficient research in positive leadership. First, the theory of change was conceptualized using social science theory, program theory, and evaluation theory that incorporates evidence-based practices from a multitude of transdisciplinary literature. The program logic is based on the validated ACS model of effective leader development by Van Velsor et al. (2010). Second, the general framework is flexible enough to be applied to any organization as activities can be modified according to specific needs and contextual considerations. Third, extensive theory and research on goal setting to increase motivation bolster the inclusion of challenging activities such as an LDP enacted through an action-learning project (Cummings & Worley, 2015; Lathum, 2018; Locke, 2009; McCall, 2010; Nowack, 2017; Van Velsor et al., 2010). Adequate research on the effectiveness of coaching and mentoring that increases self-efficacy has also been linked to performance (Cummings & Worley, 2015; Frankovelgia & Riddle, 2010; Gentry & Walsh, 2015; Locke, 2009; Stawiski et al., 2016; Van Velsor et al., 2010). Lastly, positive leadership has been associated with beneficial individual and organization outcomes such as well-being and thriving (ACP Hospitalist & American College of Physicians, 2019; Cameron, 2012; Dutton, 2003; Lavine, 2012; Warren et al., 2017).

Some limitations include mixed interpretations of the importance of a 360° assessment (Lacerenza et al., 2017) and the small amount of research linking self-awareness to performance. In evaluation studies, most assessments on the impact of LDPs have been on reactions; only 30% of evaluations measuring return on investment have evaluated the application of new leader behaviors on the job, and just 10% on the business impact (Phillips & Phillips, 2007). Another major limitation is that although positive leadership approaches are relevant to cultures across the globe (Warren et al., 2017), the concepts behind this LDP and many other positive OD interventions are in alignment with the Western values and ideals of the United States, Europe, and Canada. Some examples of this include an emphasis on individualism versus collectivism, a somewhat low power distance, a performance orientation, an intolerance for ambiguity and uncertainty, and a short-run time orientation (Kim et al., 2018; Schein & Schein, 2016). Therefore, additional consideration is warranted when considering the design and theoretical concepts behind this intervention in other parts of the globe.

Conclusion

LDPs are the most popular OD interventions because it is widely recognized that talent management is equally as important as an organization's finances and marketing when successfully adapting to internal and external change (Cummings & Worley, 2015). To improve performance, enhance the quality of consumer outcomes, and most importantly facilitate a culture that values the mental and emotional health of its members, organizations need strong, high-impact, and engaging leaders that allow the organization to fully flourish. Through assessment, challenge, and support with a positive lens, any organization can largely impact their workplace and the surrounding community in an extraordinary way.

Resources

American College of Healthcare Executives 2019 Competencies Assessment Tool. (2019). Healthcare Leadership Alliance and the American College of Healthcare Executives. Retrieved from https://www.ache.org/-/media/ache/career-resource-center/competencies_booklet.pdf

Assessments Powered by CCL Compass: Benchmarks for Managers. (2019). Center for Creative Leadership. Retrieved from https://www.ccl.org/lead-it-yourself-solutions/benchmarks-360-assessment-suite/

Gallup StrengthsFinder. (2018). Gallup, Inc. Retrieved from https://www.gallupstrengthscenter.com/home/enus/strengthsfinder?utm_source=strengthsfinder&utm_campaign=coming_soon&utm_medium=redirect

References

Avolio, B. J., & Gardner, W. L. (2005). Authentic leadership development: Getting to the root of positive forms of leadership. *The Leadership Quarterly, 16*, 315–338.

ACP Hospitalist & American College of Physicians. (2019). A deviant approach to hospital challenges. Retrieved from https://acphospitalist.org/archives/2009/11/positive.htm

Cameron, K. (2012). *Positive leadership: Strategies for extraordinary performance (selected excerpts)*. San Francisco: BK.

Cooperrider, D. L., & Godwin, L. N. (2012). Positive organizational development: Innovation-inspired change in an economy and ecology of strengths. In K. S. Cameron & G. M. Spreitzer (Eds.), *The Oxford handbook of positive organizational scholarship*. New York: Oxford University Press.

Csikszentmihalyi, M. (1997). *Finding flow: The psychology of engagement with everyday life*. New York, NY: Basic Books.

Cummings, T. G., & Worley, C. G. (2015). *Organizational development & change* (10th ed.). Cengage Learning: Stamford, CT.

Dutton, J. E. (2003). *Energize your workplace: How to create and sustain high quality connections at work (selected excerpts)*. San Francisco: Jossey-Bass.

Edmonstone, J. (2013). Healthcare leadership: Learning from evaluation. *Leadership in Health Services, 26*(2), 148–158.

Frankovelgia, C. C., & Riddle, D. D. (2010). Leadership coaching. In *The center for creative leadership handbook of leadership development* (3rd ed.) (pp. 125–146). Jossey-Bass: San Francisco.

Gardner, W. L., & Carlson, J. D. (2015). Authentic leadership. In J. D. Wright (editor-in-chief), *International encyclopedia of the social & behavioral sciences* (2nd ed., Vol. 2, pp. 245–250). Oxford: Elsevier.

Gentry, W. A., & Walsh, R. J. (2015). *Mentoring first-time managers: Proven strategies HR leaders can use.* Center for Creative Leadership white paper.

Godbole, P., Burke, D., & Aylott, J. (2017). *Why hospitals fail: Between theory and practice.* Cham Switzerland: Springer International Publishing AG.

Huang, P. H., Brafford, A. M., Austin, D. S., & Knudson, M. (2018). *Positive institutions: Organizations, laws, and policies.* In *The Oxford handbook of positive psychology* (3rd ed.). doi: 10.1093/oxfordhb/9780199396511.013.48

King, S. N., & Santana, L. C. (2010). Feedback-intensive programs. In *The center for creative leadership handbook of leadership development* (3rd ed. pp. 97–123). Jossey-Bass: San Francisco.

Kirkpatrick, D. L. (1959). Techniques for evaluation training programs. *Journal of the American Society of Training Directors, 13*, 21–26.

Lacerenza, C. N., Reyes, D. L., Marlow, S. L., Joseph, D. L., & Salas, E. (2017). Leadership training design, delivery, and implementation: A meta-analysis. *Journal of Applied Psychology, 102*(12), 1686–1718.

Lathum, G. P. (2018). *Becoming the evidence-based manager* (2nd ed.). Boston, MA: Nicholas Brealey Publishing.

Lavine, M. (2012). Positive deviance: A method for learning from the uncommon. In K. S. Cameron & G. M. Spreitzer (Eds.), *The Oxford handbook of positive organizational scholarship.* New York: Oxford University Press.

Locke, E. A. (Ed.). (2009). *Handbook of principles of organizational behavior: Indispensable knowledge for evidence-based management* (2nd ed.). United Kingdom: John Wiley & Sons Ltd.

Kim, H., Doiron, K., Warren, M. A., & Donaldson, S. I. (2018). The international landscape of positive psychology research: A systematic review. *International Journal of Well-Being, 8*(1), 50–70.

McCall, M. (2010). Recasting leadership development. *Industrial and Organizational Psychology, 3*(1), 3–19. doi:10.1111/j.1754-9434.2009.01189.x

Miller, D. L., Umble, K. E., & Fredrick, S. L. (2007). Linking learning methods to outcomes in public health leadership development. *Leadership in Health Services, 20*(2), 97–123.

Nowack, K. (2017). Facilitating successful behavior change: Beyond goal setting to goal flourishing. *Consulting Psychology Journal: Practice and Research, 69*(3), 153–171.

Peterson, C. (2006). *A primer in positive psychology.* New York: Oxford University Press.

Phillips, J. J., & Phillips, P. (2007). Measuring return on investment in leadership development. In Hannum, K. M., Martineau, J. W., & Reinelt, C. (Eds.), *The handbook of leadership development evaluation* (pp. 137–166). San Francisco: John Wiley & Sons, Inc.

Schein, E., & Schein, P. (2016). *Organizational culture and leadership* (5th ed.). Hoboken: John Wiley & Sons.

Stawiski, S., Sass, M., & Belzer, R. G. (2016). Building the case for executive coaching. *Center for Creative Leadership white paper* (16).

Stefl, M. E. (2008). Common competencies for all healthcare managers. *Journal of Healthcare Management,* (53)6, 360–374.

Van Velsor, E., McCauley, C. D., & Ruderman, M. N. (2010). *The center for creative leadership handbook of leadership development* (3rd ed.). San Francisco: Jossey-Bass.

Van Velsor, E., Taylor, S., & Leslie, B. J. (1993). An examination of the relationships among self-perception accuracy, self-awareness, gender, and leader effectiveness. *Human Resource Management, 32*(2), 249–263.

Wallace, L., & Trinka, J. (2009). Leadership and employee engagement. *Public Management, 91*(5), 10–13.

Warren, M. A., Donaldson, S. I., & Luthans, F. (2017). Taking positive psychology to the workplace: Positive organizational psychology, positive organizational behavior, and positive organizational scholarship. In M. A. Warren & S. I. Donaldson (Eds.), *Scientific advances in positive psychology*. Westport, Connecticut: Praeger.

Young, S., Champion, H., Raper, M., & Braddy, P. (2017). Adding more fuel to the fire. *Center for Creative Leadership white paper* (12 pp).

10

Evaluating Positive Organizational Psychology Interventions

Stewart I. Donaldson, Scott I. Donaldson, & Christoper Chen

> *If you can't measure it, you can't improve it.*
> — Peter F. Drucker

The first author's former professor, colleague, and neighbor, Peter F. Drucker, known as the father of modern management, strongly advocated and imprinted on his students the importance of reliable and valid measurement. He insisted that we cannot manage or manage the process of change unless we can measure it well. Positive organizational psychology interventions (POPIs) aim to generate positive and meaningful changes in the lives of workers and their organizations. In Chapter 1, we described the findings from POPI studies using the most rigorous measurement and research designs to date, which uncovered five successful intervention types:

- Psychological capital interventions
- Job-crafting interventions
- Employee strengths interventions
- Employee gratitude interventions
- Employee well-being interventions

Donaldson et al. (2019a, 2019b) provided the specific action and change models for each type of POPI, and described in detail the positive effects of each type of intervention.

The authors in this volume have used some of the most promising positive psychological science theories, principles, concepts, and empirical research findings to guide the design of the next generation of POPIs. These newer interventions are based on the science supporting flow theory, best-self interventions, job crafting, social determination theory, strengths enhancement, appreciative inquiry, and the like. We explain in this chapter the importance of rigorous measurement and strategic evaluation of these proposed POPIs as the key to achieving lasting success.

Positive Organizational Psychology Interventions: Design and Evaluation, First Edition.
Stewart I. Donaldson and Christopher Chen.
© 2021 John Wiley & Sons Ltd. Published 2021 by John Wiley & Sons Ltd.

Measurement of Positive Psychology Constructs

Ackerman et al. (2018) reviewed almost two decades of published research associated with positive psychology through the lens of its measurement. This effort was done to review how constructs in positive psychology have been operationalized, measured, validated, cited, and used to build the science. Their findings revealed that a wide range of constructs have been studied in research linked to positive psychology, including inherently positive constructs (such as well-being and happiness) as well as those with pathological undertones (such as depression and anxiety). Well-being was one of the most cited constructs, with 39 scales measuring some form of well-being, although pathology-focused scales have also been utilized extensively (see Table 10.1).

Table 10.1 Most Cited Constructs in Positive Psychological Science.

Construct	Sub-Construct (if any)	Number of Scales	Representative Scales
Well-being	General well-being	39	SPWB (Ryff, 1989)
happiness/subjective well-being		36	AHI (Seligman et al., 2005)
life satisfaction		13	SWLS (Diener et al., 1985)
Total		88	–
Emotions and mood	General emotions/all emotions	31	FEQ (Fordyce, 1988)
Mood		12	POMS (McNair et al., 1971)
Specifically positive emotions		5	DPES (Shiota et al., 2006)
Total		12	–
Personality	Non-big five	28	Eysenck I6 Junior Questionnaire (Eysenck & Eysenck, 1975)
Big five		15	BFI/BFI-44 (John et al., 1991)
Total		43	–
Self-esteem and self-efficacy	Self-esteem	17	RSE (Rosenberg, 1965)
Self-efficacy		14	GSES (Sherer et al., 1982)
Total		31	–
Spirituality, religiosity, and faith	Spirituality	18	BMMRS (Fetzer Institute & National Institute on Aging Working Group, 1999)
Religiosity and faith		11	RCI-10 (Worthington et al., 2003)
Total		29	–

(Continued)

Table 10.1 *(Cont'd)*

Construct	Sub-Construct (if any)	Number of Scales	Representative Scales
Physical/general health		28	SF-8 (Ware et al., 2001)
Depression		36	CES-D (Radloff, 1977)
Anxiety		26	DASS (Lovibond & Lovibond, 1995)
Stress (not including posttraumatic stress)		24	PSS (Cohen et al., 1983)
Affect		23	PANAS (Watson et al., 1988)
Posttraumatic stress/ posttraumatic growth		23	PTGI (Tedeschi & Calhoun, 1996)
Meaning/purpose		22	MLQ (Steger et al., 2006)
Strengths		22	VIA-IS (Peterson et al., 2005)
Relationships		21	ECR (Brennan et al., 1998)

Source: Ackerman et al. (2018).

It was also found that positive psychological science to date has predominantly used self-report measurement scales – 78% of empirical articles used some type of self-report measurement scale, with 68% using *only* self-report measurements. This includes approximately 1,279 established self-report scales along with 310 scales that were newly created or adapted from existing scales. All these scales were examined in terms of domain, constructs, positive scales, adapted or created scales, scale validation, and operationalization of popular constructs. In short, only a total of 38 scales reviewed were also further validated in later studies. However, the list of the most highly cited measurement scales in positive psychological science to date provides POPI evaluators and researchers a wide range of measurement options (see Table 10.2).

Table 10.2 Most Cited Positive Psychology Measurement Scales.

Measure	Development	Dataset Citations	Google Scholar Citations	Construct	Source of Development
Satisfaction with Life Scale (SWLS)	Diener et al. (1985)	210	20,766	Well-being	*Journal of Personality Assessment*
Positive and Negative Affect Schedule (PANAS)	Watson et al. (1988)	150	30,091	Positive and negative affect	*Journal of Personality and Social Psychology*

(Continued)

Table 10.2 *(Cont'd)*

Measure	Development	Dataset Citations	Google Scholar Citations	Construct	Source of Development
Life Orientation Test-Revised (LOT-R)	Scheier et al. (1994)	69	5,775	Optimism	*Journal of Personality and Social Psychology*
Rosenberg Self-Esteem Scale (SES)	Rosenberg (1965)	51	34,716	Self-esteem	(Book)
Psychological Well-Being Scale (PWBS)	Ryff (1989)	50	10,525	Well-being	*Journal of Personality and Social Psychology*
Hope Scale/Adult Dispositional Hope Scale (ADHS)	Snyder et al. (2003)	46	3,507	Hope	*Journal of Personality and Social Psychology*
Values in Action Inventory of Strengths (VIA-IS)	Peterson & Seligman (2004); Park & Peterson (2009)	45	7,186	Character Strengths	N/A
Gratitude Questionnaire-6 (GQ-6)	McCullough et al. (2002)	42	2,189	Gratitude, grateful disposition	*Journal of Personality and Social Psychology*
Subjective Happiness Scale (SHS)	Lyubomirsky & Lepper (1999)	39	2,643	Happiness	*Social Indicators Research*
Meaning in Life Questionnaire (MLQ)	Steger et al. (2006)	32	2,207	Meaning	*Journal of Counseling Psychology*

Source: Ackerman et al. (2018).

One of the most important aspects of designing a strong strategic evaluation of a POPI is finding or developing valid measures of the main constructs of interest. This can be accomplished by carefully reviewing relevant and appropriate measures that have been validated in previous empirical research (see Ackerman et al., 2018; Donaldson, 2019; Donaldson et al., 2020c; Donaldson & Donaldson, under review), or by developing and validating new measures that are specifically relevant to the constructs you are attempting to influence with your POPI. Donaldson and Grant-Vallone (2002) provided specific guidance about ways of using self-report measures in the workplace that minimize the problems of self-report and mono-method bias. Donaldson et al. (2020c) illustrated the importance of using collateral reports whenever possible in positive organizational psychology and POPI research and evaluation.

POPI Efficacy Evaluation or Effectiveness Evaluation?

An important distinction to make in the evaluation of POPIs is whether the purpose of the evaluation is to determine POPI efficacy or POPI effectiveness. In short, POPI efficacy evaluation typically determines whether the intervention works under controlled research conditions. Efficacy evaluations often use randomized control trials (RCTs) or quasi-experimental designs to determine if the participants in a POPI are better off on key outcomes than those in a comparison or control group. In a recent analysis of the published peer-reviewed positive psychology intervention (PPI) and POPI literature, it was found that we can now learn from more than 220 RCTs and 22 meta-analyses based largely on RCTs of PPIs and POPIs (Donaldson et al., under review). One of these meta-analyses carefully analyzed the strongest efficacy evaluations of POPIs to date and found that POPIs can have very important positive effects on constructs such as well-being, engagement, leader–member exchange, organization-based self-esteem, workplace trust, forgiveness, prosocial behavior, leadership, job stress, and calling (Donaldson et al., 2019a).

The continued development of strong evidence-based research on the efficacy of POPIs is a very important activity for the field. POPIs that do not turn out to be efficacious under highly controlled conditions should be abandoned, or at least revised and tested again to make sure they are successful before being implemented more widely in organizations and the society at large. That is, a newly designed POPI should first be able to pass the tests of efficacy evaluation before it is given to actual employees and their leaders in the diverse global workplace. However, it is important to point out that while a successful efficacy evaluation is helpful, it does not provide sufficient evidence to truly determine if the POPI is or will be effective under uncontrolled "real-world" conditions.

POPI Effectiveness Evaluation

Positive organizational psychology practitioners, including many of the chapter authors in this volume, use basic research on positive organizational psychology topics and POPI efficacy evaluations to guide the design of new or "next-generation" POPIs. But, how do we know whether or not these new POPIs will actually work in organizations, and how do we make them as effective as possible overtime? Effectiveness evaluations of POPIs are critical to ensure "real-world" success. That is, evaluating programs being implemented for clients, service recipients, or consumers in "real-world" work-related settings and organizations is the domain of POPI effectiveness evaluation (Donaldson, 2007; Donaldson et al., 2020b). Stated another way, does the POPI of interest actually make a difference in society? As pointed out above, it could be argued that all POPIs should be subjected first to efficacy evaluation, and if successful, subsequently implemented in the field and be subjected to effectiveness evaluation. However, this ideal is not always realized in practice, and POPIs will often bypass efficacy evaluation while being developed, implemented, and evaluated in the field. In fact, one might imagine that due to a variety of factors related to urgency, time, resources, and feasibility, the bulk of next-generation POPIs will be evaluated in practice (versus under controlled research conditions) using various effectiveness evaluation techniques and approaches.

Types of Effectiveness Evaluation to Consider

The great news for positive organizational psychology practitioners is there are now a wide range of approaches that can be used to measure, monitor, and evaluate the effectiveness of your practice (Donaldson, 2007, in press). In an effort to advance progress in the practice of positive psychology, we strongly encourage practitioners to use some form of measurement and effectiveness evaluation to guide and improve their work. Under great time and resource constraints, this may be limited to some minimal collection of feedback from those participating in the various aspects of your POPIs, which is much better than doing nothing (unfortunately, doing nothing is rumored to be common practice today). With a bit more time and resources, consider at least building internal effectiveness evaluation into the design of your projects and POPIs. Perhaps better yet, consider partnering with those who specialize in effectiveness evaluation to make your applications and POPIs as effective as possible under "real-world" conditions.

For example, consider using a participatory approach to effectiveness evaluation that engages all relevant POPI stakeholders in a developmental (Patton, 2010) or formative evaluation process (Donaldson, 2007, in press). Developmental evaluation is often most useful when you are developing a new POPI under complex and uncertain workplace or organizational conditions. Formative evaluation is often most useful when you begin implementing your POPI to make sure it is feasible, appropriate, and acceptable before it is fully implemented. Donaldson (2007, in press) provides both a three- (Table 10.3) and expanded six-step (Figure 10.1) participatory evaluation framework (based on the CDC Framework; National Center for Chronic Disease Prevention and Health Promotion, 2020) that can be used to help you answer formative evaluation, process/implementation evaluation, outcome/effectiveness evaluation, and impact evaluation questions.

Table 10.3 Donaldson Three-Step Participatory Effectiveness Evaluation Framework.

---

1. Engage stakeholders in developing logic models and theories of change.

2. Formulate and prioritize evaluation questions.

3. Answer evaluation questions.

Source: Donaldson, 2007, in press.

One potential positive side effect of using these participatory effectiveness evaluation frameworks is that they often facilitate the development of evaluative thinking. That is, they encourage participants to be reflective and think deeply about how to continually improve their work and the POPI you are implementing. They can also help build greater internal evaluation capacity within the organizations you are

Figure 10.1 CDC Six-Step Participatory Effectiveness Evaluation Framework.
Source: National Center for Chronic Disease Prevention and Health Promotion (2020).

developing with your POPI. Donaldson (2007, in press) expands upon these frameworks to show how you can make your effectiveness evaluation efforts culturally responsive and strengths (versus deficit) focused. Integrating more effectiveness evaluation into the practice of positive psychology and PPI work in general, and specifically into the practice of positive organizational psychology and POPI work, may be one of the most important new directions to further develop the field.

Tailoring POPIs to Needs

Another crucial new direction for the design and evaluation of POPIs is systematic needs assessment and tailoring. We now know from a wealth of data collected as part of POPI efficacy evaluations that POPIs tailored to the specific needs of workers and organizations are likely to be more effective in practice (see Donaldson et al., 2019b). The development and validation of the Positive Functioning at Work Scale is a recent attempt to provide a needs assessment instrument that can be used broadly to determine which POPI components best address employee and organizational needs (Donaldson & Donaldson, in press; Donaldson et al., 2020c). The scale builds upon and extends the PERMA profiler, and assesses nine building blocks of well-being and positive functioning:

1. Positive emotions – experiencing happiness, joy, love, gratitude, etc.
2. Engagement – absorption; experiencing flow
3. Relationships – connecting with others; loving and being loved
4. Meaning – connecting to meaning; finding your purpose
5. Accomplishment – pursuing and accomplishing goals; striving for greatness
6. Physical health – biological, functional, and psychological health assets
7. Mindset – future orientation, growth mindset, and perseverance
8. Environment – spatiotemporal elements, such as access to natural light, nature, physiological safety
9. Economic security – the perception of financial security

The results from a needs assessment like the Positive Functioning at Work Scale can help guide the design of POPIs so that they can better focus on addressing the most pressing employee and organizational needs.

Conclusion

One purpose of this final chapter is to highlight and underscore how important measurement and evaluation are to the future development of positive organizational psychology practice. It is our hope that practitioners will utilize and build upon these instruments that have been developed and validated to measure positive psychology constructs. Valid measurement is fundamental to our ability to determine employee and organizational needs, and design POPIs that address those needs, POPI efficacy evaluation, and POPI effectiveness evaluation. Sound evaluation is essential for the further development of our field and for making "next-generation" POPIs as effective as possible. We hope you end this book as excited as we are about the future of positive organizational psychology, and its potential to enhance well-being, optimal functioning, and the effectiveness of diverse workers, leaders, and organizations across the globe.

References

Ackerman, C. E., Warren, M. A., & Donaldson, S. I. (2018). Scaling the heights of positive psychology: A systematic review of measurement scales. *International Journal of Wellbeing, 8*(2), 1–21.

Brennan, K. A., Clark, C. L., & Shaver, P. R. (1998). Self-report measurement of adult attachment: An integrative overview. In J. A. Simpson & W. S. Rholes (Eds.), *Attachment theory and close relationships* (pp. 46–76). New York, NY: The Guilford Press.

Cohen, S., Kamarck, T., & Mermelstein, R. (1983). A global measure of perceived stress. *Journal of Health and Social Behavior, 24*(4), 385–396.

Diener, E., Emmons, R. A., Larsen, R. J., & Griffin, S. (1985). The Satisfaction With Life Scale. *Journal of Personality Assessment, 49,* 71–75.

Donaldson, S. I. (2007). *Program theory-driven evaluation science: Strategies and applications.* New York, NY: Routledge Academic.

Donaldson, S. I. (in press). Theory-driven evaluation science: Culturally responsive and strengths focused applications. New York NY: Psychology Press.

Donaldson, S. I. (2019). *Evaluating positive functioning and performance: A positive work and organizations approach.* (Doctoral dissertation.) Retrieved from PQDT-Global.

Donaldson, S. I., Cabrera, V., & Gaffaney, J. (under review). *Following the positive psychology intervention science to generate well-being in a global pandemic.* Manuscript submitted for publication.

Donaldson, S. I., & Donaldson, S. I. (in press). The Positive Functioning at Work Scale: Psychometric assessment, validation, and measurement invariance. *Journal of Well-being Assessment.*

Donaldson, S. I., Donaldson, S. I., & Ko, I. (2020b). Advances in the science of positive work and organizations. In S. I. Donaldson, M. Csikszentmihalyi, & J. Nakamura (Eds.), *Positive psychological science: Improving everyday life, health and well-being, work, education, and society* (2nd ed.). New York, NY: Routledge Academic.

Donaldson, S. I., & Grant-Vallone, E. J. (2002). Understanding self-report bias in organizational behavior research. *Journal of Business and Psychology, 17*(2), 245–262.

Donaldson, S. I., Heshmati, S., Lee, J. Y., & Donaldson, S. I. (2020c). Examining building blocks of well-being beyond PERMA and self-report bias. *The Journal of Positive Psychology*, https://doi.org/10.1080/17439760.2020.1818813

Donaldson, S. I., Heshmati, S., & Donaldson, S. I. (in press). A global perspective on well-being and positive psychological science: Systematic reviews and meta-analyses. In A. Kostic (Ed.), *Positive psychology: An international perspective*. London: Wiley.

Donaldson, S. I., Lee, J. Y., & Donaldson, S. I. (2019a). Evaluating positive psychology interventions at work: A systematic review and meta-analysis. *International Journal of Applied Positive Psychology, 4*, 113–134.

Donaldson, S. I., Lee, J. Y., & Donaldson, S. I. (2019b). The effectiveness of positive psychology interventions in the workplace: A theory-driven evaluation approach. In V. Z. Llewellyn & S. Rothmann (Eds.), *Theoretical approaches to multi-cultural positive psychology interventions* (pp. 115–159). Cham, Switzerland: Springer International.

Eysenck, H. J., & Eysenck, S. B. G. (1975). *The Eysenck Personality Questionnaire*. London: Hodder & Stoughton.

Fetzer Institute. (1999). *Multidimensional measurement of religiousness/spirituality for use in health research*. Retrieved from https://fetzer.org/resources/multidimensional-measurement-religiousnessspirituality-use-health-research

Fordyce, W. E. (1988). Pain and suffering: A reappraisal. *American Psychologist, 43*(4), 276–283.

John, O. P., Donahue, E. M., & Kentle, R. L. (1991). *The Big Five Inventory – Versions 4a and 54*. Berkeley, CA: University of California, Berkeley, Institute of Personality and Social Research.

Lovibond, P. F., & Lovibond, S. H. (1995). The structure of negative emotional states: Comparison of the Depression Anxiety Stress Scales (DASS) with the Beck Depression and Anxiety Inventories. *Behaviour Research and Therapy, 33*(3), 335–343.

Lyubomirsky, S., & Lepper, H. S. (1999). A measure of subjective happiness: Preliminary reliability and construct validation. *Social Indicators Research, 46*(2), 137–155.

McCullough, M. E., Emmons, R. A., & Tsang, J. A. (2002). The grateful disposition: A conceptual and empirical topography. *Journal of Personality & Social Psychology, 82*(1), 112–127.

McNair, D. M., Lorr, M., & Droppleman, L. F. (1971). *Manual for the profile of mood states*. San Diego, CA: Educational and Industrial Testing Services.

National Center for Chronic Disease Prevention and Health Promotion. (2020). Retrieved from https://www.cdc.gov/obesity/downloads/cdc-evaluation-workbook-508.pdf

Park, N., & Peterson, C. (2009). Character strengths: Research and practice. *Journal of College and Character, 10*(4), 1–10.

Patton, M. Q. (2010). *Developmental evaluation. Applying complexity concepts to enhance innovation and use.* New York, NY: Guilford Press.

Peterson, C., Park, N., & Seligman, M. E. P. (2005). Orientations to happiness and life satisfaction: The full life vs. the empty life. *Journal of Happiness Studies, 6*(1), 25–41. doi:10.1007/s10902-004-1278-z

Peterson, C., & Seligman, M. E. P. (2004). *Character strengths and virtues: A handbook and classification.* American Psychological Association; New York, NY: Oxford University Press.

Radloff, L. S. (1977). The CES-D scale: A self-report depression scale for research in the general population. *Applied Psychological Measurement, 1*(3), 385–401.

Rosenberg, M. (1965). *Society and the adolescent self-image.* Princeton, NJ: Princeton University Press.

Ryff, C. D. (1989). Happiness is everything, or is it? Explorations on the meaning of psychological well-being. *Journal of Personality and Social Psychology, 57*(6), 1069–1081.

Scheier, M. F., Carver, C. S., & Bridges, M. W. (1994). Distinguishing optimism from neuroticism (and trait anxiety, self-mastery, and self-esteem): A reevaluation of the life orientation test. *Journal of Personality and Social Psychology, 67*(6), 1063–1078.

Seligman, M. E., Steen, T. A., Park, N., & Peterson, C. (2005). Positive psychology progress: Empirical validation of interventions. *The American Psychologist, 60*(5), 410–421.

Sherer, M., Maddux, J. E., Mercandante, B., Prentice-Dunn, S., Jacobs, B., & Rogers, R. W. (1982). The Self-Efficacy Scale: Construction and validation. *Psychological Reports, 51*(2), 663–671.

Shiota, M. N., Keltner, D., & John, O. P. (2006). Positive emotion dispositions differentially associated with big five personality and attachment style. *The Journal of Positive Psychology, 1*(2), 61–71.

Snyder, C. R., Lopez, S. J., Shorey, H. S., Rand, K. L., & Feldman, D. B. (2003). Hope theory, measurements, and applications to school psychology. *School Psychology Quarterly, 18*(2), 122–139.

Steger, M. F., Frazier, P., Oishi, S., & Kaler, M. (2006). The Meaning in Life Questionnaire: Assessing the presence of and search for meaning in life. *Journal of Counseling Psychology, 53*(1), 80–93.

Tedeschi, R. G., & Calhoun, L. G. (1996). The Posttraumatic Growth Inventory: Measuring the positive legacy of trauma. *Journal of Traumatic Stress, 9*(3), 455–472.

Ware, J., Kosinski, M., Dewey, J., & Gandek, B. (2001). *How to score and interpret single-item health status measures: A manual for users of the SF-8 Health Survey.* Boston, MA: QualyMetric.

Watson, D., Clark, L. A., & Tellegen, A. (1988). Development and validation of brief measures of positive and negative affect: The PANAS scales. *Journal of Personality and Social Psychology, 54*(6), 1063–1070.

Worthington, E. L., Jr., Wade, N. G., Hight, T. L., Ripley, J. S., McCullough, M. E., Berry, J. W., ... O'Conner, L. (2003). The Religious Commitment Inventory-10: Development, refinement, and validation of a brief scale for research and counseling. *Journal of Counseling Psychology, 50*, 84–96.

Index

Positive Organizational Psychology Interventions: Design and Evaluation, First Edition.
Stewart I. Donaldson and Christopher Chen.
© 2021 John Wiley & Sons Ltd. Published 2021 by John Wiley & Sons Ltd.